Joan of Arc

THE EARLY DEBATE

Joan of Arc

THE EARLY DEBATE

Deborah A. Fraioli

THE BOYDELL PRESS

First published 2000
The Boydell Press, Woodbridge
Reprinted in paperback 2000

Transferred to digital printing

ISBN 978-0-85115-572-2 hardback
ISBN 978-0-85115-880-8 paperback

The Boydell Press is an imprint of Boydell & Brewer Ltd
PO Box 9, Woodbridge, Suffolk IP12 3DF, UK
and of Boydell & Brewer Inc.
668 Mt Hope Avenue, Rochester, NY 14620, USA
website: www.boydellandbrewer.com

A catalogue record for this book is available
from the British Library

This publication is printed on acid-free paper

Contents

To my mother
and the memory of my father

Preface

A major hurdle was overcome in the writing of this book when I realized that simplicity needed to be the order of the day. In essence, I had been trying to write a second book on a subject for which there was no first book. I planned to reread as theological debate a number of texts that, with the exception of Christine de Pizan's *Ditié de Jehanne d'Arc*, had scarcely sustained any critical reading at all, at least to anglophone audiences. Not only was there little critical literature, but in some cases there was neither an authoritative edition nor an English translation.

In the final stages of writing, therefore, I have been guided by two principles, neither of which was among my initial intentions: to introduce each text in some detail, taking little for granted, and to offer primarily the conclusions of my research at each stage in the discussion, in as succinct a manner as possible. This is not to suggest, by any means, that I feel unconditionally wedded to the ideas expressed here. I am well aware that the discovery of even a single neglected manuscript of any one of these texts could require a reshuffling of the entire picture.

In the interest of clarity and accessibility, whenever possible I have quoted from English translations, with full reference to the original in the footnotes. For the same reasons, appendices with English translations of several key texts have been included. Except where otherwise noted, all translations from the French are mine. Also, for the sake of brevity I have abridged the titles of the two crucial treatises *De quadam puella* and *De mirabili victoria* to DQP and DMV, respectively. Other titles have occasionally been less drastically abbreviated after the full title has been given.

To many people I owe considerable gratitude. In the course of rewriting, some very detailed comments and corrections offered by readers no longer found their place in my book. Their comments have, nevertheless, significantly influenced the final outcome. Those whom I wish to thank for reading the whole book include Charles T. Wood, Nadia Margolis, Marcia Colish and Thelma Fenster. My appreciation goes as well to Charity Cannon Willard and Susan Haskins, who each read and commented on one chapter. I also wish to acknowledge my debt to Kathleen Saltmarsh for providing an early sounding board for my ideas, and to Mary-Ann Stadtler-Chester and Raquel Halty for the privilege of Cambridge parking, making accessible the sanctuary of the Widener Library, where most of my research was completed. For their gracious reception during my visits to the Centre Jeanne d'Arc in Orléans, I wish to acknowledge the late Régine Pernoud and the current director, Françoise Michaud-Fréjaville. Additionally, I owe Raquel Halty thanks for her encouragement and forbearance as my department chairperson, and Caroline Palmer the same as my editor. Finally, I wish to thank my children Marc and Rebecca Fraioli for their generous understanding, and especially my husband Anthony for his unstinting encouragement and support.

NOTE

Where previously published material has been re-used, the author and publisher have made every effort to trace the copyright holders; we apologize for any omission in this regard, and will be pleased to add any necessary acknowledgements in subsequent editions.

Introduction

An important truth can sometimes be generally known, noted in passing by many writers, and still not be recognized fully. In the case of Joan of Arc, we have long understood that a civil war in France, in the midst of the ongoing conflict with England that is known as the Hundred Years War, created two images of the Maid, sharply divided along political lines. To apprise ourselves of this fact we have only to observe the clear division of opinion among the French chroniclers of the time; predictably, the royalist sympathizers wrote favorably of Joan,[1] while the Burgundian faction, supporters of the English, condemned her. English opinion, of which we have scant written record until the time of Joan's capture, can be intuited from the Burgundian sources. More striking to many minds is the exaggerated polarization of the Maid's image that emerged from her two trials: the vilification of Joan at the condemnation trial of 1431 and her subsequent exaltation at the nullification trial of 1456.

Charles Lightbody recognized that the idea of divided opinion on the Maid was not a static concept. In a sweeping vision, he wrote in *The Judgements of Joan* that the Maid "has had a whole series of trials . . . from the assembly of the doctors at Poitiers in the spring of 1429, through the long trial at Rouen and the rehabilitation proceedings twenty years later, to the canonization process dragging through half a century," and also that "she is still on trial. She still divides opinion. . . . Her life is the chosen tourney ground of fiercely contesting parties."[2] But Lightbody, who was a historian, drew primarily upon the chronicles and trial accounts in his excellent but compact overview of the debate on Joan of Arc. Unknown to Lightbody, however, was how strikingly his broad notion of 'judgments of Joan' resonates in another sector of Johannic documentation, the vast literature arising out of the debate over Joan's claim to a divine mission. It is this story that the present book seeks to relate. .

It is the premise of this book that Joan of Arc's continuing ability to create controversy, to divide her commentators into admirers and detractors, has owed not only to the obvious political fact of a divided France, but to something deeper and more essential: the debate over how one could validate

---

[1] The term "Armagnac" ceases to be an accurate name for the dauphin Charles's party after the death of the count of Armagnac in 1418. Although "Armagnac" as a word remained in circulation, "French," "royalist," or "Valois" are more accurate adjectives for the period in question.
[2] Charles Wayland Lightbody, *The Judgements of Joan: Joan of Arc, A Study in Cultural History* (Cambridge, Mass., 1961), p. 21.

1

the Maid's mission theologically. Because her divine inspiration was self-proclaimed, the problem lay in how to evaluate her declaration. Theologians use the concept of *discretio spirituum* or "the discernment of spirits" for the process of evaluating these cases, and, in fact, the celebrated theologian Jean Gerson, whose contemporary the Maid was, had codified the principles of discernment in several treatises in the years preceding Joan's arrival. The discernment procedure, conducted only by theologians, to which a minimum of attention has been paid by scholars of fifteenth-century history and thought, is unlikely to be well known to historians, and less so to scholars of literature, which is the discipline of my own doctoral training. So it came to me as a rather jarring realization that in order to understand the literary works I deemed of the greatest interest and centrality to the image of Joan of Arc – Christine de Pizan's *Ditié de Jehanne d'Arc* (1429) and Martin Le Franc's *Le champion des dames* (1440–42) – I would have to fully investigate the theological debate first mounted by the dauphin's theologians, which quickly spread to other writing, particularly literature. It now occurs to me that many texts crucial to our understanding of Joan of Arc, which were generated by the discernment question (chancellery propaganda, theological tracts, and selected literary works) which forms the basis of this book, have remained at the margins of modern scholarship. Their affinities have been unrecognized and their collective importance underestimated because we did not know how to gather them together according to the principle by which they were generated, as analyses or as polemic in the religious debate.

Writers today are less swift to denigrate medieval cultural constructs than was Ingvald Raknem when he wrote in *Joan of Arc in History, Legend and Literature* that through "deep-seated superstitions" in the fifteenth century, people "tended to interpret everything they could not understand as wonders or miracles worked by divine powers, or as witchcraft, sorcery, and devilry worked by fiends."[3] Yet we have still been too dismissive of the theme that runs like an underground current through so many contemporary Johannic texts and was clearly of central importance to Joan's contemporaries, namely, the urge to know whether or not to believe in the Maid. In a sense, the French campaign to win the theological debate (by proving that Joan was sent by God), which is the narrative of this book, was in every way as important as the military campaign. It appears certain that Joan would never have made it to the battlefield had Charles's theologians not found answers to the theological problems her mission raised. Moreover, her successes and ultimately her failure on the battlefield were seen not just as military phenomena but also as a barometer of her standing (and consequently France's standing) with God. We must fully understand that Joan's mission was able to be seamlessly integrated with France's belief in its own sacred dynasticism. As I am not the only person to point out, in a sense Joan was

---

[3] Ingvald Raknem, *Joan of Arc in History, Legend and Literature* (Oslo, 1971), p. 5.

only a minor player in a larger drama in which God and France were the protagonists.[4]

Because of her self-proclaimed supernatural mission, Joan's supporters believed that they had to use all available resources to determine exactly who and what she was. However, the fundamental difficulty inherent in such a procedure has been expressed by Régine Pernoud:

> It must be obvious that from the point of view of historical criticism, an affirmation which emanates from a single witness and cannot be checked by reference to any other source, is not tantamount to a certainty. The believer can no doubt be satisfied with Joan's explanation; the unbeliever cannot.[5]

Yet despite the magnitude and uncertainty of the task, the clergy believed it their responsibility to determine what Christians should believe in cases of self-proclaimed prophets, and the dauphin Charles, as we know from the evidence, wished his theologians to play this role in assisting in the evaluation of Joan of Arc. To make a proper assessment, theologians relied on the guidance of the Bible, on the previous literature of the discernment of spirits, and on historical precedent. History, however, offered scant precedent for a mission such as Joan's, and Charles's theologians were to remain seriously perplexed by the Maid's masculine role and its relationship to divine inspiration.

The correct chronological arrangement of the texts in the theological debate cannot be determined with certainty. Nonetheless, we know that theological scrutiny of her case began with discussions at Chinon (early March 1429), which were fortified by outside theological consultations, to which the correspondence between royal representatives and the theologian Jacques Gelu, the archbishop of Embrun, and probably the treatise *De quadam puella*, belong. Next came the formal theological inquiry at Poitiers (March 1429) whose only surviving official record is a summary known as the *Poitiers Conclusions*. Once the Poitiers commission had given tentative approval to the Maid and granted her permission to advance to Orléans, she dictated a letter on 22 March 1429, capitalizing on the positive results of the discernment investigation to report the message of her divine mission to the English enemy. Known as the *Lettre aux Anglais*, this military document, usually read as a summons to war, fills an equally important role in the religious debate, for it gives Joan's military mission God's endorsement, through the approval at Poitiers. *Virgo puellares*, a prophetic poem confected

---

[4] See, for instance, Stephen G. Nichols, "Prophetic Discourse: St. Augustine to Christine de Pizan," in *The Bible in the Middle Ages: Its Influence on Literature and Art*, Bernard S. Levy, ed., Medieval and Renaissance Texts and Studies, 89 (Binghamton, N.Y., 1992), p. 71.

[5] Régine Pernoud, *Joan of Arc, by Herself and Her Witnesses*, Edward Hyams, trans. (1962; New York, repr. 1969), p. 275.

at Poitiers, was disseminated with the *Poitiers Conclusions* and the *Lettre aux Anglais* as proof of her heavenly mission and the military power it conferred on her. Sometime in the spring or summer of 1429, Jacques Gelu wrote the *Dissertatio*, a theological defense of Joan's mission. The triad of religious propaganda documents named above, and in all likelihood also the *Dissertatio*, served Christine de Pizan as sources for the *Ditié de Jehanne d'Arc* (31 July 1429). To the summer of 1429 probably belongs the widely publicized tract *De mirabili victoria*, whose authorship has been contentiously debated, but which I prefer not to attribute to Jean Gerson, to whom it is usually ascribed, because of its divergence from a number of discernment conventions and principles codified by the chancellor himself. Each document in the final group of texts is either derived from *De mirabili victoria* or pertains to the tradition of that text. They include Jean Dupuy's *Collectarium* (summer 1429), the anonymous *Reply of a Parisian Cleric* (September 1429) and Martin Le Franc's debate over Joan of Arc's divine mission in *Le champion des dames* (1440–42). It is the purpose of this book to demonstrate the heretofore unacknowledged relationship among these works, based on their common participation in the polemical debate over Joan's supernatural inspiration.

1

Chinon and the Gelu Correspondence

When Joan of Arc arrived at Chinon asking for an interview with the dauphin, she claimed that she was sent by God to effect the recovery of France. One of the most succinct statements of her mission comes, oddly, from a skeptical Burgundian chronicler, Enguerrand de Monstrelet, who reports, understandably without mention of God, but otherwise accurately, that Joan told Charles that he had been unjustly chased (*encachié et debouté à tort*) from his kingdom and that she was sent to help him regain possession of it.[1] The heart of the problem, then, from either side of the controversy, was dynastic. Significantly, Monstrelet also relates that Joan made the restoration of Charles's dominion (*sa signourie*) dependent on whether the king decided to believe her (*se le roy la vouloit croire*).[2] Thus it is Joan who forces the major issue that faces every prophet, the need to be granted authority by those whose prophet she is to become.[3]

Modern biographers have tended to draw upon two incidents from contemporary sources to describe Joan's first days in Chinon at the court of the dauphin Charles: the Maid's identification of Charles from among his courtiers, and Joan's secret disclosure to Charles, which apparently convinced him that she knew the contents of thoughts that he had revealed only in private prayer to God. Some writers cast these two episodes as small miracles, demonstrations of the ability required of all prophets to see what is hidden, but the anecdotes are surely not of equal importance. It is customary to turn to Jean Pasquerel, Joan's confessor, for the contents of the secret, by far the more important anecdote of the two. For he claimed, although twenty-five years after the fact, that Joan had said to Charles: "On the part of My Lord, I tell thee thou art true heir of France [*vray héritier*] and son of the

---

[1] Enguerran[d] de Monstrelet in *Procès de condamnation et de réhabilitation de Jeanne d'Arc dite la Pucelle*, Jules Quicherat, ed., 5 vols., Société de l'Histoire de France (Paris, 1841–49) 4: 362.
[2] Quicherat, *Procès* 4: 363.
[3] For an excellent parallel discussion on this point for St. Bridget, see Claire L. Sahlin, "Gender and Prophetic Authority in Birgitta of Sweden's *Revelations*," in *Gender and Text in the Later Middle Ages*, Jane Chance, ed. (Gainesville, Fla., 1996), pp. 69–95.

King [*filz du roy*]."[4] This information seemingly finds corroboration in the well-known account by Pierre Sala, written at an even later date, in his *Hardiesses des grands rois et empereurs* (1516), purportedly recounted to him by the king's chamberlain, that Charles's secret prayer consisted in a humble entreaty to God for aid, specifically, for protection and defense, if indeed he were "true heir" (*vray hoir*) descended from the noble house of France and the kingdom ought "legitimately" (*justement*) to belong to him.[5]

To Charles and his intimate counselors and advisers, who had devoted more than a decade to attempting to settle the same point diplomatically, Joan's revelation that, on God's word, Charles was "true heir" must have seemed the most perfectly chosen revelation they could imagine, perhaps even a miracle. On the other hand, it did not take a diviner to know that this issue was the open wound driving the civil war between the French and Burgundian factions. Even before Charles was disinherited by the treaty of Troyes (1420), with its disparaging reference to him as "the so-called Dauphin of Vienne [*soy disant Daulphin de Viennois*],"[6] Charles himself had made repeated efforts to wrest control of the realm, strengthening his claims with potent verbal imagery. In an Armagnac ordinance of 1417, Charles annulled his lieutenancy to Queen Isabeau de Bavière or any designee and established himself as lieutenant general only to king Charles VI.[7] While the Council of Paris was still in Armagnac hands, between September 1413 and May 1418, prior to Charles's ignominious flight from Paris and subsequent exile, the archbishop of Bourges, Guillaume de Boisratier, had insisted to Henry V's face: "Sire, the king of France, our sovereign lord, is true king [*vrai roy*] of France."[8] When Charles started creating governmental bodies in dauphinist territory, parallel to those he had been forced to abandon in Paris, he continued to proclaim his rights. At Poitiers he convoked his own court, "considering that in the absence or incapacity of the king, it is his heir and universal successor [*son héritier et successeur universel*] to whom power alone belongs," and he then populated it with counselors whom he referred to as "illegally dislodged" (*illégalement destitutés*) from Paris.[9] By October 1418

---

[4] T. Douglas Murray, *Jeanne d'Arc, Maid of Orléans, Deliverer of France . . . Set Forth in the Original Documents* (New York, 1902), p. 283. English excerpts of the nullification trial can also be found in Régine Pernoud, *The Retrial of Joan of Arc: The Evidence at the Trial for her Rehabilitation, 1450–1456*, J. M. Cohen, trans. (New York, 1955), p. 161. See Pierre Duparc, ed. and trans., *Procès en nullité de la condamnation de Jeanne d'Arc*, 5 vols., Société de l'Histoire de France (Paris, 1977–89) 1: 390 where the Latin text of Pasquerel's testimony changes to French, as if quoting Joan directly: "Ego dico tibi ex parte *de Messire, que tu es vray héritier de France, et filz du roy.*"
[5] Pierre Sala, *Hardiesses des grands rois et empereurs* in Quicherat, *Procès* 4: 280.
[6] Jean Markale, *Isabeau de Bavière* (Paris, 1982), p. 265.
[7] D. Neuville, "Le Parlement royal à Poitiers (1418–1436) [Part] I," *Revue historique* 6 (1878): 5.
[8] Noël Valois, *Le conseil du roi aux XIVe, XVe et XVIe siècles* (Paris, 1888), p. 135.
[9] Neuville, "Parlement," p. 6.

Charles held himself to be no longer merely "son of the King of France, Dauphin of Vienne" (*Regis Francorum filius, dalphinus Viennensis*) but regent, and in a document of January 1419 he calls himself "Charles, son of the king of France, Regent of the kingdom" (*Karolus regis Francorum filius, Regnum Regens*).[10]

Yet for the average courtier, who judged Joan at face value, first reactions at the Valois court were characterized by a mixture of derision and disbelief, as several contemporary texts confirm. Even Charles, if indeed he did disguise himself in the crowd at Joan's first audience, as legend relates, made light of her purpose. Proving that it was not just the enemy who could ridicule the Maid, more than one French account describes how the courtiers at the dauphin's court – here in the words of Jean Chartier in the *Chronique de Charles VII*, c. 1461 – "only laughed and mocked and judged this Joan a simple person, and took no account of her words."[11] Perceval de Boulainvilliers, royal chamberlain, invents a first-person narrative in which Joan, protesting her divine calling, sees herself as she will appear to the world:

> I will be an object of derision to everyone, and rightly so. What [is] more crazy than to say to great men that it is for a Maiden to lift France up, to lead armies, to triumph over the enemy? What is more ridiculous than to see a young girl wearing men's clothes?[12]

And according to the *Journal du siège d'Orléans*, not even Robert de Baudricourt, the man who helped Joan reach the dauphin, initially took her mission seriously, unable to dislodge the notion that women in armies would be no more than camp followers:

> At the time and for several days after, he did not want to believe in her [*ne la voulut croire*]; thus he did nothing but mock her and held her vision to be fantasy and crazy imaginings, but thinking about offering her to his men for carnal sin, he retained her.[13]

[10] Neuville, "Parlement," p. 8, n. 4.
[11] Jean Chartier, *Chronique*, in Quicherat, *Procès* 4: 52. Chartier still notes, however, that "she said several other marvelous things and answered marvelously to the questions put to her," p. 53. Cf. also Auguste Vallet de Viriville, ed., *Chronique de la Pucelle ou Chronique de Cousinot, suivie de la Chronique normande de P. Cochon, relatives aux règnes de Charles VI et de Charles VII*, etc. (Paris, 1869), p. 272: "Which things master Robert reputed to be a mockery and a derision, imagining that it was a dream or a fantasy; and it seemed to him that she would be good for his men, to take pleasure in sin."
[12] For the original Latin letter from Boulainvilliers to duke Filippo Maria Visconti in Milan, dated 21 June 1429, see Quicherat, *Procès* 5: 118. A French translation appears in Jean-Baptiste-Joseph Ayroles, *La vraie Jeanne d'Arc*, 5 vols. (Paris, 1890–1902), *La paysanne et l'inspirée* 2: 240–45.
[13] *Journal du siège d'Orléans*, in Quicherat, *Procès* 4: 118. The negative sexual innuendos attached to Joan in certain chronicle accounts undoubtedly owe to this situation. That the attacks were not really personal can be demonstrated by the very indiscriminacy of the accusations, as in Bernard du Haillan's *De l'Estat et succez des affaires de France*,

Joan of Arc: The Early Debate

During the condemnation trial at Rouen, Joan's inquisitors were as interested as anybody to understand how Joan progressed beyond the stage of ridicule to the point of serious consideration and then acceptance. Prompted to make Joan give explanation in her own words, to what has been called "the primordial problem,"[14] her interrogator, Jean Beaupère, asked "how the king gave credence to her words?" Simply, and with apparent truthfulness, she replied that "he had good signs [intersignia], and through the clergy."[15] To one contemporary observer, Pancracio Justininani, whose June 1429 letter is contained in the Morosini chronicle, the event or sign which first broke down resistance to the Maid and led to a real investigation was Joan's telling her secret to the dauphin:

> The dauphin, hearing these things from the mouth of a young girl, made fun of her. He thought her crazy, possessed by the devil, and completely audacious. She, seeing that no one put any faith in her words, told him things that it is said were known only to God and the dauphin. . . . This caused the dauphin to gather together many wise men; and they began to dispute with her, to test her in all kinds of manners.[16]

Despite the uniqueness of the Maid's claims, these contemporary descriptions mirror conventional stages through which the prophet passes: unheard of wonders are greeted by ridicule, until an initial sign (here the "revealing of secret things" [manifestando occulta]),[17] recognized by Aquinas as the prophet's talent, provides the intimation of legitimacy which leads to an ecclesiastical investigation.[18]

depuis Pharamond, jusqu'au roy Louis onzième (1570), related by Pierre Lanéry d'Arc, Le Livre d'Or de Jeanne d'Arc: Bibliographie raisonnée et analytique des ouvrages relatifs à Jeanne d'Arc. Catalogue méthodique . . . depuis le XVe siècle jusqu'à nos jours (Paris, 1887), p. 68: "Some say that Joan was the w[hore] . . . of Jean, Bastard of Orléans; others say of the Lord of Baudricourt, and others of Pothon [de Xaintrailles]."

[14] P. Boissonnade, "Une étape capitale de la mission de Jeanne d'Arc: Le séjour de la Pucelle à Poitiers, la quadruple enquête et ses résultats (1er mars–10 avril 1429)," Revue des questions historiques, 3rd ser., 17 (1930): 25.

[15] W[ilfred] P[hilip] Barrett, ed. and trans., The Trial of Jeanne d'Arc: Translated into English from the Original Latin and French Documents with "Dramatis personae" by Pierre Champion, Coley Taylor and Ruth H. Kerr, trans. (New York, 1932), p. 62. Quicherat, Procès 1: 75 for Latin: "Interrogata qualiter rex suus adhibuit fidem dictis ejus: respondit quod ipse habebat bona intersignia, et per clerum."

[16] Léon Dorez, ed. and trans. and Germain Lefèvre-Pontalis, intro. and notes, La chronique d'Antonio Morosini: Extraits relatifs à l'histoire de France, 4 vols., Société de l'Histoire de France (Paris, 1898–1902) 3: 98–99. The Italian renders the phrase "seeing that no one put any faith in her words" as "e de lie vezudo, che ale suo parole, nonn iera da darli fede."

[17] De quadam puella in Dorothy G. Wayman, "The Chancellor and Jeanne d'Arc," Franciscan Studies 17 (1957): 300.

[18] See for instance, this pattern described in William A. Christian, Jr., Apparitions in Late

8

One scholar of this early period, Roger Little, has downplayed the genuineness of the investigation into Joan's divine mission. He questions whether any real exchange of opinions took place among Valois theologians and whether they lasted as long as the records claim. In Little's view, the sessions that did take place were political in nature rather than theological, and the examinations at Chinon and Poitiers mere rubber stamps to the dauphin's desire to endorse Joan for his own political benefit. To Little, because her first interrogators were "simply a clerical portion of the overall complement of the *Conseil*," the word "theologians" needs to be used in quotes, and he argues that we should view "Joan's initial sanction [at Chinon] as primarily a political act."[19] This, in turn, gives the later investigation at Poitiers "the appearance of a political *fait accompli*," in his term "duplicate proceedings," whose decision had already been finalized at Chinon.[20]

What can we say about the ecclesiastical examination of Joan at Chinon, its panel of judges, its rigor, and its purpose? First of all, it should not surprise us if Joan was interrogated by theologians, as Simon Charles alleged, even before she was allowed to see the king.[21] If true, this immediately makes the Chinon inquiry a two-tiered affair, enhancing its seriousness. But a more substantial investigation undeniably took place, conducted by a group of theologians who must already have been in residence in Chinon, some of whom were also ecclesiastical members of Charles's *Conseil*, as Little has stated. Yet this overlap in membership is an unremarkable fact. The earlier Armagnac *Conseil* in Paris had always contained prelates, in fact in greater numbers than when the Burgundians controlled the *Conseil*,[22] and the dauphin Charles, who merely perpetuated this tradition, naturally chose those close at hand for his first consultation.

The composition of this first ecclesiastical gathering for the preliminary religious investigation of Joan is known to us through the nullification trial testimony of the duke of Alençon, who states that he was present.[23] He

Medieval and Renaissance Spain (Princeton, N.J., 1981), pp. 194–95, although without as clear a notion of cause and effect from one stage to the next.

[19] Roger G. Little, *The Parlement of Poitiers: War, Government and Politics in France, 1418–1436* (London, 1984), p. 104.

[20] Little, *Parlement*, p. 104 and p. 103.

[21] Simon Charles made the following testimony at the nullification trial in 1456: "Hearing this, some of the King's Council said that the King ought not to put faith in this Jeanne; others said that, as she declared she was sent from God and commanded to speak to the King, the King ought at least to hear her. The King desired that she should first be examined by the Clergy and Ecclesiastics, and this was done; after many difficulties it was arranged that the King should hear her," Murray, *Jeanne d'Arc*, pp. 291–92.

[22] Valois, *Conseil*, pp. 132–37.

[23] The duke of Alençon said he listened to the inquiry in person, but no other evidence limits the Chinon examination to a single meeting. In fact, the probing of her spiritual nature was, as should be the case, an ongoing process, which seemed to flow almost seamlessly from Chinon to Poitiers.

identifies as those selected: the king's confessor, Gérard Machet; the future bishop of Meaux, Pierre de Versailles; the University of Paris theologian, Jourdain Morin; the bishop of Poitiers, Hugues de Combarel; the bishops of Senlis and Magdelone, most likely Jean Raffanel and Robert de Rouvres, respectively; and "several others" (*plures alii*).[24]

It is true that if ever a political intrigue lay behind the adoption of Joan of Arc's mission, in which the theologians were either instigators or instruments, it would have had to start here. The separation of France into two factions, crystallized by the murders of the duke Louis of Orléans and John the Fearless, duke of Burgundy, had colored France's whole sense of religion. And these theologians, exiles whose fate was bound up with the dauphin's, and followers of the highly politicized theologian, Jean Gerson, had the power, and perhaps the motive, to simply endorse whatever decision was most advantageous for France. Yet to take the following brief narrative, which presents the historical context in which a political conspiracy might grow, as evidence that Joan's approval belongs to the arena of political intrigue, represents an overly simplified approach to a truly complex question. It does not take into account what we can learn of the theologians themselves, particularly the one best known to us, Pierre de Versailles, or of the moral requirements by which a theologian qualified to participate in the process of *discretio spirituum* was bound.

On 29 May 1418, when Tanneguy du Châtel whisked the dauphin, in his dressing gown, from his Parisian bedchambers into the Bastille St. Antoine for safety, as the Burgundians bore down on him,[25] the dauphinist party was in effect relinquishing both its power and the city of Paris to the Burgundians. Fleeing for their lives with the dauphin were four of the masters of theology who were to judge Joan at Chinon – Gérard Machet, Pierre de Versailles, Jourdain Morin, and the future bishop of Poitiers, Jean Raffanel – as well as two others later in attendance at the Poitiers hearings – Jean Lambert and Guillaume Aimeri.[26]

Earlier, at the council of Constance in 1415, Versailles and Morin had been resolute supporters of Gerson, being identified with all his views. But Gerson, to the anger of many, had turned both the Council of the Faith of Paris

---

[24] Duparc, *Procès* 1: 381–82. Some think that Simon Bonnet is referred to here as bishop of Senlis but Raffanel, a close colleague of the others, seems more likely. Whereas Guillaume Le Roy (witness Robert Alleman; Duparc, *Procès* 5: 185) is thought to have been the bishop of Magdelone, Henri Vicomte du Motey, *Jeanne d'Arc à Chinon et Robert de Rouvres* (Paris, 1927) makes a good case that Alençon is referring to Rouvres, bishop of Magdelone at the time of his death.

[25] Clément de Fauquembergue, *Journal de Clément de Fauquembergue, greffier du Parlement de Paris, 1417–1435*, Alexandre Tuetey and Henri Lacaille, eds., 3 vols., Société de l'Histoire de France (Paris, 1903–1915) 1: 126–27. See Richard Vaughan, *John the Fearless: The Growth of Burgundian Power* (London, 1966; repr. 1979), p. 223.

[26] Henri Denifle and Emile Chatelain, *Chartularium Universitatis Parisiensis*, 4 vols. (Paris, 1889–97) 4: 343–44.

(1413), in which Machet, Versailles, and Morin had also participated, and the council of Constance, into political battlegrounds, overrunning more important considerations, like the schism, with a theologico-political debate over Jean Petit's justification of tyrannicide, the objective of which was to force responsibility for the 1407 murder of duke Louis of Orléans on John the Fearless.[27] The players were taking sides in a drama which had yet to include Joan of Arc, but already opposite Gerson in the Jean Petit case were Joan's future prosecutors, Pierre Cauchon, Jean Beaupère, Erard Emengard, Jean de Chatillon, Pierre Miget, Guillaume le Boucher, and the future grand inquisitor of France, Jean Graverent.[28]

Gerson, who had not dared return to Paris after the council of Constance because of the Burgundian takeover, lost his chancellorship of the university (although he continued to insist on the title until the time of his death), suffered the death of friends and colleagues (including close associate Jean Gentien) in the massacres following the Burgundian takeover of Paris, and endured the humiliation of Charles VI's disavowal of all that he, Morin, and Versailles, had said about the Jean Petit affair in the king's name.[29] In all that Gerson had lost, the theologians loyal to the dauphin shared. But besides their own losses, the churchmen in Chinon were surrounded by other exiles, perhaps more vengeful, who also tallied losses in human, professional, and territorial terms. Raoul de Gaucourt, then captain of Chinon, a post received from the dauphin in compensation for his losses, had suffered the assassination of his father in Rouen, and had himself been imprisoned by Henry V for ten years after the battle of Harfleur in 1415. Jean, duke of Alençon, whose great-grandfather was killed at Crécy, had at the age of eight lost his father at Agincourt, been wounded, imprisoned, and crushed financially by a ransom payment owed to his captors. Others, many of whom were displaced Normans, had similar histories, whether they were nobles like Jehan le Sec, whose losses paralleled those of Alençon,[30] or common citizens who took advantage of the terms of surrender to the English and left "with the shirts on their backs."[31] The Norman poet Robert Blondel expressed the collective indignation when he remonstrated against English "cowherds" occupying noble baronies and "wicked vagabonds"

27 As Alfred Coville observes, in *Jean Petit: La question du tyrannicide au commencement du XVe siècle* (Paris, 1932), p. 509: "At Constance, the Jean Petit affair occupied a disproportionate place if one thinks that the council had to reestablish unity in the church, restore the papacy, judge the heresies . . . of Jean Huss, Jerome of Prague, and Wycliffe, in sum, reform the church."
28 Coville, *Jean Petit*, p. 452. Coville, however, lists Jean de Chatillon as siding with Jean Gerson, p. 497.
29 Coville, *Jean Petit*, p. 559.
30 Le Sec said that he had exposed himself to "great perils," several times been imprisoned and later released after "excessive ransoms," and had seen three brothers die. See Roger Jouet, *Et la Normandie devint française* (Paris, 1983), p. 160.
31 Jouet, *Normandie*, p. 161.

11

[*méchants truands*] "now . . . fat and made over as swine, living deliciously in idleness in our own domains."[32]

But just as Gerson, tenacious and pugnacious in equal parts about the Jean Petit affair, could in those very years write the reasoned and judicious *De probatione spirituum* on St. Bridget of Sweden, in which he reminded theologians of their heavy responsibility relating to the charism of discretion, so too could the theologians at Chinon, despite political conditions, accept that responsibility, and conduct an unprejudiced examination of Joan. Versailles and Morin, devoted Gersonians who had worked in synchrony with the chancellor at the council of Constance, where Gerson's discernment treatise, *De probatione spirituum*, had been written in 1415, and Machet, who was in touch with his colleagues in Constance from Paris, were surely well-versed in the issues of faith relating to discernment. Moreover, they were undoubtedly acquainted with this landmark treatise, which along with Pierre d'Ailly's earlier *De falsis prophetis*, were important milestones in the codification of the rules of *discretio spirituum*.[33] To fail to take seriously the power invested in them to discern the word of God would have shown scorn of the constructive value of prophecy, and led to considerable conflict of conscience.

A closer view, through the study of the life of one Chinon theologian, will show how complex the interplay of politics and religion could be, and yet how ultimately the king's church advisers were moral, serious, and ethical men. For this we can turn to Alfred Coville's penetrating study of one, Pierre de Versailles, in which we also obtain glimpses of Gérard Machet and the staunch royalist Jean Jouvenel.[34] At the outset it becomes clear that Pierre de Versailles, the only prelate among Joan's first examiners for whom we have an autobiography, however brief, is not an easy man to understand. In theory, he was not above any intrigue that would further the interests of his party, even at the expense of what we would call his patriotism. In 1411 he had participated in two missions to England, initiated by the Armagnacs (in imitation, however, of a similar move made by the Burgundians), to solicit military aid from the king of France's mortal enemies for the purpose of fighting the Burgundians, promising England full rights to Aquitania and its dependencies in return.[35] But, from what we can learn about his person, it does not appear that later in his life, in his role as interrogator of the Maid, Versailles considered compromising his religious professionalism for political expediency. At the time of his evaluation of Joan, eighteen years

---

[32] Jouet, *Normandie*, pp. 173–74.

[33] Article by François Vandenbroucke, "Discernement des esprits, III. Au Moyen Age," in *Dictionnaire de spiritualité ascétique et mystique, doctrine et histoire*, Marcel Viller et al., eds., 15 vols. (Paris, 1937–67) 3: 1263.

[34] Alfred Coville, "Pierre de Versailles (1380?–1446)," *Bibliothèque de l'Ecole des Chartes* 93 (1932): 208–66.

[35] Coville, "Versailles," pp. 210–12.

later, he was a man of about fifty years, who had spent fully half his life studying theology, who, as a participant at the council of Constance, was well-versed in the heresy cases of John Huss and Jerome of Prague, and who likely had followed the controversies surrounding the recanonization of St. Bridget of Sweden, in whose case Gerson had been so closely involved. Unable to comprehend Jean Petit's defense of tyrannicide for its obvious violations of the Decalogue, his views at Constance were clear: prelates, doctors, and judges were not exempt from the standards of conduct which all Catholics, through the use of reason, could understand the need to uphold as requirements of the faith.[36] By the time of the Council of Basel, respect for his experience and, one presumes, for his reputation of integrity, caused Versailles to be designated to mount the investigation of the *De Christo integro* by Augustine of Rome for the commission on the faith at Basel.[37]

In fact, the task facing Versailles and his colleagues at Chinon was relatively simple, and at this point it would not have required a high-ranking theologian. The four university men, Machet, Versailles, Morin, and Raffanel, and their colleagues, were not being asked to conduct a formal probe of the Maid's spirit, only to provide basic confirmation of her Catholic practices, morals and purity. For this Versailles was more than qualified. He was a religious conservative who believed firmly that divine providence lay behind all human events, who returned to the Bible whenever in search of the ultimate authority, and who was impatient with those who saw shades of gray in moral cases that to him were either black or white.[38]

To Versailles, the pervasive political ills that all dauphinists felt were largely attributable to moral failures. In a revealing letter to Jean Jouvenel, a man he considered a kindred soul for their mutual "fighting spirit, zeal for the faith, and respect for law," Versailles attributed the imminent destruction of the kingdom [*imminente ejus destructione*] to three causes, oddly unbalanced, but indicative of his deep frustration: blasphemy (common swearing), tyranny, and adultery – a curious and limited selection, but a reflection of his rigid, moralistic approach to politics. Before the arrival of Joan of Arc, he had placed his faith for the realm in the young dauphin Charles, much as he must have later placed it in Joan, and perhaps partly for the same reasons. In reply to Jouvenel, he told him, after recalling the misfortune inflicted by God on Job, that one had to hope that "the heir to the throne, the dauphin, an adolescent of good character, with no hidden vices, still innocent, could find the necessary remedies for the salvation of the

---

[36] Coville, "Versailles," p. 215.
[37] Coville, "Versailles," pp. 231–32.
[38] See, for instance, his outrage that his fellow prelates, doctors, and judges at Constance made excuses for the duke of Burgundy, when the principles involved were as simple as "thou shall not kill or perjure yourself" (*non occides, non perjurabis*), Coville, "Versailles," p. 215.

kingdom."[39] Who is to say that upon meeting Joan, Versailles did not shift his expectation to the young woman who, fitting the same general moral description, offered in addition concrete promises that would revive the spirit of sacred dynasticism which, since the time of St. Jerome, had proclaimed France alone free of heresy and justified the monarch's title of "most Christian" (*très chrétien*)?[40]

Finally, an incident described at the nullification trial by Seguin Seguin, if true, gives a measure of the simplicity, sincerity, and credulousness of Versailles's faith. Versailles told how a few of Charles's men, learning of the arrival of Joan, had set out to rob her *en route*, but when they tried to execute their plan, they suddenly found themselves unable to advance, their feet nailed to the ground.[41] Many people believed in similar marvels circulating about Joan, but this episode shows the faith inspired by hopefulness of an experienced theologian. Gerson had expressed the opinion in *De probatione* that no one was capable of discerning spirits from his mere knowledge of Scripture alone. The individual needed to have personal experience with the emotions of the soul. "Unless he has flown to the heights of heaven," wrote Gerson, "then has fallen to the bottom of the abyss and has seen in the depths the marvels of God," he would be incapable of performing the task of discernment.[42] The rhetoric of Gerson aside, Pierre de Versailles appears to have held the proper credentials.

But lest the happy expectation of youth and innocence, and the artful blending of God's will with the good of the kingdom, create blind spots for those, including Versailles and Charles himself, who might have fallen under the spell of Joan's person, a further safeguard was set in place. Ecclesiastical opinions from outside the court were solicited by Jean Girard and Pierre l'Hermite, the king's counselors, from the prominent archbishop of Embrun, Jacques Gelu, who had participated in the council of Constance. Also, in all likelihood, at this time, another treatise was solicited, from an anonymous prelate who produced *De quadam puella*. It is customary, but not necessarily correct, to identify him as the Paris-educated Dutchman, Henry of Gorckum. The extent and the nature of the dauphin's parallel efforts to

---

[39] Coville, "Versailles," p. 220. For the Latin text see *Thesaurus novus anecdotorum*, Edmund Martène and Ursin Durand, eds., 5 vols. (Paris, 1717) 1: 1723–37.

[40] Saint Jerome: "Sola Gallia monstra non habuit," *Contra Vigilantium* I, *Patrologia Latina* 23, col. 339. See Dario Cecchetti, "Un'egloga inedita di Nicolas de Clamanges," in *Miscellanea di studi e ricerchi sul Quattrocento francese*, Franco Simone, ed. (Turin, 1967), pp. 54–56.

[41] Pernoud, *Retrial*, p. 100; Duparc, *Procès* 1: 471: "Non potuerant se movere a loco in quo erant."

[42] Jean Gerson, *De probatione spirituum*, in Paschal Boland, *The Concept of* Discretio Spirituum *in Jean Gerson's* De Probatione Spirituum *and* De Distinctione Verarum Visionum A Falsis, The Catholic University of America: Studies in Sacred Theology (2nd ser., 112) (Washington, D.C., 1959), p. 29.

gain outside opinions, by experts knowledgeable in the process of *discretio spirituum*, can be elucidated by examining first Gelu's correspondence and then the treatise DQP.

As might have been predicted, opinion of the Maid was significantly more guarded from a distance, and perhaps more objective than the terse, yet clearly exhilarated, preliminary report coming from Girard and l'Hermite in Chinon. It is possible to deduce the contents of their report, which we could loosely refer to as the Chinon conclusions, from our knowledge of the contents of Jean Girard's letter to Gelu, and also from the summary of facts about Joan, ostensibly the Girard l'Hermite information, forwarded to the author of DQP, with which he opens his treatise. But unlike Gelu, who only knows the Maid through the reports of the dauphin's two counselors, the author of DQP may draw some information from hearsay. However, most of his knowledge seems ascribable to specific sources, people "worthy of faith" on whom he depends to describe a person he has never met, who are most apt to be Girard and l'Hermite, or similar counselors in the dauphin's confidence at Chinon. After all, not many people would have been dispensing information to prelates on the Maid before she had given even initial satisfaction about her supernatural inspiration. And although DQP gives no positive proof of being solicited or procured by the dauphin, the assumption is altogether reasonable, since the author has apparently been asked to enumerate all the scriptural issues that would bear on a final judgment of Joan's mission, a decision whose responsibility lay with the dauphin Charles. Moreover, coming to exactly the same conclusion as Gelu, the author of DQP makes a strong recommendation in his treatise for a more extensive investigation (on the level of what would subsequently occur at Poitiers), a recommendation which could only be acted upon by the dauphin, and which therefore seems to be directed at him. The conclusion that DQP evolved from an early royal request from Chinon for outside theological consultation, parallel to the request we know was made of Gelu, seems the most compelling conclusion about the genesis of this treatise in the absence of any contextual information to guide us further. But whereas Gelu confines himself at this early stage to the advice of letters, and only later composes a theological treatise for the king, the author of DQP hastily composes a treatise at once, grounded in the principles of *discretio spirituum*, intended, to all appearances, as a preliminary guide for the Valois monarch in probing the Maid's case.

The archbishop, Jacques Gelu, whose correspondence is the first written judgment of Joan for which we have evidence, unfortunately comes down to us not in the original correspondence with Jean Girard and Pierre l'Hermite, but preserved in nonetheless authoritative seventeenth-century French

summaries by Marcellin Fornier, offering a wealth of fascinating information, which, to my knowledge, has never been described in English.[43]

The first letter to the archbishop of Embrun is written by the royal
counselor, Jean Girard, "on the command of the king, in order to have his
opinion."[44] Nothing could have been more logical than to request Gelu's
opinion. The archbishop had faithfully served the Armagnac party, and then
the dauphin, serving as counsel (*magistrum requestarum*) first to Louis, duke
of Orléans, and in 1410, three years after the duke's assassination, in the same
capacity to the dauphin.[45] He served on the king's council in 1414, where he
would have known some of the supporters and advisers residing in Chinon
with Charles in 1429, and was elected, also in 1414, "in my absence, without
my knowledge," to become director of Charles's finances as a reluctant
Général des Finances. A graduate of the universities of Paris and Orléans,
Gelu's training was in jurisprudence, but this did not deter the cardinals
convened at the council of Constance in 1414 from electing him bishop of
Tours, an occurrence he saw as an act of providence.

Gelu had more reason than the assassination of his early employer, Louis
d'Orléans, to experience malevolence toward the Burgundians. As a papal
legate, charged with a mission to work toward "internal and external peace,"
Gelu was in Paris at the time of the dauphin's flight on 29 May 1418.
Remaining in Paris in an attempt to complete his mission, he was there on
June 12, when the throats of many of Charles's supporters were cut, but had
the good fortune to flee on June 16 "escaping from the hands of impious
men."[46] Gelu was a solemn and pious man, whose high character was
validated by the signal honor of being selected, as a representative of the
French nation, to participate in the cardinals' conclave at the council of
Constance for the election of cardinal Oddo Colonna as pope Martin V.
Fiercely committed to the responsibility with which he was entrusted at
Constance, in a manner that would have made Charles confident of his
integrity regarding an opinion on Joan, Gelu's vote could not be won until he

---

[43] The summaries, written between 1626–43 by Marcellin Fornier, are preserved in
Histoire générale des Alpes-Maritimes et Cottiennes, 3 vols. (Paris, 1890–92) 2: 312 ff.
Few scholars mention this correspondence. See, however, Colonel Ferdinand de
Liocourt, *La mission de Jeanne d'Arc* (Paris, 1981) 2: 50, and Régine Pernoud and
Marie-Véronique Clin, *Jeanne d'Arc* (Paris, 1986), pp. 305–307. Jeremy duQuesnay
Adams has translated and revised the Pernoud and Clin title as *Joan of Arc: Her Story*
(New York, 1998).

[44] Fornier, *Histoire*, p. 314. A second request of a similar nature, by the counselor Pierre
l'Hermite, is not summarized.

[45] All biographical information comes from Georges Goyau, "Jacques Gelu: Ses
interventions pour Jeanne d'Arc," *Revue des questions historiques* 117 (1932): 302–20
or Auguste Dorange, "Vie de Mgr. Gelu, archevêque de Tours au XVe siècle, écrite par
lui-même, et publiée d'après un manuscrit de la Bibliothèque municipale," *Bulletin de
la Société archéologique de Touraine* 3 (1875): 267–80 which contains Gelu's short Latin
autobiography and a French translation.

[46] Dorange, "Vie," p. 272.

had completely satisfied himself about Colonna's background, perhaps himself insisting on the probe made of the candidate's background. "Since he was not well enough known to me," wrote Gelu, "I was the last, with a few others, to vote for him, after an inquiry into his life" (*post inquisitionem vitae suae*).[47] Somewhat older than Machet, Versailles, and Morin, and far removed from the milieu of the reconstituted University of Paris in Chinon and Poitiers, Gelu represented a chance through consultation for the dauphin to have a respected but entirely independent opinion.

According to Marcellin Fornier's summaries, the correspondence with Gelu proceeds in the following manner:

> Girard offers ample declaration of the wonder [*prodige*] which presented itself as Joan, maiden [*pucelle*], from the region of Vaucouleurs, raised among sheep, age 16, whom certain men [*gentilshommes*] had introduced to the king, who was reduced to the final phases of [all] the misfortune that he could anticipate. . . . This girl gave predictions [*presages*] and prophecies which were very advantageous to the kingdom. . . . Theologians, and three professors, independently examined her and heard her answers on aspects of the faith, and on the subject of the sacraments, and about [her] habits, [which answers were] so pertinent that men were only able to judge her taking into account divine power and the marvel emanating from the hand of God. All things considered, she was devout, sober, temperate, chaste, and customarily confessed and took communion once a week.[48]

Girard concludes by offering as precedents for her mission the biblical examples of Deborah and Judith, and also the sibyls.

The recourse to Deborah as exemplum is perhaps the most innovative aspect of this report, although the comparison remains undeveloped, since previous tracts on the discernment of spirits by Jean Gerson naturally did not anticipate the need for guidelines for self-proclaimed prophets who were also female warriors. No mention, however, is made as yet of Joan's bearing arms or of her male dress. Nor does he allude to her saints or her voices, or even, interestingly, to her claim to be sent by God. The question posed is only whether she deserves to be believed as a prophet.

The circumstances described support a very early date for Girard's letter, presumably sent from Chinon, yet even by then a careful theological examination (here described as the independent examination by theologians and three professors), for which we have corroboration in the duke of Alençon's nullification trial testimony, had already taken place, and an outside consultation was in the making. Given that Joan's prophecies were politically "very advantageous to the kingdom," Girard may well have hoped for Gelu's endorsement. However, by soliciting a theologian's opinion, the

---

[47] Dorange, "Vie," p. 272.
[48] Fornier, *Histoire*, pp. 313–14.

political decision became subservient to the theological one. Thus we need not read Charles's "command" for Gelu's opinion as proof that the dauphin's motive was political, but instead, that *despite* the potential for political benefit, the king knew not to make the decision without soliciting theological opinion.

The second letter that Fornier summarizes – Gelu's reply to Girard and Pierre l'Hermite – is cautious and mistrustful. In this, it reflects the same kind of circumspection regarding self-proclaimed prophets for which Gerson was known and which he expressed about St. Bridget at the council of Constance in *De probatione spirituum.* "What would be more disgraceful or incongruous for this Sacred Council," he had written, "than to declare that false, imaginary, or foolish visions are true and genuine revelations?"[49] Writing at a time when the heresies of John Huss and Jerome of Prague were fresh memories,[50] Gelu reports that "one must not readily [*aisement*] and lightly [*de leger*] be impressed [*s'arreter*] by the words of the Maid."[51] He asks for an official probe of Joan's background, particularly because he is reluctant to credit the words of a peasant girl, whose solitary life and fragile disposition make her "so susceptible to illusions."[52] It was merely sound policy to be suspicious of anyone making extravagant claims, but as Gerson had stated in *De probatione,* this was particularly true "of the young, and of women [*adolescentibus et foeminis*], whose enthusiasm is extravagant, eager, changeable, uninhibited, and therefore not to be considered trustworthy."[53] Gelu goes on to say that the king should not "make himself ridiculous in the

---

[49] Jean Gerson, *De distinctione verarum visionum a falsis,* in Boland, *Concept,* p. 28.
[50] John Huss and Jerome of Prague were condemned at Constance and subsequently burned at the stake.
[51] Fornier, *Histoire,* p. 314. Gerson, *De distinctione,* Boland, *Concept,* pp. 80–81, describes those too ready to believe, in terms worthy of Jeromian satire: "On the other hand, I do not deny that there are some who fall into the opposite error: who consider superstitions, and even the meaningless and illusory actions and dreams of delirious people, as well as the fantastic thought of the ill and the neurotic, to be revelations. Knowing that these latter are ready to believe anything, while the others are far too incorrigible and perverse, I am certain that what is written in Ovid is true, 'You will be safest in following a middle course.' " For Latin, see P. Glorieux, *Oeuvres complètes [de] Jean Gerson,* 10 vols. (Paris, 1960–73) 3: 39: "Alii sunt, nec nego, qui ex adverso in oppositum ruunt vitium; qui superstitiosa etiam et vana et illusoria delirorum hominum facta et somnia, necnon aegrotantium vel melancholicorum portentuosas cogitationes revelationibus ascribunt. Istis leve nimis cor ad credendum aliis, [etc.]" See on the subject of Jerome's satire, David S. Wiesen, *St. Jerome as a Satirist: A Study in Christian Latin Thought and Letters,* Cornell Studies in Classical Philology, 34 (Ithaca, N.Y., 1964).
[52] It appears that Gelu judges the female sex itself to be "fragile" because he uses the same term to describe Isabeau de Bavière in a letter to Henry V.
[53] Boland, *Concept,* p. 30; Glorieux, *Oeuvres* 9: 180: "Quaeritur ergo si persona sit novitia in zelo Dei, quia novitius fervor cito fallitur si regente caruerit; praesertim in adolescentibus et foeminis, quarum est ardor nimius, avidus, varius, effrenis, ideoque suspectus."

eyes of foreign nations, the French having quite a reputation for the ease with which their nature leads them to be duped."[54] To l'Hermite, Gelu reveals his deep faith in providence, recommending that the king fast and engage in acts of piety so as to be enlightened by God, and kept from error.[55] In Gelu's eyes, France, the afflicted party, may merit divine favor because the English violate "divine, natural, canon, civil, human, and moral" law. But such justification notwithstanding, in Gelu's opinion the situation still "renders this girl suspect to the king."[56]

Gelu's insistence that Joan requires further examination looks forward to the Poitiers investigation. Did this very letter in fact – seemingly a more reasonable precipitating action than a secret told by Joan to the dauphin – initiate the gathering of the commission at Poitiers? Assuming that Gelu's reply to Girard, in which he calls for further examination of Joan, allows us to date his letter as pre-Poitiers,[57] the questioning Girard describes as having already taken place confirms the testimony of those at the nullification trial who said that at Chinon testing took place by theologians, specifically on the question of Joan's faith.[58]

Gelu's next letter is written directly to the king and queen. Even in summary, this letter is a remarkable revelation of Gelu's mind and the contemporary mentality of suspicion. To the royal couple Gelu reiterates the

---

[54] Fornier, *Histoire*, p. 314. DMV seems to echo this sentiment when it states: "What a shame, indeed, if fighting under the leadership of a young woman [*muliercula*], they had been vanquished by such audacious enemies! What a derision on behalf of all those who would have heard about such an event," H. G. Francq, "Jean Gerson's Theological Treatise and Other Memoirs in Defence of Joan of Arc," *Revue de l'Université d'Ottawa* 41 (1971): 62. (See Appendix IV.)

[55] Gerson acknowledges in *De distinctione* that sometimes prophecies do not come true and this necessitates a second revelation, Boland, *Concept*, p. 95: "This is what I meant when I first said that God either disproves or contradicts false revelations and miracles, or more clearly manifests what is in His mind"; Glorieux, *Oeuvres* 3: 47: "Et hoc est quod prius appellavi Deum reclamare vel contradicere, vel de suo intellectu salubriter informare."

[56] Fornier, *Histoire*, p. 314.

[57] Pernoud and Clin, *Jeanne d'Arc*, p. 305, state that when Girard wrote, Joan had already been examined "at Poitiers." What then do we make of Gelu's request for further investigation, if Poitiers had already taken place?

[58] The resemblance of Girard's list of Joan's virtues ("she was devout, sober, temperate," etc.) to that in the *Poitiers Conclusions* ("in her is found no evil, only goodness, humility, virginity, devotion," etc.), might imply that Girard wrote after Poitiers merely reiterating that document's list of virtues. But lists of virtues merely demonstrate compliance with Gerson's admonition in *De probatione* "to investigate the personality of the individual, his education, habits, likes, associates," Boland, *Concept*, pp. 30–31. Nor should the verbal resemblance to the *Conclusions* of Gelu's warning to Girard and l'Hermite against believing too readily or lightly – "tantôt" and "legièrement" compared to "aisément" and "de leger" – be thought of as influenced by, rather than preceding the *Conclusions*. On the contrary, Gelu's call for investigation would logically precede the investigation; thus the echoing language of the *Conclusions* seems designed to show that Gelu's misgivings have been addressed and answered.

advice of his other letters of the need to test Joan thoroughly and for Charles to predispose himself to divine guidance through acts of piety. Fornier describes vividly (perhaps in Gelu's own words) how Joan must be plumbed or sounded (*sonder*) and examined (*recognoître*).[59] Then, using a curious exemplum, Gelu broaches the dangers of placing one's faith in a woman. He recounts the story of a queen "nourished in poisons" and "sent to the king," who counted on winning the emperor Alexander's love in order to kill him,[60] but this woman, whom Gelu calls a "real bottle of poisons," was ultimately thwarted and Alexander spared.[61] Gelu is so worried that Joan might harbor similar motives that he recommends that Charles "not speak with her alone at all and that she not come too close to him." Her spirit, he instructs, must be laid bare (*esplucher son esprit*) to pious and learned men (*personnes sçavantes et pieuses*), based on her words (*sa conversation*), her faith (*sa croyance*) and the novel ideas (*les nouveautez*) she advances. Significantly, however, he includes a note of optimism, acknowledging that "it is as easy for God, with few soldiers as much as with many, and by the exploits and arms of girls and women, as much as with those of men, to bring about victories," heralding two arguments that will appear in the debate at Poitiers.[62]

Tacitly acknowledging Girard's examples of Deborah and Judith by his reference to "the exploits and arms ["bras" not "armes"] of girls and women," Gelu admits that God can conquer by a woman. But not much trust is advanced for the Maid for whom three circumstances relating to her background and gender continue to make her suspect. First, she is from the region of Lorraine, a difficulty that Gelu apparently associates not with its reputation for tolerating witchcraft, but only with the potential for treason, given the region's proximity to the Burgundian border. Second, as a shepherdess, Joan can easily be duped (*aisée à estre séduite*). Finally, as a girl (*fille*), "it is as little suited to her to bear arms and lead captains as it is for her to preach, render justice and plead legal cases."[63] Here, at last, it is

---

[59] Fornier, *Histoire*, p. 315. This agrees with Gerson's *De distinctione*, Boland, *Concept*, p. 106: "For in the beginning the evil spirit often reveals many truths. Then, after a lapse of time when he has won men's confidence, he slyly stoops to deception"; Glorieux, *Oeuvres* 3: 56.

[60] The story is closer to that of Judith and Holofernes than Joan of Arc.

[61] Fornier, *Histoire*, p. 315.

[62] Fornier, *Histoire*, p. 316.

[63] Fornier, *Histoire*, p. 315: "Elle estoit fille, à qui il appartenoit aussi peu de manier les armes et conduire les capitaines, qu'à prescher, qu'à rendre justice et advocacer." Gelu perhaps draws on Justinian's *Digest* here as the Parisian cleric does. See Noël Valois, "Un nouveau témoignage sur Jeanne d'Arc: Réponse d'un clerc parisien à l'apologie de la Pucelle par Gerson (1429)," *Annuaire-Bulletin de la Société de l'Histoire de France*, Seconde Partie, Documents et notices historiques 43 (1906), reprinted by Théophile Cochard in *Bulletin de la Société archéologique et historique de l'Orléanais*, 14, no. 187 (1907): 526, n. 8. But the Bible makes similar proscriptions on roles for women.

revealed that there is a military dimension to this affair, still subordinate, however, to the discussion of other points of religious heterodoxy.

Although there had always been heresies, something in Joan of Arc's times suggested that the current age was worse than other periods of history. In *De probatione* Gerson worried about false visionaries "because of the many illusions which I know have occurred in our age, and even in this last century."[64] As one scholar expresses it, Gerson experienced anxiety over "the extent to which false mysticism was ravaging the Church."[65] And Gelu, whose concern with the testing of self-proclaimed prophets may have been heightened by the vigorous inquisitorial proceedings in his own Dauphiné region, prompting his fears that she might be "the lure [or bait], sent by some new sect" (*le leurre, envoyée de quelque nouvelle secte*).[66] Indeed, more ample documentation than usual exists in the Dauphiné region for legal proceedings against sorcery, witchcraft, and heresy.[67]

The medieval fear that Joan was a malignant force in league with the devil is sometimes unconsciously minimized by modern observers, many of whom overemphasize political motives at the expense of religious or quasi-religious ones. But this fear was real enough to make Gelu admonish the king and queen to proceed slowly, despite his recognition of France's desperate need and just cause. As for the nature of evil, Gelu shows a well-developed belief, which at first may seem entirely idiosyncratic. He believes that deception is only skin deep and that eventually evil works its way to the surface; in other words, truth eventually erupts from beneath the cloak of deceit. As Gelu explains:

> Things can scarcely continue without one's seeing some eruption [*esclat*], because cosmetics [*fard*] and things feigned [*choses faintes*] will not withstand the test of time. Let truth come out of its hiding places [*cachots*] and, just as internal maladies push themselves to the outside, [this] dissimulated evil must make some visible eruption.[68]

Gerson's treatise of 1401, *De distinctione verarum visionum a falsis*, had already described this feature of evil, in different terms, in the context of the devil

---

[64] Gerson, *De distinctione*, Glorieux, *Oeuvres* 3: 37–38, "Et in hanc quaestionem sciens incidi propter illusiones plurimas quas nostro tempore cognovi contigisse; quas etiam in hoc senio saeculi, in hac hora novissima."

[65] Boland, *Concept*, p. 113.

[66] Fornier, *Histoire*, p. 315. For those who argue that Anatole France invented the idea of a religious plot, here is evidence to place the origin of the idea much earlier.

[67] Jean Marx, *L'Inquisition en Dauphiné* (Paris, 1914) and J. Chevalier, *Mémoire historique sur les hérésies en Dauphiné avant le XVIe siècle* (Valence, 1890); see also, Gabriel Audisio, *Les "Vaudois": Naissance, vie et mort d'une dissidence (XIIme–XVIme siècles)* (Turin, 1989), who discusses MS 265, 266 "Vaudois du diocèse d'Embrun."

[68] Fornier, *Histoire*, pp. 315–16: "Que l'on ne pouvoit guères demeurer d'en voir quelque esclat, pour ce que le fard et toutes les choses faintes ne supportent point la durée du temps. Que la vérité sort de ses cachots, et qu'il fault que, comme les maladies internes se poussent au-dehors, aussi le mal dissimulé fasse quelque éruption en vue."

announcing many truths before he eventually introduces his first deception, and although Gelu's metaphors are particularly striking, the notion of outwitting the devil by outwaiting him seems to have been commonplace.[69]

Still, Gelu is aware of an opposite danger – the risk of failing to recognize true prophets. So the king must not rebuff Joan (*la rebutte*), since doing so might cause God to foreshorten his arm.[70] In Charles's case the cruelty of the enemy may have awakened God's mercy. Furthermore, incredulity, as Gerson had previously insisted in *De distinctione*, is as much a danger as over-credulity, since divine revelation is still operative:

> From the reports of well-qualified witnesses I am aware of almost incredible things . . . [but] if we deny, ridicule, or reject everything immediately, we shall appear to weaken the authority of divine revelation, which is as authoritative now as it was then, for God does not lack the power to make a revelation.[71]

That the passage of time alone was integral to the decision-making process was a concept so fundamental to Gerson that he frequently returned to it. Writing in *De probatione* in 1415, he stated:

> The first effect may seem good, beneficial, worthy, and for the edification of others, which in fact becomes a scandal in many other ways, either because the ultimate end does not correspond to the first, or because something false and erroneous was discovered about the person which previously had been reported as a sign of holiness and piety.[72]

In 1401 Gerson had described even more specifically what this meant for the examining process: "I do not think we should make a hurried investigation merely to get a result, especially in this kind of an inquiry. Instead, we should suspend judgment until the examination is completed, unless there be clear evidence of deception, or that a lie has been perpetrated in jest."[73]

---

[69] See Gerson's *De distinctione*, in Boland, *Concept*, p. 106; Glorieux, *Oeuvres* 3: 56.

[70] Fornier, *Histoire*, p. 315: "pour ce que le bras de Dieu n'est point raccourci."

[71] Gerson, *De distinctione*, Boland, *Concept*, p. 79; Glorieux, *Oeuvres* 3: 38: "incredibilia fore scripta quae idoneis testibus referentibus agnovi. . . . Si statim negemus omnia, vel irrideamus, vel inculpemus; videbimur infirmare auctoritatem divinae revelationis quae nunc ut olim potens est; neque enim manus ejus abbreviata est ut revelare non possit."

[72] Gerson, *De probatione*, Boland, *Concept*, pp. 34–35; Glorieux, *Oeuvres* 9: 182–83: "Potest itaque finis proximus apparere bonus, salubris et devotus, ad aedificationem aliorum, qui tandem prolabetur in multiplicius scandalum, dum vel non respondebunt ultima primis, vel aliud falsum fictumque deprehendetur in personis fuisse, quod reputabatur sanctitatis devotionisque."

[73] Gerson, *De distinctione*, Boland, *Concept*, pp. 105–106; Glorieux, *Oeuvres* 3: 55–56: "Debemus, meo quidem judicio, in omnibus, tamen praecipue in ista examinatione, non praecipitare sententiam; sed usque ad plenissimam examinationem suspensum tenere judicium, maxime nisi falsitas aut fatuitas cognata falsitatis aperta sit."

So it is not surprising that in a fourth letter Gelu's uncertainty over whether or not to believe in Joan (*ou de luy croire ou non*) continues, or that he reiterates the need to "keep that young girl waiting."[74] We should remember that whereas such waiting is directly contrary to notions of political and military expediency, among theologians there was agreement that the longer Joan was delayed from her mission and, subsequently, the longer she conducted it free of any indication of evil, the surer the evidence that she was not an incarnation of evil.[75] Gelu therefore judges that it would be most inappropriate for Joan to have "a lot of access" to the king, until that time when "the nature of her life and habits [has] been well ascertained."[76] In this, his remarks look toward Poitiers, not as a formal call for convening twenty-odd prelates to probe Joan's background and test her faith, as was soon to happen, but as a clear signal that she was not yet ready to be believed.

[74] Fornier, *Histoire*, p. 317: "qu'on tienne cette jeune fille dans la suspension et l'incertitude."

[75] Gelu's explanation of how time itself was a test of Joan's mission makes Roger Little's effort to reduce the number of actual investigatory sessions that took place at Chinon and Poitiers largely irrelevant. The most important factor was the overall time of observation. Anatole France, who perceives the period of testing to have been long, considers that the ecclesiastics' insistence on a very careful, time-consuming deliberation as a means of testing Joan's true purpose, is part of the scheme: "The clerics of Poitiers in the process of examining her slowly about her habits and her faith, gave her stature." And he adds: "By the duration and solemnity of their interrogations, they attracted to Joan the curiosity, interest, and the hope of marveling people," Anatole France, *Vie de Jeanne d'Arc*, 2 vols. (Paris, 1908) 1: 40.

[76] Fornier, *Histoire*, p. 317: "jusques à ce qu'on fust bien acertainé de sa vie et de ses moeurs." This statement implies that a careful investigation of her life and morals was indeed to take place.

2

De quadam puella

A second voice breaks the silence of the Chinon period, just long enough to dampen the king's enthusiasm again with a stiff measure of theological caution, and then our sources recede into silence until Poitiers. The voice is contained in the treatise *De quadam puella* (DQP), a gathering, according to its author, of all the scriptural evidence on the Maid's case, by which one can judge whether God sent Joan as a prophet for France.

The anonymous treatise lacks a salutation, or any clue, that would identify its intended audience. The author describes his treatise as reflections intended for

> those people who will look at them so that (in this case as in future similar cases) they will be capable of making an answer by themselves [*ipse aliquid respondere valeant*] to those who would ask questions similar to these.[1]

It is as perplexing a statement of intended audience as we might expect to encounter. That the treatise is destined for theologians, however, can be gathered from the future applicability of the tract alluded to here, a signal not only of the innovation involved in the act of writing it, but also of the author's stature among theologians, as he weans his inquirers of their dependence on him for "future similar cases" (*futuri consimilis*) by writing a treatise that will serve history.

The author promises in DQP to draw out the evidence from Scripture on both sides of the case, structuring his arguments as a set of twelve points, six in favor of the Maid's case and six against. As serene about the points he adduces against Joan's mission as about those in favor of it, he appears to be writing at a very early moment in the process of evaluation, prior to the endorsement of the Maid at Poitiers, a time at which his remarks would, as yet, bear no lasting consequences, since no actual investment had been made in Joan. When he writes that "people have different opinions as to the extent to which the two parties are capable of drawing evidence from the Holy Scriptures for the defense of their views," his detachment furnishes no proof

---

[1] See Appendix I for full translation of *De quadam puella*.

24

that he is a foreign author, indifferent, or emotionally detached on that account. On the contrary, the fact that the debate in DQP is specifically over Scripture, argues that we have someone on the French side, offering a private instrument of investigation destined for a still undecided French clergy, a document that no Burgundian or Englishman ever need see.

How logical it would be to assume that the theologians to be guided by this treatise were Versailles, Machet, Morin, and their colleagues, about to convene at Poitiers for an investigation. Could this, in fact, be the voice of the chancellor, Jean Gerson, whose opinion the king would have coveted above all others? From DQP's overtly pious tone and scrupulously dispassionate approach to *discretio*, one would certainly be inclined to believe as much. The author is an authoritative scholar of Scripture who, in his apparent rush to provide guidance from the Bible to help in the evaluation of Joan, writes "from sheer memory" (*memoriter commen-dando*), but nonetheless quotes Scripture accurately, alludes to the authority of the church fathers, and in one instance refers to Aquinas on prophecy verbatim. He demonstrates that he is perfectly conversant with the biblical foundations of *discretio spirituum*, and cites hallmark passages such as 1 John 4:1 ("Believe not every spirit but try them if they be of God"),[2] 2 Corinthians 11:14 ("Satan himself disguises himself as an angel of light") and Isaiah 59:1 ("Behold, the Lord's hand is not shortened, that it cannot save"), all verses that were previously adduced by Gerson in his tracts on discernment. In fact, by the time of Joan of Arc, 1 John 4:1 was so popular among discernment tracts, that its absence might even have raised questions about an author's theological credentials.[3]

But the idea of DQP as a pre-Poitiers document, sent to Charles's theologians for guidance at their assembly, is not without problems. DQP contains, for instance, the disconcerting detail that "cities, towns and castles submit to the Dauphin," information which better fits the period after the siege of Orléans than before it. Furthermore, why are there no telltale signs of DQP in the *Poitiers Conclusions*, as there are, for instance, of Gelu's correspondence and Gerson's *De probatione* (written a full fourteen years before)? If the preponderance of evidence still suggests that DQP was written at the moment of Joan's beginnings at the dauphin's court, only slightly later than the Girard–Gelu correspondence, and well before the summer of 1429

---

[2] Wayman, "The Chancellor," DQP, p. 303, offers the following variation of 1 John 4:1: "tentandi sunt si a deo sunt." But cf. Vulgate: "Probate spiritus, si ex Deo sunt."

[3] We know that the verse was cited by Alfonso of Jaén in the *Epistola Solitarii* (1375–76), Heinrich von Langenstein's *De discretione spirituum* (c. 1383), and would soon be cited in the *Poitiers Conclusions*. For the patristic writer John Cassian (c. 360–c. 435), a revered authority on discernment, the way to prevent oneself from falling dupe to a false interpretation of Scripture lay precisely in heeding the Apostle's words in this verse. See *Collationes* 1: 20–23, described by François Dingjan, *Discretio: Les origines patristiques et monastiques de la doctrine sur la prudence chez saint Thomas d'Aquin* (Assen, 1967), p. 22.

to which most critics attempt to date it, the case for this early date of composition is not cast iron.

With so little external information known about DQP – neither author, date, audience, nor historical context – a reconstruction of the context and contribution of the treatise depends in large part on internal evidence from the text. Certain inferences, however, can be drawn by comparing the treatise to the Gelu correspondence. Both ecclesiastics have been provided with biographical information on Joan. Gelu responded with letters of warning to the king, touching intermittently on the principles of *discretio*, but mainly conveying his personal concern. In his tone was the helplessness of a prelate forced to advise at a distance, who was burdened with misgivings about Charles's judgment. He advised that Joan not be sent away, but harbored serious doubts about her. The author of DQP, on the other hand, uses his biographical material to initiate the formal process of *discretio*. He lists the facts he has received about Joan, followed by the formulation of questions a theologian would need to ask in such a case. Then he organizes (drawing "from here and there") six propositions for each of the debated opinions, to facilitate the actual deliberations. In short, his treatise is organized in three parts, the biographical narrative, the formulation of pertinent questions, and the presentation of the twelve propositions.

The author of DQP provides us with the goal of his search of Scripture at various intervals in his treatise. He sees himself "inviting the finest minds to reason more deeply" (*provocans subtiliora ingenia ad intelligentiam profundiorem*),[4] giving them the possibility of "progressing even farther towards more important developments" (*ulterius etiam procedendo ad ampliorem dilatationem*),[5] so that they may discover "what lies beneath" (*ad profundiora invenienda*).[6] The treatise, then, supplies research support for those about to conduct a deeper doctrinal review, perhaps an official tribunal. Therefore the information in the treatise does not lead to a conclusion.

Admitting no first-hand knowledge of the Maid, the author of DQP says he draws on "the report which trustworthy persons [*pluribus fide dignis*] have left for the formation of the present deliberate stands."[7] At first, his very brief narrative on Joan seems to correspond to Girard's material: a young shepherdess who uses supernatural signs, makes predictions for the kingdom, and displays a number of virtues in her person. In fact, the list of Joan's

---

[4] Wayman, "The Chancellor," DQP, p. 297. One finds similar wording in the concluding remarks of Gerson's *De probatione*: "Because of this, wiser men may more easily make a judgment about these matters;" Boland, *Concept*, p. 38; Glorieux, *Oeuvres* 9: 185: "Facilius hac occasione data, sapientiores dijudicent." Whether we are faced with a reminiscence from Gerson or a clerical commonplace is unclear.

[5] Wayman, "The Chancellor," DQP, p. 301.

[6] Wayman, "The Chancellor," DQP, p. 304.

[7] Wayman, "The Chancellor," DQP, p. 298: "juxta communis famae relationem a pluribus fide dignis."

virtues in DQP is essentially the same list as that supplied by Girard to Gelu. Where Girard refers to the Maid as "devout, sober, temperate and chaste," DQP reports similarly that she "lives in chastity, sobriety and continence" and is "devoted to God." Such affirmations of virtue, as we shall see, serve a specific function in *discretio* and are therefore widespread in the literature on Joan. But among different authors there are marked variations, and the dissimilar inventory of virtues in the nearly contemporaneous *Poitiers Conclusions*, noting her "goodness, humility, virginity, devotion, honesty, and simplicity," strengthens the idea that a single source has furnished the narratives to both Gelu and the author of DQP.

Yet very differently from Girard's report, DQP describes a Maid who is already partially engaged in a military role, with all the details of that role known, including her male clothes. It might seem that Girard had withheld from Gelu, as unseemly information, the disclosure of Joan's masculine role, since Fornier's summaries of Girard's words are silent on the matter. But Gelu's disapproval in his third letter of a maid who would "bear arms and lead captains" proves that his concentration on other points is not from ignorance of the military role Joan anticipated in Charles's army. The author of DQP, on the other hand, is prepared to confront the idea of Joan as a female warrior as an attribute of her mission, and therefore germane to the problems of *discretio*. We may still be witnessing two authors in receipt of the same source material, but viewing Joan from different perspectives.

From here on, our ability to grasp the meaning and impact of DQP must rest on the analysis of the treatise itself. For clarity, a summary of the introduction and biographical narrative, the first part of the treatise, is offered. Following that, the theological questions raised by the author will be presented, part two of the treatise, and their importance discussed. Next will follow the principal and third section of DQP, a summary of all twelve propositions, focusing specifically on the nature of their theological content. Then a discussion of the authorship of the treatise, as it relates to objections to the Maid's male dress, will complete the discussion of DQP.

After a pious dedication, the author begins with a biblical citation, drawing upon Amos 7:15 ("And the Lord took me when I followed the flock, and the Lord said to me: Go, prophesy to my people Israel"), thus setting Joan's mission in the broad perspective of Old Testament history, in which God speaks to shepherds and makes them his prophets. Carrying his analogy further, the author daringly asserts: "'People of Israel [*populus israel*],' the people of the Kingdom of France can, without impropriety, be so called,"[8] thereby equating the French with the chosen people of Israel, a point to which he will return at various intervals in his treatise,[9] and reminding the

[8] Wayman, "The Chancellor," DQP, p. 296.
[9] See, for instance, the reference to "populus ille," Wayman, "The Chancellor," DQP, p. 303.

reader that divine guidance was extended to God's elect despite their transgressions.[10] To justify such a bold comparison he refers to France's perpetual faith in God and the observance of the Christian religion.[11] Interestingly, and differently from Gelu, he never mentions the justice of France's cause against England, as if firmly excluding political questions from his concern. Following this, he summarizes all the information that has come to him through his sources, who remain unidentified.

In DQP the story of Joan is told in about twenty lines: the subject is a certain young girl (*quaedam juvencula*) who came to see the dauphin. The author does not use her name and only calls her "puella" in definition, not, as Joan preferred, as her name.[12] Her father, he continues, and at times she, too, herded sheep. She claims to be sent by God (*asserens se missam a deo*), so that through her the kingdom will be brought to obedience.[13] As supernatural signs in proof of her divine mission she "reveals secret thoughts" (*revelare occulta cordium*) and "prophesies" (*futura contingentia praevidere*).[14] "It is also reported," states the author, suddenly shifting to her military role,

that she had her head shaved like a man [*rasa capite ad modum viri*] and that when she wants to perform military feats [*volens ad actus bellicos procedere*],[15] she dresses in men's clothes, takes men's weapons [*vestibus et armis virilibus induta*],[16] and then gets on horseback; and on horseback and carrying her standard, at once she becomes marvelously active.[17]

---

[10] Although a tropological reading of the Bible made comparisons with the Old Testament commonplace, a direct correspondence between France and the chosen people perhaps first occurs in the bull *Rex glorie*, written by Pope Clement V in 1311: "The King of Glory formed different kingdoms . . . and established different governments for diverse peoples. . . . Among those, like the people of Israel [*sicut israeliticus populus*] . . . the kingdom of France, as a peculiar people chosen by the Lord [*sic regnum Francie in peculiarem populum electum a Domino*] to carry out the orders of Heaven, is distinguished by marks of special honor and grace," Joseph R. Strayer, "France: The Holy Land, the Chosen People, and the Most Christian King," in *Medieval Statecraft and the Perspectives of History: Essays by Joseph R. Strayer* (Princeton, N.J., 1971), p. 313.

[11] Wayman, "The Chancellor," DQP, p. 296.

[12] The term "la Pucelle" may have become popular only after the famous *Lettre aux Anglais* of 22 March 1429. Girard refers to Joan as "Jehanne, pucelle" but "pucelle" is a description not a name.

[13] Wayman, "The Chancellor," DQP, p. 296: "quatenus per ipsam dictum regnum ad eius obedientiam reducatur."

[14] Wayman, "The Chancellor," DQP, p. 296. This exact wording is found at 1a2ae. 111, 4 in Thomas Aquinas, *Summa theologiae*, 61 vols. (New York, 1964–81) 30: 138.

[15] I have not followed Francq's translation "when she wants to leave for war," because he assumed that DQP was written at a date, after Poitiers, in late March or early April, when Joan was already involved in fighting the war, Francq, "Gerson," p. 71.

[16] Wayman, "The Chancellor," p. 296.

[17] Wayman, "The Chancellor," p. 296.

With her own men she conducts herself as an experienced chief (*quasi peritus dux exercitus*), infusing her followers with ardor, and instilling fear and weakness in her adversaries. But when she climbs down from her horse, according to the sources, she recovers "her usual feminine manners" (*solitum habitum mulierbrem reassumens*)[18] and "becomes extremely naive, inexperienced in secular matters, like a defenseless lamb" (*fit simplicissima negotiorum saecularium quasi innocens agnus imperita*).[19] After a list of her virtues, there follows a statement of the moral reform she requires of those who decide to show her obedience: she tolerates no murder, plunder or violence against women. As a consequence of these facts, writes the author, "cities, towns and castles submit to the Dauphin, pledging themselves to remain faithful" (*propter hoc . . . civitates, oppida et castra se submittunt regio filio fidelitatem sibi promittentes*). Here ends the biographical segment of DQP.

To this narrative we owe the first direct expression of Joan's claim to be "sent from God." There are no angels or saints mentioned, no references to visions or heavenly messengers, a fact which has precise theological implications. The importance of Joan's declaration is that, through the statement that she was "a Deo," she comes to inhabit a special category of inspiration. Moving away from the way most people receive direction, which Gerson describes in *De probatione* as through the teaching of Scripture, angels, the saints, and natural reason,[20] Joan becomes someone in direct communication with God. Such a person, Gerson says, receives direction "not merely from angels, but from God Himself" (*nedum ab angelis sed a Deo*).[21] The phrases "sent from God" (*missa a Deo*) and "from God" (*a Deo*), then, which are found throughout DQP, are potent affirmations of Joan's unmediated dialogue with God. At Rouen, the judges, through their relentless questioning, which seemed to plant in Joan's speech the errors that they wished to harvest, influenced Joan to talk about her saints, their bodily presence, their

---

[18] I have chosen to use Francq's translation of feminine "manners" rather than female "dress," because the latter disagrees with all the facts we know about Joan, who maintained male dress continually from Vaucouleurs, and because DQP's biographical material emphasizes behavior more than clothing. For several who translate *habitum* as women's clothes, see Anne Llewellyn Barstow, *Joan of Arc, Heretic, Mystic, Shaman,* Studies in Women and Religion, 17 (Lewiston, N.Y., 1986), p. 135; Valerie R. Hotchkiss, *Clothes Make the Man: Female Cross Dressing in Medieval Europe* (New York, 1996), p. 54; and Susan Crane, "Clothing and Gender Definition: Joan of Arc," *Journal of Medieval and Early Modern Studies* 26, 2 (1996): 308.

[19] Wayman, "The Chancellor," p. 297.

[20] Gerson, *De probatione*, Boland, *Concept*, p. 33.

[21] Gerson, *De probatione*, Boland, *Concept*, p. 33; Glorieux, *Oeuvres* 9: 181. The judges at Rouen, either in ignorance or anger, failed to distinguish among the four kinds of inspiration, claiming in article 25 against her that by affirming that she was sent from God she *usurped* the office of angels. See Barrett, *Trial*, p. 177; Quicherat, *Procès* 1: 243: "Item, dicta Johanna, *officium angelorum usurpando*, se dixit et asseruit fuisse et esse missam ex parte Dei" (emphasis mine).

odor, and their speech,[22] but the evidence of DQP argues that, from the beginning, Joan professed a private inspiration, directly from God, a prophet's inspiration.

From the very first sentence of the biographical narrative, two obstacles to Joan's claim to prophecy present themselves. The first is her youthfulness, underscored by repeated mention in DQP of the word "young girl" (*juvencula*). Maturity, sound judgment, a strong intellect, and a firm understanding of the faith were the traits of a prophet. Gerson, in fact, as we have seen, had issued a distinct warning in *De probatione* about those "new in the service of God" (*novitia in zelo dei*), who tended to be "extravagant, eager, changeable, uninhibited, and therefore not to be considered trustworthy."[23] The second problem, a detail even more damaging in its negative implications for Joan's mission, is her status as a shepherdess. Because of its implications of low social status and, as Gelu had warned, the ease with which she could be misled, this fact was a serious impediment to her claim to the high honor of divine prophet.

At first the abject condition of a girl who is the daughter of a shepherd is made especially noticeable in the text by the juxtaposition of Joan's low origins (*pastoris cuiusdam filia*) to the high condition of Charles's royalty (*regni filium*). Promptly, however, this potential liability is transformed into an asset. Making a connection which seems obvious to us today – since the image of Joan as divine shepherdess is now a cliché – yet which is overlooked by Girard (who cites only the exempla of Deborah, Judith, and the sibyls), the author of DQP likens Joan, the shepherdess, to Amos, establishing for Joan the principle that God can elect the humble to be his prophets. The divine election of Amos, the son of simple people, occurs in circumstances directly validating those of Joan. When God sought Amos as his prophet, the herdsman replied: "I am not a prophet, nor am I the son of a prophet. . . . And the Lord took me when I followed the flock, and the Lord said to me: Go, prophesy to my people Israel."[24] Not surprisingly, the English never accept this connection between Joan and the shepherd-prophets of the Bible, which we can speculate was first set down in writing in the treatise DQP. Thus, when the English author Edward Hall writes in *The Union of the Two Illustrious Families of Lancastre and Yorke* of 1548, that it is a "dispraise," a "blotte" and a "rebuke" that France fell under the sway of "a shepherd's daughter," "a beggar's brat,"[25] he testifies to the usual prejudices, unmediated by the arguments of either DQP or the Bible.

---

[22] See Barrett, *Trial*, articles 42 and 43, pp. 197–98.

[23] Gerson, *De probatione*, Boland, *Concept*, p. 30; Glorieux, *Oeuvres* 9: 180.

[24] Amos 7:14–15: "Non sum propheta et non sum filius prophetae . . . et tulit me Dominus cum sequerer gregem et dixit ad me Dominus vade propheta ad populum meum Israhel."

[25] Edward Hall, *The Union of the Two Illustrious Families of Lancastre and Yorke* [Hall's Chronicle], Henry Ellis, ed. (London, 1548; repr. 1809), p. 157.

In DQP we find no more than a partially formulated statement of Joan's mission, a sign, no doubt, of the early date of the author's biographical material, perhaps reflecting the fact that the final definition of Joan's mission only took shape at Poitiers. Yet more specifically than Girard's simple statement that "she made prophecies advantageous for the kingdom," DQP goes further: "She affirmed that she had been sent by God so that, through her own intermediary, the said kingdom should be brought to obey her" (*per ipsam dictum regnum ad eius obedientiam reducatur*).[26] While the statement leaves ambiguous in the Latin whether the kingdom is to obey Joan or Charles (the Latin *eius* meaning both *her* and *him*), in the end there is little difference. As Pius II, the author of the *Commentaries* (post-1431), relates, showing that obedience to Joan ultimately equals obedience to Charles, Joan told the dauphin:

> I have come to you, O son of kings . . . at the command of God. He bids you follow me. If you obey, I will restore to you your throne. . . . Wherever you go the people shall obey you and the nobles of their own will shall follow your standard.[27]

Nevertheless, to understand that Joan's demand for obedience meant something more significant than merely the compliance of Charles to her military demands, we must investigate briefly an incident described in other documents. Lightbody dismisses as "an unlikely story, and an obvious piece of mediaeval war propaganda"[28] the fullest contemporary account of this incident, found in Jean Dupuy's *Collectarium*, which was written in Rome in 1429 upon hearing of the victory at Orléans.[29] According to this account, Joan demanded of an unsuspecting Charles that he divest himself of his kingdom and offer it to her as a gift. "Here is the poorest soldier in his kingdom," she reportedly declared to spectators. Then, she, in turn, took the gift of the kingdom (*donataria regni Francie*) and "relinquished it to God Almighty" (*remisit a Deo omnipotenti*).[30] Finally, obeying an order from God (*Dei jussu*), she solemnly reinvested Charles with the kingdom.

Without denying Lightbody's skepticism as to the truth of this anecdote, we must recognize that the episode gains in stature and takes on sharper

[26] Wayman, "The Chancellor," p. 296.
[27] Pius II, *Memoirs of a Renaissance Pope: Commentaries of Pius II*, an abridgment, Leona C. Gabel, ed. and Florence A. Gragg, trans. (New York, 1962), Book 6, p. 203. For a Latin and Italian edition, see *Commentarii rerum memorabilium: I commentarii / Enea Silvio Piccolomini, Papa Pio II*, Luigi Totaro, ed. and trans., 2 vols., Classici, 47 (Milan, 1984) 1: 1092.
[28] Lightbody, *Judgements*, p. 57.
[29] Léopold Delisle, "Nouveau témoignage relatif à la mission de Jeanne d'Arc," *Bibliothèque de l'Ecole des Chartes* 46 (1885): 649–68. Lightbody and Delisle refer to the *Collectarium* by the title *Breviarium historiale*.
[30] Delisle, "Nouveau témoignage," p. 652 and p. 665.

contours through the information of other testimonials. The contemporary Italian *Morosini* chronicle and the German chronicle of Windecke supply additional details to Dupuy's anecdote, which we can describe as an investiture. The reason that Charles was obliged to renounce his kingdom and offer it to God was because, as Windecke noted, "he held it from him,"[31] a gesture we can now interpret as a reminder to Charles of God's omnipotence. And since it was God who spoke through Joan, his prophet, the *Morosini* chronicle explained, Charles, as a consequence, had to conduct himself according to her will,[32] in other words, obey her.[33]

This investiture, then, deftly places authority in Joan, for although God is now reaffirming Charles as his lieutenant, and Henry VI's claim to France is thus implicitly supplanted, Joan is the sole interpreter of God's will. In theory, at least, the army captains also become subordinate to Joan's leadership, not because of any military title conferred on her, but because counsel from God supercedes any judgment from a military council.[34] Moreover, with the kingdom in the direct possession of God it is no longer subject to usurpation. Although the investiture myth is a popular mechanism with no actual correlation to *discretio spirituum*, it appears to be a parallel attempt to establish Joan as direct intermediary between God and Charles, and thus "from God" (*a Deo*). Once she is thus designated, whether through myth or the proper theological channel, the next step is obvious. As St. Bridget's confessor, Alphonso of Jaén, described it (speaking only of people examined through the process of *discretio*), once we find people to whom the designation "a Deo" should be attached: "We ought to humbly believe them and totally obey them" (*debemus humiliter illas credere et eis totaliter obedire*).[35] Taken in this light, Joan's demand for obedience in DQP may carry rather specific theological implications.

---

[31] Germain Lefèvre-Pontalis, ed. and trans., *Les sources allemandes de l'histoire de Jeanne d'Arc*, Société de l'Histoire de France [Eberhard von Windecke] (Paris, 1903), pp. 152–53.

[32] Letter of 9 July 1429, Lefèvre-Pontalis, *Sources* 3: 95.

[33] Further precisions, related years later at the nullification trial by Jean Pasquerel and Bertrand de Poulengy, can be found in Murray, *Jeanne d'Arc*, p. 283 and p. 230, respectively. For the Latin, see Duparc, *Procès* 1: 390 and 1: 305.

[34] Joan's conscious distinction between kinds of counsel is related in Jean Pasquerel's nullification testimony. According to him, a knight told Joan that the military had held counsel together, and had come to different conclusions from hers about their strategy for the next day, but Joan replied: "You have been to your Counsel, and I have been to mine; and believe me the Counsel of God will be accomplished and will succeed; yours on the contrary will perish," Murray, *Jeanne d'Arc*, p. 288. See Duparc, *Procès* 1: 394 for the play on *consilium* in the Latin.

[35] Arne Jönsson, ed., *Alphonso of Jaén: His Life and Works with Critical Editions of the* Epistola Solitarii, *the* Informaciones *and the* Epistola Serui Christi, Studia Graeca et Latina Lundensia, 1 (Lund, Sweden, 1989), p. 122. The full citation is: "Ait enim apostolus: *Probate spiritus, vtrum a Deo sint. Et si tunc in examine inuentum est, quod a Deo sint, debemus humiliter illas credere et eis totaliter obedire.*"

By our expanding the meaning of obedience in DQP through the investiture myth, DQP advances the definition of Joan's mission over Girard's version, but most of the well-known goals of her mission are still wholly absent. Importantly, DQP contains no mention of Joan's first objective, the raising of the siege of Orléans. If DQP was written prior to the Poitiers deliberations, where the advance on Orléans was approved, this would naturally explain the author's silence about Orléans. It may be hazardous to base any theory on the limited evidence of one witness, but Pius II, a generally trustworthy authority on Joan,[36] suggests that Orléans may never have been among Joan's original goals. According to Pius, her first intention was to crown Charles at Reims, and it was only when the dauphin told her she was "promising something very difficult to perform" because the city of Orléans, which lay between, was under siege by the English, that she quickly assimilated what she had just been told, and replied: "Do not talk to me of the siege of Orléans. First of all I will raise the siege."[37] In any event, failing any reference in DQP to Orléans, we have in this treatise only a rudimentary expression, even if accurate for that date, of Joan's divine mission. Rudimentary as it may be, however, it is enough to raise a number of theological issues, which form the second part of the treatise.

In part two of his treatise, the author of DQP proceeds to the formulation of the pertinent questions, based on the facts in the biographical narrative, that will aid in the determination of the origin of the Maid's revelations. The preparation of such questions is not original to our author, since anyone embarking on the task of *discretio* was required, by the nature of the task, to do as much. What these questions call to our attention, however, is that the challenge presented by Joan was not simply a choice between actions done by her or actions by God. One had to consider the various spirits, construed slightly differently from theologian to theologian, that could govern actions, and in which, as Gerson wrote "much similarity is discovered."[38] In the simplest terms, certain theologians (Cassian, John Climacus) signaled angels, demons, and our own human nature as the three spirits; others, including Gerson, speak of four: divine, angelic, diabolical, and natural or human.[39]

---

[36] Nadia Margolis, *Joan of Arc in History, Literature, and Film: A Select, Annotated Bibliography* (New York, 1990), p. 84, calls him the "most insightful, nuanced, 15c. commentator on J' (even among [the] French . . .)."

[37] Pius II, *Memoirs*, Gabel and Gragg, p. 203. As an argument through silence, we also have Jean Pasquerel's testimony that Joan reportedly predicted, on God's word, that Charles would be "consecrated and crowned at Reims," adding that God had sent her to lead him there. She did not, however, according to his report, predict the taking of Orléans. See Murray, *Jeanne d'Arc*, pp. 282–83; Duparc, *Procès* 1: 390.

[38] Gerson, *De probatione*, Boland, *Concept*, p. 37.

[39] See Gerson, *De probatione*, Boland, *Concept*, p. 37, where he lists: "the Spirit of God, the good angel, the evil spirit, and the spirit of man"; Glorieux, *Oeuvres* 9: 184: "spiritus Deus, spiritus angelus bonus, spiritus angelus malus, spiritus humanus." In DQP, the reduction of the categories to three, found also in such theologians as Pierre d'Ailly

DQP, which passes over any mention of the angelic spirit in its discussion of Joan – just as its biographical data remains silent on the subject of angels, saints, or angelic voices – considers that for Joan's case there are three spirits to consider, human, diabolical, and divine, and three tiers of judgments to be made. First, was the Maid herself of truly human nature? Second, if Joan were human, and not a ghostly spirit, were her actions human, and therefore accomplished by herself, or supernatural? As a third point, if her actions were found to be supernatural, then, and only then, would one ask whether she was sent "through the intermediary of . . . a good spirit, or . . . of an evil spirit" (*per . . . spiritum bonum, an . . . per spiritum malum*). In other words, the question of Joan's being "sent from God" could not arise unless she first proved herself "of divine origin" (*divinitus*), by showing proof of modes of knowing that, in Gerson's words, "surpass the ordinary way of obtaining knowledge."[40] Finally, as a fourth point, comes the question on everyone's lips:

> Should one really have faith in her words [*an eius verbis fiducia sit exhibenda*], approve her actions as if their origin were divine [*tamquam divinitus*], or should one consider them as fabricated and misrepresented [*an phitonica et illusoria*]?[41]

The importance of the distinctions among the different spirits articulated here was universally understood. This was not an exercise concocted by the French party, but a practice one prepared for in a school of theology. It was, in fact, part of a theologian's contribution to society. For a sense of perspective, we can turn briefly to the evidence of Joan's judges at Rouen to prove that they too comprehended the issues raised in our treatise, even if they had never read DQP and did not draw the same conclusions about the Maid as members of Charles's party. Jean Beaupère, for instance, was asked in 1452 for his opinion on Joan. Recognizing exactly how devastating his reply was for Joan (because by judging her actions human, he precluded her being sent by God), he replied:

> With regard to the apparitions mentioned in the Trial of the said Jeanne, I held, and still hold, the opinion that they rose more from natural causes [*cause naturelle*] and human intent [*invention humaine*] than from anything supernatural [*cause surnature*].[42]

and the earlier John Climacus, directly bypasses any discussion of Joan's inspiration coming through angels, which agrees with other early evidence.

[40] Gerson, *De probatione*, Boland, *Concept*, p. 31; Glorieux, *Oeuvres* 9: 181: "excedant . . . communem intelligendi modum."
[41] Wayman, "The Chancellor," p. 297.
[42] Murray, *Jeanne d'Arc*, p. 176; Quicherat, *Procès* 2: 20: "Dit que au regard des apparicions dont il fait mencion au procès de ladicte Jehanne, qu'il a eu et a plus grant conjecture que lesdictes apparicions estoient *plus de cause naturelle et intencion humaine, que de cause sur nature.*" (Emphasis mine.) Paul Doncoeur and Yvonne

Similarly, Zanon de Castiglione, bishop of Lisieux, also conversant with the requirements of *discretio*, dismissed the possibility that God had sent Joan in the judgment he wrote for bishop Cauchon at Rouen, admitting for consideration only the two negative possibilities of *discretio*: either that these were "deceptions and phantasms on the part of devils" (diabolical spirit) who, he noted, could "usurp the form of angels" or "they are lies humanly conceived" (human spirit).[43]

Three other assessors at Joan's trial, however, pointed to the crucial importance (and the extreme difficulty) of determining precise answers through *discretio* before taking any action, and balked at the bishop's violation of theological procedure at Rouen. To these men – Pierre Minier, Jean Pigache, and Richard de Grouchet – if the true origin of the spirit of Joan were not determined, neither approval of Joan nor her condemnation would be valid, since the very same actions would appear in different lights depending on the spirit from which they originated.[44] These three men fared very badly with Pierre Cauchon for their opinion, as can be judged by Cauchon's reply upon reading their judgment. According to Grouchet, Cauchon exclaimed: "So this is what you have done, is it?" (*Est hoc quod fecistis?*),[45] apparently sensing his neatly constructed trial suddenly threatened by Catholic orthodoxy.

The framework for a deep investigation of the spirit that motivated Joan, which the three assessors who angered Cauchon at Rouen looked for in vain at the trial he conducted in 1431, was to be found, had they known, in the third section of DQP, to which we now turn. This is the body of the text, the twelve propositions which, through the important medium of Scripture,[46]

Lanhers, eds., *Documents et recherches relatifs à Jeanne la Pucelle*, vol. 3: *La réhabilitation de Jeanne la Pucelle. L'enquête ordonnée par Charles VII en 1450 et le codicille de Guillaume Bouillé* (Paris, 1956), p. 56, give "invention" instead of "intention." The original of this text was in French. See Murray, *Jeanne d'Arc*, p. 156.

43 Barrett, *Trial*, p. 278.

44 Their judgment is as follows: "It appeared to us then as now, that a formal answer on these statements . . . is dependent upon a positive distinction [*certitudine discretionis*] which our insufficiency cannot attain, concerning the origin of the revelations. . . . Because, if these revelations proceed from an evil spirit or demon [*a malo spiritu vel daemone*], or are imagined by her own efforts [*propria industria confictae sint*], it appears to us that many statements are suspect. . . . If on the contrary these revelations come from God or a good spirit [*a Deo vel bono spiritu*], which is, however, not clear to us [*quod tamen nobis non constat*], they cannot in our opinion be interpreted in an evil sense," Barrett, *Trial*, p. 281; Quicherat, *Procès* 1: 369–70.

45 Pernoud, *Retrial*, p. 182; Duparc, *Procès* 1: 230.

46 Gerson describes Scripture in *De distinctione* as "the place or workshop where the royal master-mold of the spiritual mint is hidden," Boland, *Concept*, p. 93. Since it is through Scripture that God speaks, if a genuine revelation is to be distinguished from the "counterfeit coin of a diabolical illusion" (Boland, *Concept*, p. 76), anything that deviates "in its design or inscription in any way . . . even though only slightly" from the royal master-mold "is sure to be counterfeit" (Boland, *Concept*, p. 93).

apply the author's four abstract questions to the concrete facts of her case.

As we turn to a description of the twelve propositions in DQP, we must remember that the spirit of the process of *discretio spirituum* in which our author is engaged, is that of a quest for truth based on Scripture. At first glance, however, the two sets of strictly antithetical propositions seem to cancel each other out, with no possibility of real knowledge possible, as if the charge brought against Abelard's *Sic et non* (a plausible model for DQP), that of a skeptical tract, could be leveled against DQP. If God speaks through Scripture, why does no single message clearly emerge? According to François Dingjan, the paradigm is a natural one, even for the example of Christ. "The gospel," he observes,

> presents Jesus to us from the moment of his arrival in this world as a sign of contradiction, a subject of discernment; some will attribute to him a divine origin, others a diabolical origin.[47]

It is the obscurity of the word of God, according to the theologians, that suggests a variety of interpretations which are then pondered and ranked by man. Above all, the point is that this is not a document that likes or dislikes Joan, and therefore the details of her life hold no genuine interest *per se.* Rather it is a treatise that addresses the theological divisions among men that her case creates, which the author of DQP holds to be acceptable differences, at least for now.

Propositio one, perhaps the most curious proposition to the modern mind, addresses the question of whether Joan is a genuine human being (*veram humanae naturae personam*). In fact, the author also questions whether she is a "true maid" (*veram puella*) but he does not argue this point. That Joan is in fact human is demonstrated experientially by her human behavior. The point must be established for the sake of future argument; it also desensationalizes her case, helping to remove it from the grasp of inquisitors enthralled by demons, clerics preoccupied with deception, or prelates who believe in magical transformation.

Propositio two is informational and not directly about Joan. It establishes why there were prophets in the age of the Old Testament (to prefigure the coming of Christ) and in the age of the New Testament (to aid the early church as it "took root"). But, importantly, it describes the predictions of prophets as prognostications "which go beyond any understanding of human faculty" (*quae omnem humanae facultatis cognitionem transcendunt*) and explains the indispensability, therefore, of confirming these sayings by adding signs and miracles. At Poitiers, the doctors will tackle this issue only to conclude that by then nothing had as yet occurred "above human understanding" (*par dessus euvre humaine*).

[47] Dingjan, *Discretio*, p. 229.

Propositio three demonstrates the purpose of the first two propositions. Through the testimony of Matthew 28:20 ("And behold I am with you all days, even to the consummation of the world") and Isaiah 59:1 ("The hand of the Lord is not shortened that it cannot save") the author establishes God's continuing use of prophets as "remedies and succor," even in the present time. Their specific purpose is to awaken human nature (*genus humanum . . . excitari*), the mechanism by which they operate "the revelation of what is concealed" (*revelatione occultorum*) and "the performance of miracles" (*operatione miraculorum*). Since the gift of the prophet shows itself "now in one people, now in another," the author concludes: "One must believe with piety that such advantages are not denied to us."

Propositio four gives the most important argument in support of Joan, the grounds for proving that women can be prophets. In this proposition, the author invokes Paul's authority: "God chose what was weak in the world to confound all that which was strong" (1 Corinthians 1:27). Until the Middle Ages, women do not seem to have entered the literature of *discretio spirituum* separately from men. That is why Alphonso of Jaén's emphatic avowal in the *Epistola solitarii* (where he cites Esther, Judith, Deborah, and others), that God makes use of women to carry out his divine plan, and Gerson's more sober consideration of the same possibility in *De probatione* and *De distinctione*, may be considered innovative with regard to women in the history of *discretio spirituum*, and therefore important for Joan. To Alphonso, who as Bridget's confessor is invested in the notion of female prophets, it is a source of anger that simple people and women are dismissed as "ignorant and light-minded" (*ignarum et leuis capacitatis*), and therefore reputed to be unworthy of prophecy.[48] The more detached Gerson admits in principle that women can be prophets, but urges the examining prelate to scrutinize such cases much more painstakingly than for men. The reputation Gerson has earned among modern scholars for hostility toward women mystics, however, can more accurately be defined as caution and suspicion.

In future theological opinions on Joan, Paul's verse from 1 Corinthians becomes an obvious and popular citation. It is contained in Jacques Gelu's *Dissertatio*, six of the eight nullification trial extra-judicial opinions,[49] and is alluded to in chronicle and poetry. We do not know whether discussions at Poitiers focused specifically on the topos of the power of the weak to confound the strong, and if so, how it came to be introduced. Pius II, at least, maintained that the exemplum of Judith, which was associated with

---

[48] Jönsson, *Alphonso of Jaén*, p. 120.
[49] In addition to the Latin texts of the eight *consilia* entered into the nullification trial (Duparc, *Procès*, vol. 2), see Jane Marie Pinzino, 'Heretic or Holy Woman? Cultural Representation and Gender in the Trial to Rehabilitate Joan of Arc,' unpublished doctoral dissertation (Ann Arbor, Mich., 1996). I wish to thank the author for the specific references and for providing me with access to her dissertation.

this topos, was invoked. Yet we have no assurance that DQP was the source of any such discussion at Poitiers.

Propositio five treats an area not well-enough known to the author, that is, the true life of the girl Joan. He has just argued, however, that it should be more extensively investigated. Although bad men have sometimes prophesied, the author explains, God does not send bad men in the guise of the present young girl, who "possesses at her discretion, the power of supernatural gifts to manifest what is concealed and to predict the future." Such a conclusion is backed by the Apostle's declaration that there is no accord between Christ and Belial (2 Corinthians 6:15). Furthermore, calling upon the biographical narrative, the author uses the allusion to the moral reform she instills in her followers as proof of her goodness, stating that she "encourages people to acts of virtue and to other achievements of honesty in which God is glorified." This concern of the Maid's with an objective outside herself, and the observation also noted that she works for peace, are very positive criteria, for according to Cassian, a prophet's mission must have an end goal (*finis*) that gives form and value to everything done to accomplish it,[50] as he put it: "a good intention which works not for oneself, but for the glory of God and the common interest."[51] Thus the author is able to observe already in *propositio* five that the Maid is a person "whom it is not inopportune to count among the good people especially sent by God" (*hanc juvenculam non est incongruum connumerari bonis specialiter a deo missis*).[52]

Propositio six draws its conclusions from the preceding points, yet it is in effect a reiteration of the statement in *propositio* five, that Joan can be granted credit as someone "sent on purpose by God" (*a deo specialiter missa*). This result is not to be confused with the author's opinion; it is only the conclusion of the first set of propositions, and an utterance still subject to contradiction. Before turning his attention to the case of the "opposite party," the author makes a surprisingly original statement without any apparent precedent or any known sequel in Johannic documents. As a counter-proposal to the criticism of the masculine guise that Joan has adopted, the author daringly suggests (asserting, however: "one should not be surprised" [*nec mirum*]) that propitious circumstances for receiving divine revelation may lie in Joan's condition as a rider. Just as David wore the ephod to consult with God, and Moses accomplished miracles when he carried his rod, so Joan, "as a rider" (*in statu equestri*) might be "more enlightened by a second light than in her usual feminine condition" (*sit alterius luminis quam in solito statu muliebri*).[53]

At the end of this proposition, the author turns with an almost unnerving

---

50 Dingjan, *Discretio*, p. 18.
51 Cassian, *Collatione* 1: 21: 2. Cited by Dingjan, *Discretio*, p. 24.
52 Wayman, "The Chancellor," DQP, p. 300.
53 Wayman, "The Chancellor," DQP, p. 301.

even-handedness from bolstering the case of the partisans of Joan (*huius viae amicus*) to providing grist for "others who feel more inclined to the opposite side" (*alii in oppositam partem magis inclinati*). Scripture is clearly a tool able to serve both sides.

Propositio one against Joan calls into question the seemingly obvious argument that Joan is a human being, since Matthew 24:5 ("For many will come in my name saying, I am Christ: and they will seduce many") and 2 Corinthians 11:14 ("For satan himself transformeth himself into an angel of light") teach that it is impossible to make a judgment solely on the basis of appearances. This is a proposition that it would have behooved Joan to know at Rouen when her artful inquisitors, who were specifically targeting this point, asked her how she would tell, when St. Michael appeared to her, "if he were a good or bad spirit if the Enemy put himself in the form and guise of an angel." She answered that she would "certainly know whether it was St. Michael or a counterfeit in his likeness" – discriminatory talents that she could not have realized, even the most well-trained clerics knew, in their wisdom, that they did not possess.[54]

Propositio two continues the point made in the previous proposition, stating that because the evil spirit has greater intelligence than humans, it too can "reveal secret thoughts" (*pronuntiant occulta cordium*) and announce "the issue of events . . . [in] the immediate future" (*effectus futurorum contingentium*). Thus the very signs by which one distinguishes true prophets can be counterfeited by the devil. Consequently, the biographical-narrative claims about her supernatural powers, when taken in isolation, are inconclusive.

Propositio three is less an argument against Joan than the statement of a truism – in fact, the most basic truism of *discretio* – that from neither external appearances (*propositio* one) nor signs (*propositio* two) can the discernment between a true and a false prophet be easily made.[55] For this reason, and because false prophets often try to give second interpretations to prophecies that do not come true, and also because, confusingly, true prophets occasionally prophesy events that never occur, one should test the spirits. Here the author makes reference to 1 John 4:1: "Believe not every spirit, but try the spirits if they be of God."

Propositio four against Joan returns to the subject of *propositii* three and four in support of Joan, God's direct involvement in nations. Contrary to those propositions, it is argued here that the offer of temporal happiness to a people by God reveals nothing of divine favor, because God grants temporal

---

[54] Barrett, *Trial*, p. 123.

[55] Although Gerson makes it clear that "there is no general norm or natural ability for distinguishing always and infallibly the revelations that are genuine from those that are false or illusory" (*De distinctione*, Boland, *Concept*, p. 78), because it would negate the purpose of faith, through *discretio spirituum* he believes that we can arrive at a "healthy certainty" (*bonae spei certitudo*), Boland, *Concept*, p. 102; Glorieux, *Oeuvres* 3: 53.

goods equally to the good and the bad. Moreover, since God scorns attachment to transitory possessions, temporal happiness (for example, victory) might even be an unfavorable sign. Once again, however, the author draws upon the analogy between the people of France and the people of God to describe the possibility of a single but significant exception: "Yet, in the Old Testament, as long as the celebrated people were the servants of God, they had in exchange such temporal goods."

Propositio five exposes the most damaging argument in the treatise against Joan, and it was, as we know, the indictment that led to her condemnation and death as a relapsed heretic: the accusation that her clothes and her shorn hair were prohibited by Scripture; specifically, that she violated Deuteronomy 22:5 and 1 Corinthians 11:6. As Pius II wrote, she dressed as a man, "not knowing that she was putting on death."[56] To anyone involved in *discretio*, it was understood that genuine prophets would exhibit an uncommon saintliness, but the perceived indecency of a woman riding and wearing male clothing (since this was unfeminine) brought Joan's moral character into question. The author of DQP recognizes that Esther and Judith could be considered culpable for what Ambrose called their "robes of allurement"[57] (the seductive clothing as necessary to their missions as Joan's male attire was to hers), but to our author these women at least maintained their femininity. In order to excuse the impropriety of Judith's adornment, Jerome had emphasized its temporary nature, distasteful to Judith herself: "Quickly changing her garb, she puts on once more in the hour of victory her own mean dress finer than all the splendours of the world."[58] A similar compartmentalizing of potentially censurable behavior is described in the biographical narrative of DQP, perhaps offering our author a measure of reassurance, for his source relates that upon dismounting from her horse she recovered her usual femininity and became "extremely naive, inexperienced in secular matters, like a defenseless lamb."

Propositio six against Joan comes to the exact opposite conclusion as *propositio* six in favor of Joan, namely that whether the Maid was "sent on purpose by God," or whether God acts "through her as an intermediary" (thus making her worthy of trust), "cannot be shown with satisfactory evidence"; and in fact the circumstances of her arrival are "contrary to divine orders" (*contra divina mandata*) – an allusion to her male clothes.

At this time the author has discharged his responsibility as far as the scriptural aspect of Joan's examination is concerned. He has revealed all that

---

[56] Pius II, *Memoirs*, Gabel and Gragg, p. 208.
[57] Bernard F. Huppé, ed. and trans., *The Web of Words: Structural Analyses of the Old English Poems: Vainglory, the Wonder of Creation, the Dream of Rood, and Judith* (Albany, N.Y., 1970), p. 141.
[58] *The Principal Works of St. Jerome*, W. H. Fremantle, trans., A Select Library of Nicene and Post-Nicene Fathers of the Christian Church, 2nd ser., vol. 6 (Grand Rapids, Mich., repr. 1983), p. 108.

De quadam puella

he has to say about Joan on such short notice and has prepared the way and offered the arguments for those who would "lean on" his work to defend their point of view.

To the end of the treatise, he maintains that he has done no more than provide a "gathering" (*collectio*), and so he distances himself slightly from a work that he must offer, more or less, as is. His desire to render service to the proponents of each side, however, is genuine, even earnest. They will judge him not for his opinions on Joan, for he has not offered them to his readers, but on whether he has brought forward the appropriate scriptural passages for the case. He cannot be praised or blamed for what he has found in Scripture, having simply identified what is there.

Having presented each of the three parts of DQP, the facts about Joan, the questions on the nature of spirits, and the twelve propositions, we are at liberty to step back from the details and judge the treatise's impact. This is a treatise about prophets. Its task is to measure the merits of Joan against the requirements of Scripture in order to judge the validity of her words as those of a prophet. Yet France comes under as much scrutiny as Joan, since the idea of God sending a prophet to one of his peoples, while it occurs as a reprimand to a nation neglectful of God, is still primarily a sign of divine caring toward that people, caring that must nonetheless be earned. The real question, then, is whether France could be so positioned, in its history and in its faith (forgiving previous error), to merit the gift of a prophet sent from God. The subject of DQP, then, may be construed as nothing less than the salvation history of France, which explains the author's indifference in DQP to politics and to England.

It is likely that the reputation of the entire treatise, however, came to rest on its fateful mention of Deuteronomy 22:5, and that, especially since the only men named as putative authors were either Valois-supporter Jean Gerson or his student and disciple, Heinrich von Gorckum, this treatise has gone down in history as a Valois embarrassment. We are limited to two facts from which to draw our understanding of DQP's contemporary role. In 1484, DQP was included in the *editio princeps* of Gerson's works.[59] In 1514, however, in a new edition of the chancellor's *Opera*, the text of DQP was still printed, but the treatise *De mirabili victoria* (DMV – which receives full treatment in a later chapter) replaced DQP as Gerson's opinion on the Maid, a substitution justified only by the following editorial comment added to DQP: "ascribed to Jean Gerson but seems more the style of Heinrich von Gorckum."[60] To understand this replacement we must consider briefly the existence of this "other" Gerson treatise, a tract whose author was as committed to an unequivocal defense of Joan as was the author of DQP committed to impartiality.

---

[59] Wayman, "The Chancellor," p. 283.
[60] Wayman, "The Chancellor," p. 284.

We have testimony from as early as November 1429 from a *Morosini* chronicle correspondent confirming the existence at that date of DMV, describing it as a defense of Joan written by Gerson.[61] The correspondent's exhilaration that Joan is being defended by "an important man, a doctor of theology" shows how potent the idea was, even for a foreigner, that Gerson would champion the Maid's cause. In the same spirit, Guillaume Bouillé included DMV, ascribing it to Gerson, among the extrajudiciary treatises at the nullification trial; he even copied portions of it into his own contribution without attribution to its author, which we should undoubtedly take as a sign of respect. So when printer–editor Geiler von Kaysersberg placed DMV in the new edition of Gerson's works in 1514, evidently he was only realigning his information to agree with a tradition of long duration already.

It is not without a certain irony that Gerson's authorship of DQP has been generally discredited, for the treatise exhibits the same watchful caution that is found in Gerson's other discernment treatises, Gelu's recommendations to the king, and, as it will soon appear, the *Poitiers Conclusions*. Moreover, DQP clearly subscribes to the orthodoxy of refusing to endorse a female prophet lightly, a view entirely compatible with Gerson's reputation and written record. As has often been observed, however, the endorsement of Joan in DMV is out of character for Gerson.

But the problem lies in the relationship between the two treatises. For critics in general draw very significant theories and substantial claims about Joan's fate from their ascription to Gerson of one or the other treatise. In deciding the highly controversial question of Gersonian authorship, an overwhelming desire exists, not unnaturally, to show that the respected and authoritative Gerson supported belief in the Maid. However, since Joan's judges at Rouen used her male clothing as the technicality on which they ultimately condemned her, any treatise ascribed to Gerson that challenged those objections, like DMV, would be eagerly embraced; but any treatise, like DQP, which preferred Esther and Judith's femininity to Joan's evident masculinity, or worse yet, which was the first document to draw attention to the biblical prohibition against male dress in Deuteronomy 22:5 (as DQP seems certain to have been), could expect to find disfavor. For to adopt DQP as a treatise by Gerson makes it impossible to say that Gerson held no serious objection to the Maid's attire. Whereas in the case of DMV, with its defense of male dress, some have even argued that if the treatise had been allowed as evidence at Rouen, as it was at the nullification trial, Joan's fate could have turned out differently.[62] No such claim can be made for DQP.

Moreover, since most historians (including some of Joan's contemporaries) have wanted to view the accusations against male dress as a desperate invention confected at Rouen (and at the very least an English invention),

---

[61] Dorez and Lefèvre-Pontalis, *Morosini* 3: 234–35.
[62] See the chapter on DMV for these citations.

DQP is troubling to their argument, for it tells us that in Joan's own party controversy surrounded her attire virtually from the beginning. And if Gerson is credited with the authorship of DQP, it lays at least part of the blame at his feet. No longer viewed as a mere consideration for Charles's theologians to ponder, even though the point is very cautiously introduced in DQP, with the words "it would seem at first glance" (*videtur prima facie*), the fateful *propositio* five has become a poignant reminder of its use as ammunition for the Rouen judges.

We must be very careful to reject the idea that the English could not have produced the charges against Joan's male dress without DQP. There is no sign that DQP ever reached Anglo-Burgundian France, and the English were quite capable of making the accusation on their own, as they did, in fact, several times before 1431. Oddly, however, there is no absolute sign of DQP in Valois France either. To explain this absence, Wayman suggested that the treatise lay unnoticed among the chancellor's papers in Lyon until his works were published by Johann Koelhoff in 1484.[63] This idea is as possible, barring any new evidence, as the assumption which one might wish to draw from the evidence, that DQP was suppressed for citing Deuteronomy 22:5.

Yet if DQP was available in those years, the treatise offered no value as propaganda for the French, irrespective of the Deuteronomic citation, since it was nonpartisan. It would have made no sense to use the neutral and inconclusive DQP for propaganda, a purpose which DMV, on the other hand, quite obviously served well. In fact, we will see that DMV enjoyed a dissemination commensurate with or even surpassing that of the widely publicized *Poitiers Conclusions* and *Lettre aux Anglais*, and therefore had a profound effect in shaping future Johannic debate.

Clearly DQP fails as political propaganda because it was written as a guide for the church. And yet, its invitation to debate the Maid's case further is, in fact, taken up at Poitiers, whether at our author's urging or not. After Poitiers, the idea of Joan as a subject for debate persists. The pros and cons of Joan's case continue to permeate the contemporary literature, but with a very significant difference. After the commitment of the Poitiers doctors to Joan, nonpartisan evaluations, the bedrock of *discretio spirituum*, fade away as if inappropriate, unpatriotic, or otherwise culpable. The *Poitiers Conclusions*, however limited the endorsement, in fact swelled the ranks of believers in Joan, owing partly to their rather wide dissemination. On the other hand, the hypothetical objections raised against Joan in the early period started to give way to a panoply of genuine accusations against the Maid, whether by the enemy or detractors from her own party. Neutrality no doubt became difficult to maintain, and perhaps was even actively discouraged.

Until that time, at least for theologians, suspicion was a virtue and a duty. As Régine Pernoud observed about the prelates at Poitiers: "The apostolic

---

[63] Wayman, "The Chancellor," p. 286.

commissioners were compelled by their office to distrust the hypothesis of a miracle."[64] The author of DQP, as we know, wished to make no decision on Joan and was engaged only in executing one of the phases of *discretio spirituum*. The ultimate decision-makers were the prelates gathered at Poitiers, to whom we now turn.

---

[64] Pernoud, *Retrial,* p. 115.

3

The *Poitiers Conclusions*

At Poitiers, the requests of the archbishop of Embrun and the author of DQP were fulfilled and a comprehensive examination of the Maid took place. This was the decisive stage of the investigation because it was here that the churchmen, no longer permitted the luxury of reserving judgment, had to approve or disapprove Joan's mission. Perhaps a Latin poet, who speaks to us in verse appended to nullification trial manuscript B.N. lat. 5970, and whose account has the ring of the eyewitness, accurately describes how the decision to test the Maid at Poitiers was taken. The anonymous poet's words are the very epitome of what the task set for Poitiers was to be, and why it would be so. He relates that standing before the gathered counselors at Chinon, in an impassioned plea designed to break the impasse over what to do about the Maid, one man (*unus vir*) spoke up:

> O king, o race of Franks, lest anybody commit a sin, now this soul must be probed [*nunc spiritus iste probetur*] as to whether it be supernatural [*an sit de superis*], as sacred writ expects it to be done.[1]

Was this rebuke, referring precisely to the "probing of the spirit," delivered to restrain enthusiasts of Joan by demanding that they conduct a proper religious hearing or, on the contrary, to restrain skeptics eager for her dismissal? Whichever the case, the stage was perfectly set by his remarks for the upcoming phase of Joan's evaluation. The matter of deciding would be prolonged, contrary to the wishes of those advocating expediency, whether they be endorsers, detractors, or Joan herself.

The expedition from Chinon to Poitiers, in which the king, his retinue and Joan made the journey together, demonstrated to Joan that, as far as Charles was concerned, she was still on trial. The Maid may not have entirely understood the purpose of this trip to a larger city, the new capital of France, where the king had reconstituted his parliament, but he had decided that she would not be granted men-at-arms without it. Reportedly, Joan learned only

---

[1] Du Motey, *Jeanne d'Arc*, p. 31. For the full text of the anonymous poem, see Quicherat, *Procès* 5: 24–43.

en route where the king was leading her and why. "In God's name," she is said to have declared, "I know that I will be challenged there [*je y auray bien affaire*]; but God [*Messires*] will aid me."[2]

Impatience more than dread seems to have characterized the Maid's perception of this new obstacle, the testing at Poitiers. To Joan, the ceaseless questioning on the part of the doctors, so unnecessary to her way of thinking, simply kept her from obeying what she already knew was God's command. As Joan's confessor Pasquerel later confirmed: "She was not pleased at so many examinations, [since] they prevented her carrying out the work for which she was sent."[3] On the other hand, Joan did get a chance she had been waiting for – the opportunity to have her words fully heard and taken seriously. That these words had become important to the doctors is evidenced by the keeping of a register, the minutes of the Poitiers hearings, which, whether lost or intentionally destroyed, has not come down to us.

Because the "Book of Poitiers" is now lost, what went on during Joan's interrogation is not formally known.[4] The absence of this written record has encouraged some to believe that at Poitiers a political faction of discontented exiles, who wished to be restored to their former titles, privileges and territories, overruled the hesitations of the clergy and forced the approval of Joan. Seeing her simply as a temporary expedient in an obvious predicament, they silenced the doubts of her theological examiners so that she could advance to Orléans. Thus, according to the proponents of the political-intrigue theory, *discretio spirituum* was not the operative procedure at Poitiers. As Anatole France summed up the main idea, Joan's interrogators "knew the rules for judging in matters of faith, without a doubt," but "at that hour it was not a question of curing heresy, it was a question of chasing out the English."[5]

As a reply to those who believe that politics held sway over the theological imperative to probe Joan's spirit at Poitiers, we must refer to the *Poitiers Conclusions*, a summary of the decision reached by the prelates themselves. A mere thirty lines in length, it is all that remains of an official nature to instruct us about the interrogation. Regret over the loss of the full minutes of the proceedings, however, should not obscure the quantity of valuable information contained in this short synopsis. Certainly there is enough evidence here to justify the rejection of the extreme view of political

---

[2] *Chronique de la Pucelle*, Quicherat, *Procès* 4: 209. Cf. *Journal du siège d'Orléans*, Quicherat, *Procès* 4: 128: "En nom de Dieu, je sçay bien que je auray beaucoup affaire à Poictiers où on me meine; mais Messires me aydera; or allons, de par Dieu!"

[3] Murray, *Jeanne d'Arc*, p. 283.

[4] For the fullest discussion to date of the disappearance of this register, see Charles T. Wood, "Joan of Arc's Mission and the Lost Record of Her Interrogation at Poitiers," in *Fresh Verdicts on Joan of Arc*, Bonnie Wheeler and Charles T. Wood, eds. (New York, 1996), pp. 19–29.

[5] France, *Jeanne d'Arc* 1: 258.

conspiracy held by Roger Little, who finds in the *Poitiers Conclusions* (which
he calls the *Résumé*) "the clear lack of reference to any regular doctrinal
examination" and goes so far as to maintain that "it seems impossible to
view the document published by Quicherat [the *Poitiers Conclusions*] as a
résumé of those proceedings."[6]

Part of the conviction that Poitiers was merely an exercise in politics rests
on the belief by some that the Maid's interrogators were not primarily
theologians. It is therefore important, before demonstrating the strong
theological basis of the *Conclusions*, to dispel this notion, especially because
for a proper discernment trial to take place, not only ecclesiastics, but elite
clergy were required. St. Paul had said that these men must possess the
charism; the theologian and author of DQP called them "those wiser men"
(*sapientiores*) and Gerson referred to them as the "spiritual moneychangers"
who weighed and rendered judgment on "the precious and unfamiliar coin
of divine revelation."[7] Therefore, the background and ecclesiastical credentials of these men is pertinent information.

Approximately eighteen ecclesiastics gathered in Poitiers for the second
examination of the Maid. It is possible to reconstruct a fairly complete roster
of the participants, their degrees, titles, and religious affiliations, and to
conclude, at a minimum, that they were men of religion. Presiding over the
inquiry was an archbishop, Regnault de Chartres, archbishop of Reims and
chancellor of France. He was joined by a Carmelite, Pierre Seguin,[8] who held
a doctorate in Sacred Scripture, an obviously crucial talent relative to
discretio spirituum. There were at least three Dominicans, Guillaume
Aimeri, Brother Seguin Seguin, and Pierre Turelure, thought to be at that
time Inquisitor General of Toulouse, and later to become bishop of Digne.[9]
In addition to the Carmelite and Dominicans, were deputed a Franciscan,
Jean Raffanel, confessor to the queen, Marie d'Anjou, and a Benedictine, the
renowned Pierre de Versailles. Among their numbers were professors of
theology, masters and bachelors of theology, and licentiates in civil and
canon law.[10] Some were former professors of theology at the University of
Paris, and several were bishops or would be so elected in the future. In fact,
we can go further than merely verifying that these men were prelates.
Arguably, they were the flower of the Valois clergy.[11] In only a few years,
the University of Poitiers would be founded on the basis of their numbers

---

[6] Little, *Parlement*, p. 112.
[7] Gerson, *De distinctione*, Boland, *Concept*, p. 80; Glorieux, *Oeuvres* 3: 38.
[8] Ayroles distinguishes between Pierre Seguin and Seguin Seguin, whom he believes was a Dominican. See Ayroles, *Jeanne d'Arc* 1: 11.
[9] Ayroles, *Jeanne d'Arc* 1: 7.
[10] This information comes from the nullification-trial testimony of François Garivel (Duparc, *Procès* 1: 328) and Seguin Seguin (Duparc, *Procès* 1: 471).
[11] Octave Raguenet de Saint-Albin, *Les juges de Jeanne d'Arc à Poitiers, membres du parlement ou gens d'église?* (Orléans, 1894), p. 39.

and distinction. It is likely that at Poitiers we are witnessing a gathering of the finest clergy in non-occupied France.

It is a problem for us in trying to understand the Johannic debate that by the nature of the document, the *Poitiers Conclusions* are designed to show consensus, rather than debate. In the unified view of this document the proponents of conspiracy see the silencing of dissent. Yet the reason for the need for consensus was that once the theological decision was taken, a recommendation went to the king's council, so that the military approval, which was in its jurisdiction, could be made. But this does not exclude the airing of opposing views, even at great lengths, beforehand. Many scholars have used references in chronicle sources to the king's council, or *Conseil*, as evidence that the decision made regarding Joan was secular, not ecclesiastical. Instead, the truth seems to be that the decision was two-tiered: ecclesiastical first, and then secular and military. The testimony of Joan's steward, Jean d'Aulon, who said that he was present when the decision of the doctors was read aloud to the king's council, bears this out.[12]

If we can dispense with the general charge that politicians, not theologians, determined Joan's fate at Poitiers, by the demonstration that the opinions rendered by clergy and council were separate, there is still the difficulty of knowing whether a real theological debate took place there – the debate that would prove that uppermost in the minds of the French was the genuine desire to know whether or not Joan was sent by God. Predictably, there are two divergent schools of thought on how the theologians conducted their probe of Joan. In theory, clergy conducting an investigation of Joan's spirit would be preoccupied only by the fear of rendering an improper theological judgment. But both camps of analysts allow for strong political impulses even in the sphere of religion. Two graphic quotations from scholars on either side demonstrate how distinct the opposition is between the views. To Anatole France, the masters at Poitiers wanted to use Joan, and so when the clergy examined her, to employ his colorful imagery, they "retracted their theological claws."[13] Taking the opposite stance is Salomon Reinach, who holds that the hearings were seances conducted by ecclesiastical jackals. To him, Joan's Poitiers judges were cut from the same cloth as her later judges, making Poitiers "a kind of rehearsal for [the trial] at Rouen."[14]

Joan herself offers a certain validity to both views. It is true that she

---

[12] In response to a request by Regnault de Chartres that he send a deposition for the nullification trial, d'Aulon declared that "he was present at the said Council when the Masters [Poitiers commissioners] made their report on what they had found in the Maid," Murray, *Jeanne d'Arc*, p. 309. For the original French see Quicherat, *Procès* 3: 209.

[13] France, *Jeanne d'Arc* 1: 258.

[14] Salomon Reinach, "Observations sur le texte du procès de condamnation de Jeanne d'Arc," *Revue historique* 148 (1925): 211: "une sorte de répétition de celui de Rouen."

acknowledged at her condemnation trial that before the clergy knew her sign, there was "trouble arising from [their] opposition."[15] But at the same time, she referred at Rouen to "the clergy of my party," not only to contrast them with their counterparts at Rouen, one suspects, but with a measure of affection. A sampling of the questions asked during the Poitiers hearings has survived, with seeming accuracy, in the form of nullification-trial testimony. Much of that information does not have a bearing here, but some questions may have been deemed hostile by Joan, whether at Rouen or Poitiers, and consequently led to the belief that her interrogators at Poitiers were hostile, when in fact the questions were merely designed to fulfill the dictates of *discretio spirituum*. At Rouen, when Joan was asked whether members of her own party firmly believed that she had been sent by God, for instance, she answered: "I do not know whether they do, and I refer you to their own opinion; but if they do not, nevertheless I am sent from God."[16] And when Seguin Seguin asked her if she believed in God, she snapped: "Yes, better than you."[17] It was this defiant, almost retaliatory way Joan had of answering questions, which she demonstrated both at Poitiers and Rouen, a blend of self-confidence and self-defense, that tends to make people see her as a victim at Poitiers. Her situation conjures up archetypal images, and did so even for her contemporaries. Alain Chartier wrote a letter about the Maid in which he hastened through the list of images: "a woman against men" (*foemina cum viris*), "an analphabet against scholars" (*indocta cum doctis*), "one against many" (*sola cum multis*), "the lowly against the exalted" (*infima de summis*).[18] It was this perception of unequal odds that led a *Morosini* chronicle correspondent to consider Joan "a second Saint Catherine [of Alexandria]" (*altra santa Catarina*) for her apt handling of the masters at Poitiers.[19]

It is by examining the *Poitiers Conclusions* document itself, however, that we are actually able to determine that a discernment trial took place at Poitiers, with Joan's claim to a divine mission its sole and exclusive subject. Based on misinformation, a *Morosini* chronicle correspondent claimed that at Poitiers "it was concluded that this creature could only be a saint and a servant of God."[20] If he mistakenly believed that Joan had been validated as a

---

[15] Condemnation trial, March 10, Barrett, *Trial*, p. 93.
[16] Barrett, *Trial*, p. 82; Quicherat, *Procès* 1: 101: "Interrogata utrum illi de parte sua, credant firmiter ipsam esse missam a Deo: respondit: 'Ego nescio utrum credant, et me refero ad animum ipsorum; sed si non credant, tamen ego sum missa a Deo.'"
[17] See Pernoud, *Joan of Arc*, p. 55; Duparc, *Procès* 1: 472.
[18] Alain Chartier, "Letter to a Foreign Prince," in Quicherat, *Procès* 5: 133.
[19] Dorez and Lefèvre-Pontalis, *Morosini* 3: 52–53: "But nothing is so evident as her victory without contest [in the discussion] with the masters of theology, such that it seems she is a second St. Catherine arrived on earth" (*vegnuda in tera*). Recourse here to St. Catherine for reasons of exemplarity in no way suggests that Justiniani knew St. Catherine to be one of Joan's saints.
[20] Dorez and Lefèvre-Pontalis, *Morosini* 3: 98: "questa tal criatura nonn eser altro che santa."

saint, the procedure, at least, was by and large the same. And yet, as anybody could recognize, there were deep distinctions to be made between the process of probing Joan's spirit and a canonization trial, that would spell caution to her evaluators. As if it were a discernment trial in reverse, Joan was tested before she acted rather than after. Most prophets were sponsored in these inquiries by a confessor, a religious house or an entire religious order. A prophet's life usually provided writings that could be examined, their miracles were primarily cures or other humanitarian aid, and they themselves were frequently already dead. So it goes without saying that for Joan to arrive accompanied only by men-at-arms, with no confessor, envisioning for herself a military mission, based on the authority of her own word, we are witnessing a categorical deviation from the norm.

The *Poitiers Conclusions* tell us that in order to perform their investigation, the doctors adopted as their guiding principle the directive of 1 John 4:1: "Try the spirits if they be of God." In order to accomplish this, they were required to probe the prophet in two ways, through the examination of the life and by demanding a sign. The object of the first part of the probe was to verify that the prophet harbored no vices and was free of heretical practices. The purpose of the second part we can understand best as it was cogently put to Joan by Seguin Seguin. "And then I told Joan," he related at the nullification trial,

> that it was not God's will that she be believed if nothing appeared by which it should seem that she ought to be believed, and that the king could not be advised, on her mere assertion, to entrust her with soldiers . . . unless she had something else to say.[21]

The *Poitiers Conclusions* demonstrate how delicate a tightrope one walked to make a decision through discernment. The document opens with the proposition that the king must neither "turn away nor reject [*debouter ne déjetter*] the Maid who says she is sent by God,"[22] nor, the text continues, "believe in her immediately or lightly." But the proponents of a political conspiracy are drawn to the reference in the first line stating the king's "necessity." Therefore, to them the decision to employ the Maid looks not like the result of prelates carefully weighing the theological circumstances, but like a sheer political tactic employed in a time of need to extricate themselves from a calamity. Thus Roger Little uses this indicator to show the prelates "shifting the emphasis away from the more specific matter of Joan's spiritual credibility and onto the question of Charles VII's immediate political necessity."[23] But sometimes the natural tendency of modern analysts

---

[21] Pernoud, *Joan of Arc*, p. 55; Duparc, *Procès* 1: 472.
[22] See Appendix II for a translation of the *Poitiers Conclusions*.
[23] Little, *Parlement*, p. 108.

to recognize political causes obscures other interpretations, namely theological ones.

We must not overlook that in the same sentence as the appeal to the "necessity" of Charles's realm, the *Conclusions* also mention "the continuous prayers of his poor people to God." Bowing to an axiom of medieval belief, we should interpret the relationship between prayer and the direct intervention of God as holding out genuine promise to Charles and the members of his party. Moreover, there is another point to be made. The concept of necessity is as theological as it is political. The term carries a distinctive meaning in Christian theology, which is quite likely to be the meaning intended by the prelates who framed the *Poitiers Conclusions*, and it is a sense which largely removes the term from susceptibility to being interpreted as political opportunism, and situates it instead in the realm of salvation history, specifically, that of France.

It was a widely reported fact in French sources on Joan that prior to her arrival France had reached the nadir of its fortunes. Average people, not theologians, testified to the desolation of the kingdom, the withdrawn obedience of the knights, the penury of the treasury, as Joan and others put it, the "pity" that was the kingdom of France. To a historian, the accuracy of the description may be debated,[24] but to a theologian the situation takes on a different hue. It was an accepted Christian principle that one did not ask God for a miracle unless every human avenue to a solution had already been pursued; to do so would be to tempt God. But if France had tried and tried, and still fallen to its lowest point, it was theologically possible that the kingdom had been brought so low that the anticipation of divine intervention had been made feasible. A variation of the principle stresses the need for correction in an errant people.[25] Thus the report of many, that prior to the raising of the siege of Orléans there was "no succor but from God," gives understanding to the otherwise incomprehensible arrival of Joan as divine envoy.

The first of the two ways to test a prophet is the examination of the life, specified in the first paragraph of the *Poitiers Conclusions* as an inquiry into her life, habits, and intention. It is referred to as a probe "by human means" (*par prudence humaine*) in contrast to the supernatural properties of a miracle. Here arises a new opportunity for confusion, which might feed the idea of political opportunism. A mistaken reading of the list of virtues associated in the *Conclusions* regarding Joan sees this list primarily as biographical items, signs of whether she would or would not be a good

---

[24] See M. G. A. Vale, *Charles VII* (Berkeley, 1974), p. 54, for a challenge to Régine Pernoud's statement that France was "desperate" and that this "is attested by all the writings of the times."

[25] Bossuet stated that "when [God] wishes to show that an action is done by his hand alone, he reduces everything to impotence and despair; then he acts." Cited by Gaston du Fresne de Beaucourt, *Histoire de Charles VII*, 6 vols. (Paris, 1881–91) 2: 203.

ally. In fact, such a list is standard in the process of *discretio spirituum*. It is not so much an enumeration of the personal attributes of the girl Joan, as an inventory of attributes – "goodness, humility, virginity, devotion, honesty, [and] simplicity" – whose presence, in each case, implies a counterpart in evil, any one of which, if found in Joan, would reduce her case to nothing. That true debate went on at Poitiers seems more obvious if we consider that the antitheses of these virtues – iniquity, pride, dissolute living, apostasy, dishonesty, and artifice – were mainstays in the litigation against Joan at Rouen. Although it is not in the nature of this document to raise controversy, on one very important point, at least, we should listen to Pius II. As far as the deliberations at Poitiers were concerned, Pius related that "they found in her no trace of deceit or guile or evil intent. The only difficulty was her dress."[26] Either with or without the prompting of the author of DQP, if Joan's male clothing did not lead the debate at Poitiers, it appears to have at least sustained it for a time. Her masculine attire was not a charge trumped up at Rouen.

When the *Poitiers Conclusions*, regarding the second point, call for Joan to produce a sign, what is referred to is the need of every prophet to produce a miracle. We must not think, when the document states that, so far, her promises are "only human works," that the theologians knew she was a mere ordinary mortal but decided to employ her anyway. Instead of a cynical proclamation that Joan did nothing divine even though they were approving her, this phrase seems, once again, to be part of the theological framework of the document. Some confusion over slightly different wording in the *Registre delphinal* of Mathieu Thomassin obfuscates the matter by rendering the phrase as "although the promises . . . of the said Maid are *above* human works" (*par dessus euvres humaines*).[27] (Emphasis mine.) But the doctors can only mean one thing here, which we know in any case to be true: that she had not yet satisfied them as to the second requirement, the production of a miracle. All the record of minor marvels attached to Joan up to this point – including the alleged identification of Charles among his courtiers and her telling him a secret – do not count to earn her their support.

In the second paragraph of the *Conclusions*, the doctors are at pains to demonstrate how utterly thorough the king's probe of the Maid has been, which they manage to convey almost to a ridiculous degree. Giving six weeks for the length of the examination, the longest duration of any source, they date its inception to "the coming of the said Maid." Far from implying that no theological interrogation of Joan took place, the *Conclusions'* enumeration of all the people who have been brought into the investigation – "clerics, churchmen, pious people, men-at-arms, women, widows [and] others" –

---

[26] Pius II, *Memoirs*, Gabel and Gragg, p. 203.
[27] Quicherat, *Procès* 4: 306. As Quicherat points out, this rendering creates a misinterpretation.

simply confirms that, to an exaggerated extent, the king refused to rely on his own judgment. And it does not erase the existence of a theological examination if others examined her too. This was done so that "all people" (*toutes gens*) could be shown the Maid and converse with her, as an added precaution, both "publicly" and "secretly." Finally, when the disclosure is made that there has been found in her "no evil" (*point de mal*), the *Conclusions* mention an additional prong to the investigation, not enumerated in the first paragraph: an investigation into her birth. This we can take as a reference to the expedition of investigators to Domrémy, perhaps added at the behest of Gelu or DQP's author. But although "marvelous things . . . related as true" were uncovered, they, no more than any other rumored wonder from the early days of Joan's mission, can be taken as her sign, as the next sentence of the *Conclusions* explains.

It is here that the *Conclusions* provide a momentary glimpse of the exchange that took place at Poitiers over Joan's miracle. Based on what we know about Joan's insistence that she listen to nothing but her own divine guidance, the remark rings true, for, according to the *Conclusions*, when asked about her sign, she replied "that before the city of Orléans she [would] show it, *and not in any other place* [*et non par ne en autre lieu*]: for this was ordered by God." (Emphasis mine.)

At this point the king might have wished the Maid and her insistent imperatives away from him and out of his sight. She had provided no miracle and demonstrated her indifference to one of the crucial tenets of *discretio spirituum* by saying that "with her men-at-arms," if allowed to go to Orléans, she would make a miracle there of her promised victory. The *Conclusions*, by an earlier reference to the miracle of the victory of Achaz, seem to adopt her idea that a military victory could count as a miracle. And what the local citizens did to help at the nullification trial, was to insist one after another, that Orléans could not have been retaken barring a miracle. But the fact is that Joan was asking the commissioners to wave the second precondition for belief in her mission (the furnishing of a miracle). What she demanded, in essence, was that they act on their belief in her before she was able to secure it from them.

The prelates' dilemma at this point was considerable, especially given that there was another influence to consider. Joan had shown them no evil; the fact is noted three times in the course of the *Conclusions*. This being the case, the *Conclusions* stated that "doubting her or dismissing her without appearance of evil, would be to repel the Holy Spirit, and render one unworthy of the aid of God." The theologians were under considerable pressure in making a decision, both because her highly unusual mission demanded extra caution and because the political situation cried out for immediate action. In these difficult circumstances, the commissioners did not purport to have the final answer. Knowing also that discernment was never a secure science, they approved her, but did so only "as far as [the king] is able" (*en tant que luy est possible*) to know, thus protecting themselves on both accounts. At this point they might have joined in with Gerson, who declared in *De probatione* targeting the predicament of *discretio spirituum*: "Truly there is danger here, either in approving or in disapproving."[28] They arrived at a solution, however, once again open to false interpretation as a sign that the investigation was a mockery as far as discernment was concerned. For in the statement that the king probed Joan insofar as it was possible, some might think his challenges to the Maid lacked rigor. Moreover, the idea is heightened by several allusions to her own persistence. Yet in reality, Christian dogma has always denied that humans can be perfectly certain about the decisions they make in cases of discernment. The reason was made clear by Gerson when he asked: "What reason would there be, then, for faith?" And so Charles's theologians took the safe course: they approved Joan only provisionally, allowing her the latitude to show her miracle at Orléans. The doctors never said what Joan would have liked, that she was indeed sent by God. Although they allowed her to advance to Orléans, their statement on her mission never went further than declaring that she said she was sent by God. The fact that they decided they must "not prevent her" and must "have her led there . . . placing hope in God" is a tepid and limited endorsement at best. In the end the masters did what Seguin Seguin promised they would never do, they sent her to Orléans based on her words alone, instead of requiring proof. On the other hand, what they were doing was to place the onus of proof on Joan. The endorsement she coveted of her mission would depend entirely on what she could do at Orléans.

What then of the theological investigation that took place at Poitiers, as the document known as the *Poitiers Conclusions* reveals it? When compared to Gerson's two cornerstone texts on judging visionaries, *De distinctione* and *De probatione*, which were as authoritative as anything written on the subject in that time,[29] there are no glaring discrepancies. It is likely, moreover, that since several of the Poitiers doctors had worked with Gerson, they may well have deliberated with Gerson's very treatises before them.[30]

But nothing suggests that when the opinion of those favoring the Maid prevailed, dissent had been unfairly suppressed or a solely political decision had been made. Therefore, viewed in the context of the requirements set by Gerson's discernment treatises, the *Poitiers Conclusions* deserve final assessment as an orthodox, if unusual, theological investigation.

---

[28] Gerson, *De probatione*, Boland, *Concept*, p. 28; Glorieux, *Oeuvres* 9: 179: "Est autem utrobique, vel in approbatione vel in reprobatione, periculum."

[29] Boland, *Concept*, pp. 153–54.

[30] Two men had been with Gerson at the 1413 Council of Paris, and Pierre de Versailles was a member of the French delegation at the council of Constance where Gerson first began to codify the criteria for discernment.

4

Prophecy

The handing down of a favorable opinion on the Maid by the Poitiers commission opened the door to her military career, ecclesiastical action having finally coincided with her own desires. The commission had been an impediment to what Joan euphemistically called her desire to be "set . . . boldly to work."[1] In fact, the prelates' very need to question her seems to have caught her off guard. She had lost time at Domrémy seeking escorts for her journey to the king, and Poitiers became a further delay. From the beginning, Joan operated with a divine script dictating a tight chronology. As related by Pius II, at the walls of Reims when the citizens sought momentarily to defer their surrender, Joan showed this impatience, saying that "there must be no delay; everything must be done at the time God had appointed."[2] It is in this context that we can understand the exuberance unleashed in Joan with the announcement of the decision at Poitiers.

From the period of brisk preparation between the conclusion of the hearings and the Orléans campaign, there are only two documents extant, and they are military in nature, a just measure of where all attention at the time was focused. Of the two surviving texts, the first is an appeal for military recruits written in Latin verse as a prophecy, known by its opening words *Virgo puellares*; the second a military summons to the English, known as the *Lettre aux Anglais*, by far the more important document of the two. Neither text has attracted the attention of military historians. *Virgo puellares*, if it is known at all, must seem of slight value as a military recruitment tool, which was indeed its purpose, and the *Lettre* deviates so dramatically from conventional military summonses that it could easily be dismissed as peripheral to military operations.

For Joan's mission, however, the importance of these two texts resides in their function in promoting her theological agenda. We should interpret the genesis and the religious focus of both documents as due to the Poitiers hearings; they are the result of the earliest benefit Joan gained at Poitiers, the permission to broadcast the message that she had been sent by God. Each text

---

[1] Barrett, *Trial*, p. 168.
[2] Pius II, *Memoirs*, Gabel and Gragg, p. 206.

seeks, in its own way, to extend the notion of Joan's divine mission into the military realm, but because the prophetic poem *Virgo puellares* emanated from Poitiers – indeed, was composed there[3] – and the *Lettre* was but a consequence of the probe, attention should first focus on the notion of prophecy at Poitiers.

The granting of the gift of a prophetic spirit to certain individuals has always been recognized as consistent with the Christian faith, and that it was still possible at the time of Joan of Arc we have seen insisted upon by the author of DQP. Women were always part of the prophetic tradition, perhaps chiefly because persuasion was one avenue of authority open to them, but although Christine de Pizan could claim that "our Lord has often revealed his secrets to the world through women,"[4] the example of St. Bridget and other contemporaries proved that female prophets did not always find an easy route to acceptance. In its purest form, prophecy, according to the theologian J.-P.-J. Ayroles, works "to prepare . . . [our] minds, without knowing it, to accept a marvel when it is produced."[5] He calls it the testimony that providence renders to itself.[6] Looked at from a secular and psychological perspective, prophecy seeks to eliminate the arbitrary, and to demonstrate by foreseeing and foretelling events, that they are, in the words of H. W. Parke, "really part of a pattern of happenings" rather than uncontrollable, random acts.[7] Thus the task of Joan as prophet was to create a narrative in which the restoration of monarch and monarchy was neither random nor uncontrollable, but an expression of divine will.

In Joan's case, her entire mission could be considered a prophecy, her own role an integral part of the divine narrative she announced. Therefore, the ecclesiastics at Poitiers handled their investigation of her according to the dictates of the church, as an occurrence appropriate to the application of *discretio spirituum*, and, in order to judge the presence of the prophetic spirit, as the example of DQP illustrates, they turned to the Old and New Testaments.[8]

Nonetheless, the investigators took an unusual step during the Poitiers hearings and examined rumors relating to popular prophecies that were said

[3] Quicherat, *Procès* 4: 305.

[4] Christine de Pizan, *The Book of the City of Ladies*, Earl Jeffrey Richards, trans. (New York, 1982), p. 108.

[5] Jean-Baptiste-Joseph Ayroles, "La vénérable Jeanne d'Arc, prophétisée et prophétesse," *Revue des questions historiques* 79, n.s. 35 (1906): 28–29.

[6] Ayroles, "La vénérable Jeanne," p. 32.

[7] H. W. Parke, with ed. B. C. McGing, *Sibyls and Sibylline Prophecy in Classical Antiquity*, Croom Helm Classical Studies (London, 1998), p. 18.

[8] In a letter on Joan of Arc, the Italian Franciscan friar, Cosma Raimondi, specifically describes how his doubts about the Maid's mission led him to examine more diligently the Old and New Testaments. See G. Mercati, "Una lettera di Cosma Raimondi Cremonese sulla Ven. Giovanna d'Arco," *Studi e documenti di storia e diritto* 15 (1894): 306.

to have predicted Joan. For the theologians to have claimed that Joan's arrival had been prophesied, as prophets had predicted the birth of Christ, would have been an impressive claim, separating her from other medieval prophets who, like Saint Bridget and Saint Catherine of Siena, prophesied but were not themselves prophesied.[9] However, the evidence suggests that the focus at Poitiers was mainly on folk prophecies useful for political propaganda, in which many people including theologians may nevertheless have still believed. This literature, which treated sophisticated themes such as the ebb and flow of realms, often flourished in times of political instability. In Joan's case, the six or seven prophecies to which she became connected, dealt either with French and English political relations, the state of the monarchy, or French dynastic issues, the three most influential among them infusing religious themes into the realm of politics.[10] Oddly, we have no concrete evidence linking to Poitiers any of these three important prophecies – a prophecy announcing a virgin redeemer, a prophecy from the Second Charlemagne cycle, and a Birgittine prophecy. But they must be explained briefly, since the case for their sporadic circulation appended to Johannic texts is persuasive, and their spirit permeates attitudes about Joan.

The first prophecy, that of a virgin redeemer, casts the Maid in the role of a second Mary, a move as bold as the parallel in DQP comparing the French to the people of God, and with similar accents. Although lacking a written source, the origin has been convincingly located in cathedral art as a transposition to fifteenth-century France of the topos of Eve transformed into Mary (*eva mutans nomen*).[11] In its most sanguine iteration, related in the *Morosini* chronicle by Jean de Molins, the prophecy states that "just as through a woman, through Notre-Dame Saint Mary, [God] saved the human race, so through this young girl, pure and unsullied, he saved the most beautiful part of Christianity."[12] But this version has been cleansed of half the original prophecy. Depicted in cathedral sculpture was not only the angel proclaiming "AVE" but frequently a representation of Eve (EVA), whose name had been transformed into that of the salvific virgin. This is the version we find related twice by nullification witnesses. Durant Laxart, a relative of

---

[9] I would discount small claims that someone's life had been prophesied, which emerged at the time of canonization. For St. Bridget, see Catherine Moitessier, comtesse de Flavigny, *Sainte Brigitte de Suède: Sa vie, ses révélations et son oeuvre* (Paris, 1892), p. 7.

[10] A few surviving prophecies are so meaningless that they are without impact. Such is the case with a prophecy attributed to Merlin recounted by Walter Bower: "Lofty fame, glowing red from a mound of salt, will cause mackerel to well up at Orléans in the waters where they have been sunk," *Scotichronicon*, D. E. R. Watt et al., eds. and trans., 9 vols. (Aberdeen, 1987–98) 8: 131.

[11] France, *Jeanne d'Arc* 1: 275. Cf. also Eustache Deschamps *Autre Balade* 252: "Through Eve was our perdition, through Mary our recovery," in *Oeuvres complètes d'Eustache Deschamps*, Auguste Queux de Saint-Hilaire and Gaston Raynaud, eds., 11 vols., Société des Anciens Textes Français (Paris, 1878–1903) 2: 79.

[12] Dorez and Lefèvre-Pontalis, *Morosini* 3: 80–81.

Joan's through marriage, recalled her saying: "Was it not foretold formerly that France should be desolated by a woman, and should be restored by a maid?"[13] and Joan's host at Vaucouleurs, Catherine Le Royer, related an already more pointedly "Johannic" version: "Do you not know the prophecy which says that France, lost by a woman, shall be saved by a maiden from the Marches of Lorraine?"[14] Everyone understood that Isabeau de Bavière was designated by the prophecy as the woman who had ruined France, for signing the treaty of Troyes, but drawing attention in this prophecy to the purity of Joan's virginal body was hazardous, for it implied a negative contrast with Isabeau, a potential allusion to her rumored adultery, which needed no emphasis, if Charles, as everyone wished, was to be judged true heir.[15] Reference to Isabeau, therefore, often goes no farther than this in Johannic prophecy. *Virgo puellares*, as we will see, makes no reference to the queen, limiting itself to the image of Joan's virgin innocence, the symbol of a fresh beginning.

A more potent way of dealing with the specter of illegitimacy, whether personal or political, and an excellent way to argue the just cause of Charles's involvement in the war, appears in a series of prophecies referred to collectively as the Second Charlemagne cycle. One of these prophecies is transcribed in the archives of Côte-d'Or, written in honor of Charles VI in 1380 when he acceded to the throne,[16] which was the first time that the reign of one Charles followed another, thus *Karolus filius Karoli*. Although a woman savior was never implicated in the cycle, there were promises of new beginnings similar to those of the virgin redeemer prophecy: Jerusalem retaken, a Christian king raised to the status of emperor, his jurisdiction encompassing all of the Christian world, and his reign one of peace. Medieval rulers all harbored to some degree the dream of spearheading the crusade that would set these events in motion.

For an explicit reference to the Second Charlemagne prophecy in a Johannic context, we must wait until Christine de Pizan's *Ditié*. But it is doubtful that the association of Joan with a crusade undertaken by Charles is an idea original with Christine, considering her extensive use of written sources, including prophecies. When royal counselors were groping for myths of legitimacy to apply to Charles VII's kingship, it was an easy conversion to change Charles VI to the father and make Charles VII the

[13] Murray, *Jeanne d'Arc*, p. 226; Duparc, *Procès* 1: 296: "Nonne alias dictum fuit quod Francia per mulierem desolaretur, et postea per virginem restaurari debebat?"

[14] Murray, *Jeanne d'Arc*, p. 227; Duparc, *Procès* 1: 298: "Nonne audistis quod prophetizatum fuit quod Francia per mulierem destrueretur, et per unam virginem de marchiis Lotharingie restauraretur?"

[15] Charles T. Wood discusses legitimacy in *Joan of Arc and Richard III: Sex, Saints, and Government in the Middle Ages* (New York, 1988). Wood's comments bring precision to several commonly held erroneous views on a complicated and controversial subject.

[16] Maurice Chaume, "Une prophétie relative à Charles VI," *Revue du Moyen Age latin* 3 (1947): 31.

son. The process was similar to, and perhaps also echoed, the melding of Charlemagne's name with the sibylline prophecy of Constantine as world emperor.[17] Such craftsmanship, with the sense of order and inevitability it created, provided a legitimacy trope which we saw exploited earlier by the French chancellery in royal documents emphasizing "Karolus filius Karoli." It would require little effort to add to this tradition of France's glorious destiny a virgin for whom every battle felt like a crusade and whose king was to her indubitably the "true heir" signaled for greatness.

The last of the three major prophecies pertinent to Valois affairs in 1429, the St. Bridget prophecy, is the most elusive but potentially the most significant. It deals with themes very basic to Christianity, which were so ingrained in medieval thought that one cannot be sure whether to credit Bridget specifically, yet some Birgittine influence on French thinking seems likely. In essence, Bridget's prophecy warns that the desolation of France is due to sin and the kingdom can only be led to recovery through contrition and reform, a corollary to a simple insight of Bridget's that kingdoms reaped what they deserved and so only good kingdoms could acquire peace.

Only one contemporary source, Walter Bower's *Scotichronicon*, specifically mentions this prophecy in conjunction with Joan, placing it directly after *Virgo puellares* in the text. Bower, a friend and ally of the French, gives a version of the prophecy which he found in a source he calls "Bridget's book *On the French.*" His version is seriously abbreviated with most of the anti-French sentiment of the original expunged. Bower refers momentarily to France's "many sins and flashy ways"[18] but focuses mainly on the banal message that peace requires appeasing God by piety and humility.

The original prophecy, dating from 1360, preserved in Book Four, chapters 104–105 of Bridget's *Revelations*, contributes nothing to French glory. Easily recyclable owing to its general terminology, the prophecy's appearance in connection with Charles VII was perhaps its third incarnation, interpolations having in all likelihood already entered the prophecy by that time.[19] No one in France was apt to propagate the harsh words of Bridget from these two chapters of the *Revelations*, but they must have been known, especially by those doctors at Poitiers previously at the council of Constance,

---

[17] Gabrielle M. Spiegel, "The *Reditus Regni ad Stirpem Karoli Magni*: A New Look," *French Historical Studies* 7 (1971): 158–59; see also Chaume, "Prophétie," p. 41, for the oracle of the three Cs.

[18] Bower transcribes the text as follows: "There will never be such firm and quiet peace in France that the inhabitants can in any way rejoice together there in full security and harmony until the people of the kingdom have appeased God my son by some great works of piety and humility, for they have hitherto provoked him to indignation and wrath by their many sins and flashy ways," *Scotichronicon* 8: 133.

[19] The first revision of *Revelations* IV, 104–105 may have taken place in 1379–80 after the death of the Black Prince. See Eric Colledge, "*Epistola solitarii ad reges*: Alphonse of Pecha as Organizer of Birgittine and Urbanist Propaganda," *Mediaeval Studies* 18 (1956), p. 32.

where Bridget's *Revelations* were scrutinized in anticipation of her canonization.

The prophecy begins with the Virgin Mary asking Christ to "have pity on the unhappy realm of France" (*miserere isti regno*) since he has commanded generally that sinners should be forgiven.[20] The French and English kings appear as "two ferocious beasts" bent on destroying one another. Peace is to be achieved *per matrimonium* – because "the other king has justice" (*quia alter regum habet iusticiam*) – which is the mechanism by which the French can have a legitimate heir (*ad legittimum heredem poterit peruenire*).[21] In 1429, this would likely have been read as an allusion to the union set by the treaty of Troyes between Catherine of France and Henry VI, and therefore an affront to Charles VII's claim to legitimacy. After the outlining of a bland three-point reform for both kings, suddenly Bridget threatens that if the French king, who is designated only as "that king who now holds the kingdom" (*ille rex, qui nunc tenet regnum*) refuses to obey (*obedire*) "his life shall end in misery [*dolore*], his kingdom will be given over to tribulations [*tribulacionibus*], and his line held in such detestation that all shall be amazed [*obprobrio et confusione ita, quod omnes ammirabuntur*]."[22] Furthermore, Bridget grants just cause in the war to the English king, he "who has justice on his side" (*qui iusticiam habet*) and she promises that Christ will aid and fight for England (*adiuuabo eum et pugnabo pro eo*).[23] The only hope for France comes in the final line, which for obvious reasons is the only accent heard in Bower: "When the French acquire true humility, the kingdom will devolve to the true heir [*legittimum heredem*] and experience a good peace."[24]

Although Bridget's prophecy originally designated John II rather than Charles VII and was transcribed around the time of the treaty of Brétigny in 1360, the prophecy gave concrete and immediate expression to the idea that French sin and French kingship were causally connected, a judgment of special significance because it looks inwardly to moral reform as a way of controlling the outside forces of war. The idea that the outcome of war owed to divine favor rather than military strength was commonplace, its biblical bases numerous and well known. But in Bridget's prophecy the moral solution to France's political problems touched upon specific points of French vulnerability (union through marriage with the enemy, the lack of a true heir, a kingdom given over to tribulation, and the lineage of the king "held in such detestation that all shall be amazed"); the emphasis on

[20] For the Latin text see *Sancta Birgitta Revelaciones, Lib. IV*, Hans Aili, ed., Samlingar utgivna av Svenska Fornskriftsällskapet, 2nd ser., Latinska Skrifter; bd 7: 4) (Göteborg, 1992). Colledge, "*Epistola*," p. 31, gives a useful English summary of chap. 104–105.
[21] Aili, *Revelaciones*, p. 299.
[22] Aili, *Revelaciones*, p. 299.
[23] Aili, *Revelaciones*, p. 299.
[24] Aili, *Revelaciones*, p. 299.

correcting personal behavior may also have seemed to forecast Joan's own special insistence on moral reform.

Here then are the three prophecies which furnished the broad prophetic backdrop against which Joan's mission took place. It matters less that each prophecy either assimilated Joan or came to be associated with her – for all three definitely predate Joan – than it does for us to recognize that they created a sense of order for events in France, whether good or bad, into which Joan's mission could be blended.

MERLIN, BEDE, AND THE SIBYL

It is from a tantalizing but elusive stanza in Christine de Pizan's *Ditié* that we have our most precise information on the prelates' search at Poitiers for written sources predicting the Maid. The prophets named are the two most venerable English prophets, the eighth-century Bede and the fictional Celtic bard Merlin, as well as "the Sibyl" of classical antiquity, a very authoritative collection of names. In stanza 31 Christine writes: "For more than 500 years ago, Merlin, the Sibyl and Bede foresaw her coming, entered her in their writings as someone who would put an end to France's troubles, made prophecies about her, saying that she would carry the banner in the French wars and describing all that she would achieve."[25] In a letter of 9 July 1429, a *Morosini* chronicle correspondent, writing twenty-two days before Christine, with less explicit and less accurate information, locates the success of the quest for prophecies in Paris: "In Paris, Master Sasidis's mission found numerous [*molte*] prophecies mentioning this young girl [*damixela*]; among others a [prophecy] by Bede in Alex[andro]."[26] But Christine, who adheres closely to her sources, places this stanza between two stanzas clearly referring to Poitiers, as if the prophecies were uncovered at the Poitiers hearings. At any rate, logic prohibits us from thinking a search of codices could have taken place behind enemy lines in Paris.

Of the three prophets, only for Bede and Merlin can we find actual prophecies associated with Joan. The Sibyl's impact at Poitiers is undocumentable. But in the Middle Ages the names of Bede, Merlin, and Sibyl were usually uttered in the same breath, and the venerable pre-Christian origins of the sibylline tradition enhanced the authority of Bede and Merlin. The prophecies of Merlin were well known by the late twelfth century and translated into French by the thirteenth,[27] and already in 1385 the poet Deschamps in *Autre Balade 26* (*Contre l'Angleterre*) had invoked the three names to predict the imminent destruction of England.[28]

[25] Angus J. Kennedy and Kenneth Varty, eds., *Ditié de Jehanne d'Arc*, Medium Aevum Monographs, n.s. 9 (Oxford, 1977), p. 45.
[26] Dorez and Lefèvre-Pontalis, *Morosini* 3: 126–27.
[27] Rupert Taylor, *Political Prophecy in England* (New York, 1911), pp. 140–41.
[28] Deschamps, *Oeuvres* 1: 106–107.

Evidently the French drew satisfaction from finding English prophecies predicting the downfall of England, prophecies to gainsay the anti-French prognostications of St. Bridget, and so it should not startle us that both prophecies identifiable with Poitiers, those of Bede and Merlin, are Anglo-Saxon in origin. Since someone other than Joan had to demonstrate that she had been prophesied, it fell to a so-called Bede prophecy, recorded in a Bridlington poem about the Black Prince, written between 1362 and 1364, and later recast by the French, to offer signs that Joan had been heralded.[29] The prophecy is astrological in nature, a trait making it compatible with the scientific reputation of Bede. Applied to Joan it pretends to be a chronogram, whose roman numeral letters calculate the date of the Maid's arrival, although it must have seen more service in commemorating the event than in predicting it. Due to the necessity of refabricating the verse to give evidence of a date associated with Joan, it is impossible to give a meaningful translation of the Bede chronogram.[30] But the key element in the prophecy for the French – beyond the signaling of a noteworthy date – was the terse message that a young girl would carry a banner. Thus, at Poitiers the prophecy's allusion to a young girl (*puella*) immediately became a specific reference to Joan (*la Pucelle*).[31]

Perhaps Christine has conflated the Bede chronogram with the second prophecy advanced for Joan's early prediction – the verse credited to Merlin. The limitation of Bede's verse for those at Poitiers was precisely its inability to predict the outcome of the war, once an aura of mystery and expectation had been brought to bear on a decisive year. Thus the detection of a 200-year-old cryptic "merlinesque" verse, found in Geoffrey of Monmouth's *Historia Regum Britanniae*, must have generated a certain excitement, despite the need to draw its declaration of victory out of a highly enigmatic statement: "A virgin ascends the backs of the archers / and hides the flower of her virginity."[32] Everyone knew that the longer-lasting prophecies were those that lent themselves to multiple interpretations (the

---

[29] Olivier Bouzy, "Prédiction ou récupération, les prophéties autour de Jeanne d'Arc dans les premiers mois de l'année 1429," *Bulletin de l'Association des Amis du Centre Jeanne d'Arc* 14 (1990): 39.

[30] Watt translates the version in Walter Bower as follows: "Force with force twice-seven buttocks will mingle; The French colts will prepare new battles with the bull. Behold, battles resound, the maid carries banners," Bower, *Scotichronicon* 8: 133. Philippe Contamine, "Jeanne d'Arc et la prophétie," in Contamine, *De Jeanne d'Arc aux guerres d'Italie: Figures, images et problèmes du XVe siècle* (Orléans, 1994), p. 54, translates a different version as: "Two times six, two times seven, the cuckoos will join with one another. The French chickens will prepare new wars for the bull. And now the wars create blissful happiness. In those days the maid carries banners."

[31] See for instance, Christine de Pizan, *Ditié*, line 242: ". . . foresaw *her* coming." (Emphasis mine.)

[32] Acton Griscom, *The Historia Regum Britanniae of Geoffrey of Monmouth* (New York, 1929), p. 397.

cause in fact of their longevity), and that among contemporaries different readings were possible.[33] Interpretation was understood to belong to the prophetic process. The meaning given the Merlin prophecy in official Valois circles is most likely that of a French translation found in a contemporary manuscript, Berne 205. The manuscript contains two clusters of Johannic documents at fols. 62–69 and again at fol. 133, where the Poitiers-composed *Virgo puellares* (fol. 133a) is directly followed by the Merlin text and translation (fol. 133b), a fact which quite securely identifies the French translation with a royalist environment. As can be seen, the translation takes sizable liberties with the text,[34] both in placing the virgin on horseback and in armor, and in identifying the archers as English: "There will be a virgin who will ride in arms against the backs of the English archers and her sex and the flower of her virginity will keep secret."[35] Those in search of prophecies announcing the advent of the Maid were probably satisfied when they came upon the Latin original of this prophecy merely by its reference to a maid, but those who read the translation found additional reasons, in the interpretive accretions, to believe that Joan had been forecast by Merlin.

A more popular oral version of the Merlin prophecy, in which a new line beginning *Ex nemore canuto* had been added from a different part of Monmouth's *Historia regum Britanniae*, is attested several times at the nullification trial.[36] Fascinating nullification-trial testimony by Gobert Thibault, a squire of the king, tells us that Gérard Machet, the king's confessor and later bishop of Castres, believed Joan to have been prophesied. According to Thibaut, Machet said that he "had discovered in a writing that

---

[33] Thus a 9 July 1429 letter in the *Morosini* chronicle alluding to prognostications about Joan states that "some interpret them one way, some another," Dorez and Lefèvre-Pontalis, *Morosini* 3: 126-27.

[34] Originally, this prophecy may have implied only the interaction between two zodiac signs, *Virgo* and *Sagittarius*. See, however, the use of "PVeLLa" rather than *virgo* in the zodiac prophecies of the *Chronique du Mont-Saint-Michel (1343–1468)*, Siméon Luce, ed., 2 vols. (Paris, 1879–83) 1: 28–31.

[35] See Charles de Roche and Gustave Wissler, "Documents relatifs à Jeanne d'Arc et à son époque, extraits d'un manuscrit du XVe siècle de la Bibliothèque de Berne," in *Festschrift Louis Gauchat* (Aarau, 1926), p. 366: "Que vne virge sera qui cheuauchera en armes contre le dos des anglois archiers et son sexe et la fleur de sa virginite tendra secrez."

[36] The Monmouth line reads: "Ad hec ex urbe canuti nemoris eliminabitur puella," Griscom, *Historia*, p. 390. The new line about the oakwood was grafted onto the other line, as their separate locations in the *Historia* quite clearly prove. Olivier Bouzy, "Prédiction," p. 42, is right in noting that there is no meaningful rapport between the verse *Ex nemore . . .* and *Ascendit virgo*. He is unable to date the union any more closely than between the twelfth and fifteenth centuries. Of the few written instances of this popular prophecy (Berne 205, Kaerrymel, Thomassin) none of them starts with the line *Ex nemore canuto* as if the graft occurred after an initial dissemination of the short *Ascendet virgo* version.

there should come a maiden who would aid the Kingdom of France," and furthermore, Thibault testified, Machet and the other doctors "believed it was she of whom the prophecies spoke."[37] But although the Merlin prophecy has strong ties to Poitiers, we cannot be sure that either version from Monmouth is the one Machet knew.[38]

The advantage for the interests of the French party of the added line beginning *Ex nemore canuto* was that people equated the oakwood in the prophecy with the *Bois Chenu* of Joan's native province. It is clearly this longer version that her judges at Rouen were asking her about when she admitted that

> when she came to the king, several people asked her if there were not in her part of the country a wood called the oakwood; for there was a prophecy which said that out of this wood would come a maid who should work miracles.[39]

Machet could indeed have been among the "several people" who asked. Joan's simple reply at Rouen, however, was that she "put no faith" in the prophecy.[40]

Bringing the names of the revered ancient prophets – Merlin, Bede, and the Sibyl – to bear on the Maid's case seemed to give historical weight to her mission. And the Merlin prophecy, expanded in translation, was particularly effective by interpreting the mention of the Maid's hidden virginity as a reference to her riding in armor, a seeming authorization of her controversial request to ride armed. But the moment came at Poitiers when the prophecies uncovered in the ancient books were deemed too imprecise to be useful. It was then that the sixteen-line Latin prophecy *Virgo puellares* was composed. Even if the Bede chronogram had been restructured to publicize the arrival of Joan, the Merlin prophecy, while a good discovery, was too vague to be useful for the monumental task of strengthening Charles's army, which by most accounts was inadequate to the venture at Orléans. Whereas the *Lettre aux Anglais* would divulge everything that Joan had held in her heart since she left Domrémy, *Virgo puellares* was crafted by members of Charles's royal circle to address specific practical problems. But if a prophecy is degraded when it becomes too specific, it also becomes more efficacious and this is certainly true of *Virgo puellares*.

No one claimed that the new verses of *Virgo puellares* owed to Merlin, but a rare insight into the process of reconstructing prophecies is offered by

---

[37] Murray, *Jeanne d'Arc*, p. 266; Duparc, *Procès* 1: 369.

[38] Bouzy, "Prédiction," p. 42, assumes that the prophecy uncovered or remembered by Machet is the Merlin prophecy, but Thibault's version seems too vague to provide proof.

[39] Barrett, *Trial*, p. 55; Quicherat, *Procès* 1: 68.

[40] Barrett, *Trial*, p. 55; Quicherat, *Procès* 1: 68.

Mathieu Thomassin in the *Registre delphinal*. There he records the two-verse Merlin prophecy *Descendet virgo* stating that "on the said verses others were constructed [*furent faictz*] whose contents follow below,"[41] whereupon he transcribes the sixteen-line poem. Quickly, *Virgo puellares* became the reigning Johannic prophecy in print – with eleven separate transcriptions, either extant or attested, and three vernacular translations, two in French and one in German – although the oral version of the Merlin prophecy continued to circulate by word of mouth. We can surmise that the Merlin lineage of *Virgo puellares*, demonstrated in Thomassin, was rapidly lost, since the only other manuscripts containing both the Merlin prophecy and *Virgo puellares* (Berne 205 and Kaerrymel 979) transcribe the Merlin original after, rather than before, *Virgo puellares*, and not until ten years later in the Kaerrymel manuscript (in 1439), without any acknowledgment of a connection. However, even when the relationship between the Merlin original and its new rendition was lost, the poem's contemporary rather than ancient composition was still grasped. We learn this from the far reaches of Germany, where the Dominican chronicler Hermann Korner makes an illogical attribution of *Virgo puellares* to members of the University of Paris (since the poem's politics are clearly not Anglo-Burgundian) but proves by this his recognition of its contemporary production.

If the unique testimony of Thomassin, that *Virgo puellares* is based on *Descendet virgo*, seems slender evidence on which to establish the derivation, the context of the passage implies a possible motive for its composition that weds the two texts together, giving Thomassin's statement considerable authority. It appears that while Joan sought primarily to bring the message of her divine mission to a larger audience, Charles's counselors were more worried about how to publicize the two most troublesome facts about the upcoming Orléans campaign: that authority had been granted to a woman, and that the woman would don male armor. Although the gender issue was perhaps more important, Thomassin admits to the disruptive effect of Joan's demand for armor. In his account, arming Joan is on a par with her promise to chase away the English ("to do this [Charles] had to arm her"), and it is related as news that left everyone "astonished" (*esbahy*).[42] Several contemporary sources even see the primary effect of the *Poitiers Conclusions* as the permission granted Joan to equip herself, specifically, the right to acquire her own armor and wear men's clothes.[43] Some accounts even characterize the

---

[41] Quicherat, *Procès* 4: 305.
[42] Quicherat, *Procès* 4: 305.
[43] [Jean de Mascon?] follows a reference to the *Poitiers Conclusions* immediately by this statement: "Then they made her a complete coat of armor and also a banner and she was granted permission to be dressed as a man" (*eut licence d'estre habillée comme ung homme*), *La délivrance d'Orléans et l'institution de la fête du 8 mai, chronique anonyme du XVe siècle*, M. Boucher de Molandon, ed. (Orléans, 1883), p. 27.

king as bestowing men's clothes, armor, and a mount on Joan, practically as soon as the words of her mission had left her mouth.[44]

The French translation of *Descendet virgo* introduced the idea, hardly implied in the original, that the Maid in the prophecy was armed. *Virgo puellares* goes further, specifically featuring the detail of Joan's male dress (*induta virili veste*) – once again demonstrating the centrality of the issue long before the trial at Rouen – even before the poem discloses her claim to a divine mission (*Dei monitu*), a prioritization with which Joan would certainly have disagreed. Apparently deciding that the best defense is an offense, the pseudo-prophets at Poitiers, drawing on the new spirit of humanism, portrayed the Maid in these lines as an armed feminine Mars, designed for the French soldiery as a challenge for them to match, and for the English (should the poem come into their hands) a formidable mythological figure. Also in evidence is the imagery, used almost mandatorily in the months before Joan's arrival, depicting the French monarchy as a trampled lily, a lily that would now be raised up through the Maid's exertions. But in case we take this Latin prophetic poem to be a key part of the theological debate surrounding Joan's mission, instead of the unadorned propaganda piece that it is, we must realize that the depiction of the utopian French peace in the poem's last seven lines, christianizing a poem of otherwise pagan allure, may have come to the poets as an afterthought. Walter Bower's *Scotichronicon* omits precisely these seven lines.[45] Although the other ten examples of *Virgo puellares* offer the full sixteen-line text, reasonably confirming their version to be the original, nevertheless, the last seven lines denote religious festooning of a largely secular text, but one likely to generate enthusiasm either way for Joan.

Whatever message the French took from *Virgo puellares* – and there is no surviving evidence that, in the final analysis, this internal document did not convey to the French, as the external *Lettre aux Anglais* was designed to do to the English, the dominant message of Joan's supernatural mission – the poem eventually came into English hands, with predictably different results. Through the chance preservation of an English reply to *Virgo puellares*, a harangue not focused exclusively on points made in that poem but addressing a number of them, we learn which were the salient points of *Virgo puellares* to its English contemporaries.

The English reply to *Virgo puellares* (hereafter the *English Reply*) understandably makes little of Joan's claim to a divine mission. The "lying" claim that the Maid has been "sent by God" (here: *ab ethere mitti*) is not presented as Joan's own avowal, but has been transferred to Charles – ambiguously

---

[44] For instance, an extract from the *Tableau des rois de France*, preserved by the dean of St. Thibaut de Metz, in Quicherat, *Procès* 4: 326: "Et incontinent le roy la fist habiller et s'armer et monter en son plaisir."

[45] Bower, *Scotichronicon* 8: 132–33.

termed "her host" – who is acting out of self-interest. The Maid is an "insolent whore" (*procax meretrix*) and "pythoness" (*phitonissa*)[46] believable to the French only because they are a superstitious people (*fatidice gentis . . . gensque supersticiosa*). More sympathetically stated, this is the flaw of overcredulity. Turning the tables on Joan's claim to virginity, the author of the *English Reply* portrays her as a "prostitute disguised as virgin" (*meretrix quoque dicta puella*), but achieves a double insult by adding the opposite accusation that she is mannish ("virago disguised as a virgin" [*virgo viraginea*]).

The core communication of the *English Reply*, however, is the author's desire to deliver motivational direction to English troops, just as *Virgo puellares* seeks to motivate actual or potential French soldiers. And the leitmotif of the verses is that of permanence, the durability of the English presence in France, now suddenly threatened by Joan's victories. The English are warned not to yield to her terror, but to "stay with the task begun" (*non vos a ceptis divertat*). The successes of this long-fought war for possession of France – which the author carefully identifies as a just war ("this France to which you rightly hold title" [*quos equo jure tenetis*]) – are at risk. The danger of the Maid is viewed as potentially cataclysmic, as powerful as "pulling out the roots" (*antique collidere semina*) of something that has lasted for a long time. In effect, Joan is accused of rekindling war where a measure of peace and quietude had been won at a price (*longum pacare laborem*). The *English Reply* looks toward total English victory, but seems almost content to bargain for maintaining the *status quo*. In particular, it states that the "artful words" (*presagia*) of the Maid must not deflect the English from their assignment. The *English Reply* lays bare the Maid's strategy, but, ironically for the architects of *Virgo puellares* at Poitiers, who designed their verses to announce Joan's entry into the world of action, the English portray Joan's tactic as one of purely verbal propaganda. She is not an actor ("this pythoness . . . can do nothing for herself" [*phitonissa quidem sibi nil eadem valitura*]), but an artful and cunning purveyor of words. Joan's prophecies are degradingly termed "the presages of that prophetic people," but it is evident that her verbal arts present a genuine danger to the English. "Fear her omens not at all, Englishmen," the writer warns. "Let them not sway you, these presages that will haul you over the coals with a lance in the gut,"[47] he continues, appealing to the efficacy of actions over words. Finally, the diatribe ends with the warning that the English soldiers must continue to place their trust in the sword, since the French will reap no benefit from their spells and predictions.

---

[46] For the origins of this word, meaning "prophetess," first applied to the priestesses of Apollo at Delphi and its derogatory application to St. Bridget by her enemies in Rome, see Sahlin, "Gender," in Chance, *Gender and Text*, p. 82.

[47] From notes taken 18 November 1993 by the author at the *Centre Jeanne d'Arc*, Orléans, from draft of new edition of Quicherat.

In turning from *Virgo puellares* to the *Lettre aux Anglais*, we turn from a pragmatic tract, written in undistinguished verse, but rhymed to enhance its prophetic mystique, to a document which may also have had its origins in the expedient – as a summons to enemy captains at the walls of Orléans – but which, if so, is nonetheless a powerfully written open letter to the English, as magnetizing as its counterpart *Virgo puellares* is pedestrian. For its blend of military efficiency, patriotic spirit, and religious substructure, the *Lettre aux Anglais* has been justly celebrated. But for our purposes, it is, without a question, one of the seminal, defining documents in the theological debate over Joan's divine mission. The *Lettre*, as we shall see, is Joan's manifesto of her spiritual vocation, a document therefore standing in stark contrast to the clerics' prosaic *Virgo puellares*.

5

Lettre aux Anglais

The first step Joan took as a result of the favorable, although limited, outcome of the investigation at Poitiers was to compose the *Lettre aux Anglais*, a summons to the English currently holding Orléans in a blockade, which it is reasonable to believe was the document through which the English gained their first knowledge of the Maid's presence.[1] Looked at from the point of view of discernment, the sequence of events by which the prelates identified the probable source of Joan's inspiration, in order that she be allowed to write the *Lettre* and announce her divine mission publicly, is curiously backwards. Generally, discernment commissions held the prophet's writings in their possession before they passed judgment, in fact their charge was to scrutinize the writings for the presence of error as a significant part of the process. The contrast is plain when we consider that for St. Bridget at Constance the process revolved around the orthodoxy and theological validity of spiritual writings already in existence, while for Joan the decision at Poitiers opened the possibility and granted her the privilege of writing for the first time.

In a sense Joan was dictating her own letter of accreditation, much as a gathering of prelates would testify in writing to certify the sanctity of a person authorized for canonization. Joan's newly won approval did not confer sainthood, as had been the outcome of *discretio* for Bridget, but the Poitiers doctors' judgment did authorize her to announce publicly, not only who she was, but more importantly, her sacred mission. Thus, with the confidence in her that the drawing up of the *Poitiers Conclusions* implied, a confidence ·vhose implication Joan's judges at Rouen demanded, without success, that she swear to explicitly,[2] Joan was finally able to pronounce unchecked and to the outside world the name of her sponsor: she was sent by God (*envoyée de par Dieu, le Roi du ciel*). Again, just how different this scenario is from a discernment procedure leading to canonization can be realized by noting that in a normal case of canonization, approval decorated

---

[1] Pernoud, *Joan of Arc*, p. 71.
[2] In article 21, concerning the *Lettre*, it is noted that "asked if her own party firmly believed her to be sent from God, she answered she knew not whether they did, and referred us to their opinion," Barrett, *Trial*, p. 175; Quicherat, *Procès* 1: 240.

someone already dead, whose body was exhumed once canonization was authorized, whose feast day was assigned, and whose name was added to the local calendar of saints.[3] For Joan, approval allowed her to go to war. Furthermore, and ironically, the feminine docility, whose evidence as a theological proof was so sought after in examining Joan at Poitiers, was now supplanted by a warrior's assertiveness.

In order to understand this atypical circumstance theologically, we must remember that the premise underlying Joan's approval by the commission was that she would demonstrate a miracle at Orléans. The fulfillment of the victory she promised, whereby she would in effect transform words into deeds, answered the challenge of Matthew 7:16: "By their fruits you shall know them," and hence would constitute her sign. The ecclesiastics at Poitiers may have balked at Joan's assertion that the political nature of a military victory could constitute a miracle, as we can surmise from the objection in the *Poitiers Conclusions*: "although her promises involve only human deeds," but once the premise of Orléans had gained their support, regardless of their hesitations, the way was clear for a victory to prove a miracle. As was so often true in Joan's case, whether it worked for or against her, the Old Testament offered pertinent testimony. Thus, the *Poitiers Conclusions* allude to the miraculous victory of Gideon, and we will later see Christine de Pizan name a series of Hebrew battle-miracles as parallel in an authorizing way to Joan's actions.

Because of the determinative nature of Joan's campaign at Orléans, she must have felt a significant investment in the nature and wording of the *Lettre*.[4] Any impact she could have through words alone reduced the burden of what had to be done through arms. Thus the *Lettre* is rich in points crucial to the debate over Joan's spiritual mission which can be briefly listed to demonstrate their amplitude: first, God has sent Joan; second, the news she brings comes from God and Joan (*de par Dieu et la Pucelle*); third, she is sent to chase the English out of all France (*pour vous chasser hors de toute la France*); fourth, she proposes the option of retreat and makes two overtures of peace; fifth, the English departure from France is inevitable (*n'ayez point une autre opinion*, etc.); sixth, death is the consequence of noncompliance (*s'ils ne veulent obeir, je les ferai tous occire*); seventh, mercy will be the reward for obedience; eighth, Charles is true heir (*vrai héritier*); ninth, he will rule because God wants him king (*car Dieu . . . le veut*); tenth, this revelation comes through Joan (*cela est révélé par la Pucelle*); eleventh, Paris will be (re)taken; twelfth, numbers of soldiers are irrelevant because God is giving Joan supernatural strength (*le Roi du ciel enverra plus de force à la Pucelle*, etc.); thirteenth, fighting will demonstrate God's preference by the outcome (*aux*

---

[3] Kenneth L. Woodward, *Making Saints: How the Catholic Church Determines Who Becomes a Saint, Who Doesn't, and Why* (New York, 1990), p. 65.

[4] See Appendix III for a full English translation.

horions on verra qui aura meilleur droit); finally, the English have a choice between "self destruction" (*que vous ne vous fassiez mie destruire*) and joining the French in a glorious deed, an allusion to a crusade against the infidel.

This was no ordinary military summons, as a rapid look at the summonses in the fourteenth and fifteenth centuries reveals. In essence, the military summons, if it was issued at all,[5] was no more than a declaration of war. The hostile intention was generally accented by the accompaniment of a lacerated, bloody glove, the *guantum pugnae*.[6] One extant summons from Italy in 1372 speaks directly to the military aggression intended, amid the other formalities of the letter: "We invite you to war. . . . Come forth, therefore, you bellicose men!"[7] Once a provocation of this nature had been made, a second type of summons requested in writing the establishment of a time and place for battle.[8] The details at this point could become exceedingly complicated. Sometimes peasants were enlisted to cut down trees and fill in ditches that might impede the movement of the armies, or a number of experts from each side were assigned to search out terrain that was properly configured and close enough to both camps to prevent one army from arriving more refreshed than the other. Furthermore, a summons was far from guaranteeing a battle. In one instance, in 1346, Philip VI gave Edward III a choice of the next Thursday, Sunday, or Tuesday as battle date, but Edward simply refused.[9] Nor was Jean II any more successful in engaging Edward III's son, who simply backed out of an engagement saying "that he had come to those parts to do certain business, which he had managed to accomplish, thank God, and was returning to where he had [other] business."[10] Indeed, the necessary conclusion from the evidence is that summonses had little actual effect on action.

The vast difference between the *Lettre* and the conventional summonses just described can be easily judged by comparing them to the fourteen points made in Joan's missive as enumerated above. But four factors, in particular, especially merit our attention: first, the promise of the *Lettre* to be effective; second, the option to retreat and two overtures of peace; third, the introduction of God's will through the words of the Maid; and fourth, the broad concerns taken up in the *Lettre*, which go well beyond the engagement at Orléans.

---

[5] Jean Glénisson, "Notes d'histoire militaire: Quelques lettres de défi du XIVe siècle," *Bibliothèque de l'Ecole des Chartes* 107 (1947–48): 244, notes that no summonses were issued at either the battles of Poitiers or Crécy.

[6] Glénisson, "Lettres de défi," p. 240 and p. 250.

[7] Glénisson, "Lettres de défi," p. 250: "Vos invitamus ad bellum. . . . Venite igitur, viri bellicosi!"

[8] Glénisson, "Lettres de défi," p. 236.

[9] Glénisson, "Lettres de défi," p. 243.

[10] Glénisson, "Lettres de défi," p. 244: "qil est venuz en yceles parties pur certains busoignes feares, lez quels il avoit bien comply, Dieu mercy, et fust en returnaunt la ou il avoit affaire."

First point: The obsessive interest in battle locations seen in the conventional summons, based on the fear of one side gaining a modest advantage, shows that the soldiers on the field actually saw the outcome of battle as directly related to temporal circumstances. Joan, on the other hand, scoffs at this notion in the *Lettre*, making numbers of soldiers involved in battle as irrelevant as stumps or hollows on the battlefield: "The King of Heaven will send greater strength to the Maid and her good men-at-arms than you in all your assaults can overwhelm." Through this sentence she states the superiority of divine over human strength, thereby creating the sense of inevitability that the *Lettre* projects.

Second point: For some readers of the *Lettre*, those wedded to the image of Joan as simple, humble, pious, and appropriately feminine – an image without question intentionally projected by the *Poitiers Conclusions* – it is as though Joan owed her supporters an apology for leaving them with the embarrassment of explaining the *Lettre*. Critics usually conclude that the scribe, Jean Erault, a prominent theologian, or other clerics, modified the originally dictated text. This would account for three expressions in the *Lettre* which Joan denied when it was read to her at Rouen.[11] But Joan insisted on taking full credit for everything else in the text, stating in the fifth session of her trial on 1 March 1431 "that none of the lords ever dictated these letters, but she herself dictated them . . . though they were indeed shown to certain of her party."[12]

A more fruitful way to justify Joan's *Lettre* would be to acknowledge that her document offers mercy in the case of retreat and makes two proposals for peace, which goes counter to the medieval notion of a summons as a declaration of war, earning the *Lettre* the paradoxical designation, by one critic, of "pacific" and "menacing."[13] The "if . . . then" configuration so marked in the syntax of the *Lettre* identifies Joan's source as Deuteronomy 20:10–12, the prototype of all summonses:

If at any time thou come to fight against a city, thou shalt first offer it peace. If they receive it, and open the gates to thee, all the people that are therein, shall be saved. . . . But if they will not make peace, and shall begin war against thee, thou shalt besiege it.

Whether taught the value of the summons by prelates or through some instinctive sense of her own that an offer of peace should always precede a challenge to war, Joan was firm about the need to issue summonses.[14] That

---

[11] Barrett, *Trial*, p. 71: "Surrender to the Maid," "body for body," and "chieftain of war"; Quicherat, *Procès* 1: 84.
[12] Barrett, *Trial*, p. 71; Quicherat, *Procès* 1: 84.
[13] Anatole France, "Le siège d'Orléans (1428–1429) [pt. 4]," *La revue de Paris* 15 Feb. (1902), p. 742.
[14] Mathieu Thomassin, *Registre delphinal* in Quicherat, *Procès* 4: 306: "Avant qu'elle voulsist aller contre les Anglois, elle dist qu'il falloit qu'elle les sommast et requist, de par Dieu, qu'ilz vuydassent le royaume de France." [Not quite an offer of peace!]

she understood the function of the summons in establishing a just war emerges from her condemnation trial testimony. At Rouen, she replied to the accusation of article 18 (inciting to murder and shedding blood): "that she summoned the Duke of Burgundy . . . to make peace," admitting, however, that to her the only peace with the English would come from their return to their own country.[15] Her *Lettre* departs in its proposal of peace from medieval chivalric convention in order to conform to biblical precept. To do so cradled the lamentable fact of war in a theological justification.

Despite the openings for peace, few would deny that, looked at through slightly more cynical eyes, the *Lettre* can be read as a mere license for aggression and violence. Deuteronomy 20:13, in fact, provides a model for violence as well as peace, by directing that all the subjugated males be pierced through by the sword after God grants victory. Moreover, although Joan denied having dictated the aggressive term "body for body," she never disputed the phrase "I will have them all put to death." As has been observed by one of Joan's biographers, the offers of mercy in the *Lettre* "are made very much as afterthoughts."[16] But this is not to say, as her Rouen judges would claim, that Joan gloried in the spilling of human blood.[17] She issued no less than three summonses to the English at Orléans before taking action, concluding the third in this way: "That is what I write to you for the third and last time, and shall write no more."[18] There was virtually no chance that the English would accede to the young girl's orders, or that Bedford would order a retreat. The understandable natural antipathy of the English to such a proposal may have been correctly summed up in modern times by Vita Sackville-West: "Solid English sense could say nothing but 'Rubbish.'"[19] Yet peace, although under her conditions, appears to have been Joan's sincere wish. Had Bedford, against all likelihood, accepted her offer, Joan would doubtless not have returned home to "spin with [her] poor mother," as the knight Jean de Novelonpont, known as Jean de Metz, testified in 1456,[20] but would have joined Charles on the great crusade, which she alludes to in the *Lettre* itself, to her mind, the final war before the true and lasting peace.

Third point: The ordinary summons was no more than a piece of diplomatic writing whose words owed to its author, whether the knight himself or a clerical draftsman.[21] By comparison, in the *Lettre* Joan purported to reveal God's will, stating that the tidings from the Maid came from God (*de par Dieu les nouvelles de la Pucelle*). This meant that while the English

---

[15] Barrett, *Trial*, p. 170; Quicherat, *Procès* 1: 234.
[16] Edward Lucie-Smith, *Joan of Arc* (1976; New York, repr. 1977), p. 79.
[17] Article 25, Barrett, *Trial*, p. 177; Quicherat, *Procès* 1: 243.
[18] Pernoud, *Joan of Arc*, p. 87.
[19] Vita Sackville-West, *Saint Joan of Arc* (1936; New York, repr. 1991), p. 136.
[20] Murray, *Jeanne d'Arc*, p. 223; Duparc, *Procès* 1: 290.
[21] Glénisson, "Lettres de défi," p. 237.

might not take orders from Joan, they were obliged to listen to the counsel of God, interpreted through her in the *Lettre*. The *Lettre* made it appear that God, whether previously wrathful, preoccupied or indifferent, had abruptly recommitted himself to France, and that for this purpose he had sent Joan. There is no mention of voices, no naming of saints in the *Lettre*. The only voice heard dictating the divine will is that of the *Pucelle*. She is there in person, as if God himself stood in her boots.

As Pierre Champion stated, the *Lettre* is "the most important document that we possess on the thinking of Joan of Arc,"[22] but Joan herself would have argued that the *Lettre* represented divine thought, not her own. In fact, at her condemnation trial, when her judges tried to insist that she had written this letter "incited by her temerity and her presumption" (*sive temeritate et praesumptione ducta*), thus arguing her motivation, she retorted that she wrote it "through the bidding of the King of Heaven" (*par le Roy du Ciel*), twisting their focus into an argument of agency.[23] This was what made the *Lettre*, in Joan's mind, a prophecy, not a mere plan of her military intentions. Her role as divine messenger dictated the self-assured tone. As Anatole France noted: "She seeks not to persuade the adversary. . . . Her reasons are not of this world. . . . Speaking in the name of the King of Heaven, she commands."[24]

Fourth point: The broad scope of the *Lettre* is evident from the moment of the salutation, and is expanded further by the end. Instead of only addressing the captains conducting the siege at Orléans, Joan writes an open letter and includes as addressees the seven-year-old king, Henry VI, and the duke of Bedford, regent of France, neither of whom was present at Orléans. Instead of asking only for the surrender of Orléans, Joan's demand is for the keys to all the captured cities. In fact, she orders that the English abandon all France. She even weaves the dynastic question into her summons, declaring that Charles is "true heir" and adds the promise that he will take Paris. The *Lettre* also extends its purview in time, by Joan's threat to produce "so great a *hahay* [tumult] that none so great has been in France for a thousand years," as well as in geographic space, by her allusion to a crusade to retake Jerusalem. Thus the *Lettre* reads more like Joan's theological and political platform than it resembles an exercise in the formalities of battle diplomacy. Moreover, it appears that Joan felt her entire mission was spelled out in prophetic terms in the *Lettre*. When the text was read out to her at Rouen, she implied that the *Lettre* was a prophecy needing seven years to be fulfilled, with or without her: "To this article . . . Jeanne answers that if the English

[22] Pierre Champion, ed. and trans., *Procès de condamnation de Jeanne d'Arc*, 2 vols., Bibliothèque du XVe siècle, 22, 23 (Paris, 1920–21; Geneva, repr. 1976) 2: 400.

[23] Article 21, Barrett, *Trial*, pp. 174–75; Quicherat, *Procès* 1: 239.

[24] France, "Le siège," p. 741. Jehanne d'Orliac, *Joan of Arc and her Companions*, Elisabeth Abbott, trans. (Philadelphia, 1934), p. 144, says approximately the same thing: "far from arguing, the letter declared."

had had faith in her letters they would have been wise men, and within seven years they will perceive what she wrote."[25]

The claim has been made, and there is limited documentation to corroborate it, that the *Lettre* as we know it, and as Joan acknowledged it at Rouen, is a composite text and that originally she sent only a series of short, perfunctory summonses to various members of the English party. According to this interpretation – strengthened by Mathieu Thomassin's division of the *Lettre* in the *Registre delphinal* into four separate letters, and by a similar breakdown in the *Journal du siège d'Orléans* (combined, however, in a single letter) – Henry VI, the men-at-arms, the captains at Orléans, and Bedford all received separate, basically non-redundant letters, varying in length from six to seventeen lines. This reading helps account for the repetitions in the full-length *Lettre*, and excuses Joan of the charge of filling her letter with the "repetitions used by illiterate people when most in earnest,"[26] but the chronicles which divide the *Lettre* into separate missives were composed late – both of them after the nullification trial. In contrast, the evidence between 1429 and 1431 validates the issuing of a single letter. Furthermore, certain divisions make little sense, the exhortation to the men-at-arms, in particular, because it includes the sentence better directed at Henry VI, stating: "You will not hold France . . . but Charles will."

The most important objection to the theory of a four-part *Lettre* is that it destroys the unity of thought in the full text, eliminating, for instance, from Bedford's and the captains' letters the crucial proposition that Joan has been sent by God, and extending the invitation of a crusade only to Bedford. This is to say nothing of the harm that chopping the text in fourths causes to the raw magnificence of the text itself, a beauty which countless readers of the *Lettre* have observed; for instance, Mark Twain summed it all up in understated admiration when he declared that she had "a capable tongue."[27] There are, in fact, in the *Lettre*, deep accents not tapped by comparing the document to the summons prototype alone, but which come into view especially when we consider a broader range of texts and ideas with bearing on the French monarchy.

As the final part of our discussion of the *Lettre*, these elements, not all of which exist in written texts, will be examined, first treating concerns to which the *Lettre* represents, knowingly or unknowingly, a response: Joan's self-designation as the Maid (*la Pucelle*), her alleged secret to the king, the treaty of Troyes, and Saint Bridget's prophecies on France. Second, we will examine specific reactions to the *Lettre* by the English: responses from the rank-and-file soldier, a letter of 7 August 1429 from the duke of Bedford to Charles VII, evidence from the condemnation trial, and finally, the letter of censure

[25] Barrett, *Trial*, p. 176; Quicherat, *Procès* 1: 241.
[26] Francis Cabot Lowell, *Joan of Arc* (Boston, 1896), p. 70.
[27] Mark Twain, *Personal Recollections of Joan of Arc by the Sieur, Louis de Conte (Her Page and Secretary)* (New York, 1896; repr. 1926), p. 172.

written in 1431, following the Maid's condemnation and burning, on behalf of the young Henry VI.

Joan did not sign her name to the *Lettre*, as she would later affix it to letters sent to the inhabitants of Reims, Troyes, and Riom.[28] But, if the document that introduced Joan to the enemy could be termed her calling card, in the body of the text she clearly gives her "signature," identifying herself with her *nom de guerre, la Pucelle*, which was the name she preferred to use and considered more relevant than her given name. In fact, the word *Pucelle* occurs six times in the course of the text. The *Lettre* also identifies Joan as chieftain of war (*chef de guerre*), but the term appears only once, and during her trial she denied having dictated the phrase. The terms *pucelle* and *chef de guerre* epitomize the dual image of the Maid, which we have seen so often, the clashing figures of gentle femininity and masculine bravery, which most writers mark as separated by her presence on the field or off it, but are here merged, in their inherent contradiction, in the same document. It is the same contradictory depiction found in the aggressive four-stanza poem "Ariere, Englois" ("Retreat, you Englishmen"), which pauses from its threats and insults to call Joan, the instigator of the violence, "the gentle Maid" (*la douce Pucelle*).[29]

One can validly argue that Joan's bias in favor of the term *pucelle* derived from a wish to prove her dedication to God through the preservation of her virginity. Yet in the military context of the *Lettre*, Joan's insistence surely serves another important purpose as well. To imprint the term "virgin" on the minds of the enemy was to make a preemptive strike against being seen as a camp follower or prostitute, essentially the only historical explanation for women on the battlefield in the fifteenth century. Joan was recreating in real life a justification for a woman's presence in war, just as the author Benoit de Sainte-Maure had settled the question in fiction for his Amazon heroine Penthesilea in the well known twelfth-century *Roman de Troie*.[30] In Benoit's verse, Penthesilea makes an impassioned speech to insist that men understand the correct image of the Amazons:

> You believe us to be like other common women, who have flighty and changing hearts: that is not our business. We are virgins [*puceles somes*]: we have no interest in evil deeds or sexual indulgence.[31]

---

[28] See her signature in a letter to Reims in Quicherat, *Procès* 5: 160, and in a letter to Riom in Quicherat, *Procès* 5: 148. Pernoud and Clin, *Jeanne d'Arc*, p. 377, also list a letter of 28 March to Rheims, but Quicherat, *Procès* 5: 162 shows no signature.

[29] Paul Meyer, ed., "Ballade contre les Anglais (1429)," *Romania* 21 (1892): 51.

[30] Benoit de Sainte-Maure, *Le roman de Troie*, Léopold Constans, ed., 6 vols. (Paris, 1904–12).

[31] Benoit, *Troie*, 4: 53, lines 24,091–24,096: "Tu cuides que nos seions taus / Come autres femmes comunaus, / Que les cors ont vains e legiers: / Ço n'est mie nostre mestiers. / Puceles somes: n'avons cure / De mauvaistié ne de luxure."

To this need to establish her legitimate business in the theater of war, we can attribute Joan's bristling hostility towards *filles de joie*, related in several chronicles and depicted in a miniature in *Les Vigiles du roi Charles VII*.[32]

Although much publicity has surrounded the secret Joan told the king, by which he is said to have come to believe in her, we have seen how the process of *discretio spirituum* was actually the mechanism for placing faith in the Maid, and that the discernment procedure was not considered complete without the demonstration of a sign, the miracle at Orléans. It is important to separate the theological requirement of a sign from the secret, the latter being just that, despite confusion over the distinction from Joan's judges during the condemnation trial.[33] Astonishingly, however, the gist of the secret – either as it is gleaned from Jean Pasquerel's nullification-trial testimony or Pierre Sala's sixteenth-century chronicle, two sources previously discussed – receives prominent consideration in the *Lettre*, amounting, in essence, to a public expression of the secret.

To the extent that a real secret might have touched on Charles's doubts about his legitimacy or guilt regarding his sins, any reference to those problems in a missive directed at the enemy would obviously be omitted. But Pasquerel states, as we have already seen, that Joan told Charles, as she now told the English in the *Lettre*, that God accepted Charles as true heir. Even the wording of Pasquerel's testimony and the *Lettre* is the same, both using the term *vray héritier*, which is only verifiable given the unusual shift in Pasquerel's testimony from Latin to French at this point: "Ego dico tibi ex parte *de Messire, que tu es vray héritier de France, et filz du roy*."[34] Naturally, there was no need to raise doubts among the English about Charles's blood legitimacy by including in the *Lettre* the confirmation that Charles was son of the king, so the words *filz du roy* never appear. The slightly longer, non-contemporary version, reported to Pierre Sala by the king's chamberlain, includes the request for succor, in the form of protection and defense, if the kingdom were his legitimately (*justement*) and he were true heir (*vray hoir*). The *Lettre*, in proclaiming divine intervention, promising the expulsion of Charles's enemies, and declaring his just cause and status as true heir, amounts to just that. The talk during Joan's trial of a crown that was the "sign" likely owes to Joan's giving in to fatigue made of her judges' questioning. If a secret existed, it must have been roughly as Pasquerel and Sala told it. There seems to be no other message that she could have given her king that would have been relevant or interesting.

The influence of the treaty of Troyes can be felt from the first words of the *Lettre*. There may be reason to believe that Joan's classic declaration of her

---

[32] The miniature is reproduced in Marina Warner, *Joan of Arc: The Image of Female Heroism* (New York, 1981) as illustration no. 28.
[33] See the session of 10 March. Reference from Warner, *Joan of Arc*, p. 55, n. 6.
[34] Murray, *Jeanne d'Arc*, p. 283; Duparc, *Procès* 1: 390.

illiteracy, that she knew "neither A nor B,"[35] deserves reconsideration, since it has been noted that during her trial she asked to retain certain documents in her prison cell to read at her leisure.[36] There is, of course, not the least necessity that she should have read the text of the *Treaty of Troyes* to know its contents. Moreover, as reported by Gobert Thibault at the nullification trial, she dictated the words of the *Lettre* to Jean Erault, a supportive prelate among Joan's examiners at Poitiers, who transcribed, and may have edited, her message.[37] This process, as previously stated, would not have been unusual. Alphonso of Jaén, for instance, seems to have shared a similar relationship with Saint Bridget for the transcription, editing, and translating of her prophecies,[38] as did other seers and prophets, and even conventional military summonses underwent literary enhancement.[39]

In any event, Joan calls into question the entire illusion of the lawfulness of the English presence in France by denying her letter's designees their right to the titles they claim to bear. Thus Henry VI is termed only King of England, not king of the double monarchy of England and France; Bedford only "calls himself" (*qui vous dites*) regent, as William Pole, John Talbot, and Thomas Lord Scales "call themselves" (*qui vous dites*) his lieutenants. This act of verbal defiance belongs to a series of such challenges in French and English correspondence over the course of the war, but is intended in all probability to reply to the most outrageous of previous instances, nine years before: the specification at the end of the *Treaty of Troyes*, when the document finally deigns to refer to the blood heir and dauphin, of Charles as "so-called [*soy disant*] dauphin of Vienne."

Since Joan announces that God has confirmed Charles as true heir, this casts the English in the role of illegal landholders, without title, who therefore owe compensation to the French (*payant pour ce que vous l'avez tenue*). This point begins to establish the case for Charles's just cause, sanctioning his use of force to regain his possessions. In contrast to the *Treaty of Troyes*, which portrays the linkage of the two kingdoms as the means to "reinstate peace and eliminate dissensions,"[40] Joan invokes in the *Lettre* the clear logic of the principle of national sovereignty, suggesting that to the English belongs one country, and to the French another, each to be ruled by its proper king. Joan proclaims that now the English must return to their country (*allez-vous-en en*

---

35 Nullification testimony of Gobert Thibault relating a reply to Pierre de Versailles at Poitiers, Murray, *Jeanne d'Arc*, p. 265; Duparc, *Procès* 1: 368.

36 Pernoud and Clin, *Jeanne d'Arc*, p. 377. No reference given.

37 Murray, *Jeanne d'Arc*, p. 265; Duparc, *Procès* 1: 368. See Pernoud, *Joan of Arc*, p. 66, who believes it possible that Joan's words were edited.

38 See, for instance, Flavigny, *Sainte Brigitte*, p. 565.

39 Glénisson, "Lettres de défi," p. 237, describes a letter in a style "one would think taken from a novel," calling these letters "small *chefs-d'oeuvre* of war literature" that one could imagine being read and commented upon at different courts.

40 For the text of the treaty of Troyes see Markale, *Isabeau*, pp. 259–66 or Eugène Cosneau, *Les grands traités de la guerre de cent ans* (Paris, 1889), here p. 102.

votre pays) as a French king, at God's will, is to rule over France. Implying that she has a clear sense of France's geographical borders, Joan notes that the English must leave "all France."

Both the framers of the *Treaty of Troyes* and the author of the *Lettre* are well aware that the war between France and England pits one Christian nation against another, a questionable proposition even when the rules of war and the weight of the Bible and the church could be brought to bear in its defense. One of the grounds used in the *Treaty of Troyes* to authorize the double monarchy is that the evils of the division between the two countries have spread "to the entire church militant."[41] But the *Lettre* outdistances the Lancastrian formulation of unity, which yoked together the two dissenters and outlawed further dissent, by proposing, in its final lines, an even more compelling configuration, the invitation to the English to join in a crusade against the infidel, a form of unity which was destined to advance the entire church. Alluding to the thoroughly cosmic vision of Christian peace embodied in the Second Charlemagne prophecy, which Warner has called "the collective fantasy" of the late-medieval crusading ideal,[42] Joan asks the English to lay down their arms against the French and "join her company, where the French will do the fairest deed ever done for Christianity." The proposal for a joint crusade was not new. The desire to substitute an expedition against the Turks for wars between Christians had been a fundamental theme of Saint Catherine of Siena.[43] But the idea allows the *Lettre* to greatly intensify the justification of the French cause. The thrust of the *Lettre*, then, is to consider the delivery of the French from the yoke of the English as no more than a "preliminary act."[44] It is the first stage only in a wider effort to exalt the faith.

Of the prior sources bearing an intertextual or dialogic relationship to the *Lettre*, it remains only to examine the prophecies of Saint Bridget, chapters 104–105 of Book Four of the *Revelations*, already introduced in an earlier chapter. It is at least as unlikely that Joan had read the *Revelations* as the *Treaty of Troyes*, but we do not need her to have been familiar with the texts for the chapters in question to be useful in our efforts to understand the *Lettre*. A brief review of the pertinent points in the prophecies is in order. First, Bridget spoke of the tribulations that the king would suffer and the desolation that would befall the kingdom of France due to sin (not a point, as

---

[41] Cosneau, *Traités*, p. 103.
[42] In a letter written by Joan to the duke of Burgundy on 17 July 1429, reproduced in Quicherat, *Procès* 5: 126, she expressed the same idea in much different terms: "If fighting is your desire, then go after the Sarrasins." Cited by Warner, *Joan of Arc*, p. 177.
[43] Paul Rousset, "Saint Catherine de Sienne et le problème de la croisade," *Schweizerische Zeitschrift für Geschichte / Revue Suisse d'Histoire / Rivista Storica Svizzera* 25 (1975): 506–507.
[44] Chaume, "Une prophétie," p. 36.

previously stated, to emphasize to the enemy, and there is no trace of this theme in the *Lettre*). Then Bridget proclaimed that the English had just cause, a condition amply refuted by points in the *Lettre* already discussed. Finally, Bridget prophesied that Christ would aid the English and fight for them. But after the unexpected death of the talented military commander, the earl of Salisbury, and the disastrous conclusion for the English at Orléans, the aid of Christ for the English cause might not have seemed self-evident. In fact, Bedford was later to look back on Orléans as the critical moment at which the English received "a great blow" (*a greet strook*) from which they never recovered, and he murmured, without any apparent allusion to Joan's mission, that they had undertaken the siege of Orléans "God knoweth by what advis."[45]

In a sense the problem with the prophet Bridget was the same one that troubled the doctors at Poitiers; Bridget's promises were only words. In Joan's *Lettre*, however, there is more than the mere pledge of words. For Joan is there not only to speak for God, as Bridget does in her prophecy, but, crucially, to also perform any fighting that God requires. Thus she is not only divine messenger but executrix of the divine will.[46] Christ might have taken the English side, as Bridget said, but he remained in heaven. Joan, on the other hand, to use the ambiguous and powerful term she used herself, was "sent" to France. The implication of her physical presence was the promise of action.

We can appreciate how unusual this circumstance is among prophets, whose calling, of course, is based on words, through an episode involving a minor Johannic prophecy attributed to the seer Marie d'Avignon. As recounted by Jean Barbin at the nullification trial, Marie d'Avignon was frightened by a vision in which a quantity of arms was presented to her. Fearing that she would have to don the armor and become a warrior, she was relieved to find that "a maiden [*quedam Puella*] who should come afterwards should bear these arms and deliver the kingdom of France from the enemy,"[47] a circumstance allowing Marie to remain solely a prophet and to continue to behave within the restricted parameters of a prophet's behavior.

However, the *Lettre* discloses more than the fact of Joan's dual role. First, it promises more strength to Joan than any army can produce, an oblique reference to the power of the weak (through God) to confound the strong.

---

[45] Fragment of a letter by the duke of Bedford in Quicherat, *Procès* 5: 136.

[46] This double role is noted by Jacques Cordier, *Jeanne d'Arc: Sa personnalité, son rôle* (Paris, 1948), p. 187, who calls her "messagère céleste" and "executrice directe."

[47] Murray, *Jeanne d'Arc*, p. 270; Duparc, *Procès* 1: 375: "Sed quedam Puella, que veniret post eam, eadem arma portaret et regnum Francie ab inimicis liberaret." This dichotomy was suggested to me by Colette Beaune, "Prophétie et propagande: Le sacre de Charles VII," in *Idéologie et propagande en France*, Myriam Yardeni, ed. (Paris, 1987), p. 70.

Then it states clearly, in a sentence that has often been misread, that "by the blows (*aux horions*) one would see who has the greater favor of God." By reading the word "horions" as "horizons" (at dawn?), a recent rendering,[48] the essential idea that divine strength is to be exhibited in battle "through the blows" is entirely lost, and with it disappears one of the prime theological concepts of the *Lettre* and of Joan's mission itself.

An examination of the English response to Joan's military summonses, particularly the *Lettre aux Anglais*, again places us in the realm of the debate over the inspiration driving Joan's mission, but the debate broadens at certain moments to include her effect on the whole Christian world. Obviously having nothing positive to say about the Maid, the English make protest on the following grounds: the renewal of war, the refusal to negotiate, the creation of commotion, the refusal to acknowledge the church militant, the upheaval to Christianity, the seduction by the Maid of ignorant and simple people, her violence and cruelty, her boasting and presumption, and her dissolute life.

From Anglo-Burgundian chronicles, we see that the rank-and-file soldier saw Joan's summonses as frightening and novel. An astonished Norman chronicler observed, for example, that the Maid was "much feared [*crègnoit l'en mout*] . . . because she used summonses, and said that if they did not surrender, she would take them by assault,"[49] as if her practice of summoning the enemy were unusual. Fear, then, rather than the claim of divine intervention, was the message of the *Lettre* on this chronicler's page. Ironically, however, the combative language that the English so condemned at Rouen[50] may have partly stemmed bloodshed during Joan's campaign, because the stunned enemy began to offer less and less resistance at the announcement of Joan's arrival and the threatening words of her decrees. We learn this from the *Chronique des cordeliers* which credits her successes, at Sens, Auxerre, Troyes, and elsewhere, as much to these summonses as to her deeds. Conveying a sense of what men in official positions termed her crime of seducing the people, the anonymous author claims that "there was not a fortress which did not wish to surrender at her simple utterance and summons [*à sa simple parolle et semonce*]" and describes the surrender of Troyes as "instantaneous and bloodless" (*incontinent, sans cop ferir*).[51]

Whether a more generalized fear, which created recalcitrant recruits and

---

[48] Pernoud and Clin, *Jeanne d'Arc*, p. 380.

[49] P. Cochon, *Chronique normande* in *Chronique de la Pucelle ou Chronique de Cousinot, suivie de la Chronique normande de P. Cochon, relatives aux règnes de Charles VI et de Charles VII*, etc., Auguste Vallet de Viriville, ed. (Paris, 1869), p. 457.

[50] See Barrett, *Trial*, p. 248, for instance, for article 6 of the final articles of condemnation, which quotes a fragment of the letter: "by the blows would the favor of the God of Heaven be seen." In Quicherat, *Procès* 1: 333: "Ad ictus percipietur quis habeat potius jus a Deo coeli."

[51] *Chronique des cordeliers*, extracts in Jules Quicherat, "Supplément aux témoignages contemporains sur Jeanne d'Arc," *Revue historique* 19 (1882): 73.

led to desertions in the English army, arose from the terror generated by her verbal challenges would be difficult to prove. Nonetheless, at least two extant English edicts dated 3 May 1430 and 12 December of the same year address such refractoriness for which the Maid might bear responsibility,[52] although a different letter by Bedford ascribes responsibility for diminished troops and lost courage jointly to the arrival of Joan and to the death of the earl of Salisbury.[53] Not all the English responded to Joan with fear, of course. The other predominating emotion was anger, which led to an English response of willful insolence. This can be seen in the highly uncharacteristic retention of the herald who delivered the *Lettre* to the English at Orléans, and the insults hurled at the Maid from the walls and trenches, marked by words such as "trollop" (*ribaude*), "cowherd" (*vachère*), and, as recounted by Jean Pasquerel, "the Armagnacs's whore" (*la putain des Armignacz*).[54]

A letter of 7 August 1429, sent by the duke of Bedford to Charles VII from Montereau (the site of the murder of John the Fearless), provides an ostensible response from the English side to the *Lettre*. Bedford writes three weeks after Charles's coronation at Reims, perhaps with the *Lettre* specifically in mind. This occurs only eight days after Christine de Pizan completed the *Ditié*, which draws on the *Lettre*. Although we must assume that Bedford, an addressee of the *Lettre*, had mulled over its contents long before Christine obtained a copy, it is surprising that the *Lettre* was generating these contradictory discourses, almost simultaneously, so long after its composition. Perhaps knowledge of the document was increasing in Burgundian territory at that time.

The duke's letter, like Joan's, is more than a summons. At various moments it seems to reflect or contradict the *Lettre*, its greatest difference being the sense of genuine weariness from Bedford at the prospect of a continuing war, and thus the duke's greater willingness than Joan to negotiate peace. Bedford never wavers from his ironclad commitment "to defend and guard the right of our said lord the king [Henry VI],"[55] but he proclaims his willingness to do "everything that may be expected from a Catholic prince," to obtain a true peace.

Building on the fiction of peace and unity that the wording of the *Treaty of Troyes* created before him, Bedford displays indignation that Henry, "by the grace of God true and natural lord of the kingdoms of France and England," should find the peace in "his territories" broken by force of arms mounted by the French. Cloaking himself in the mantle of righteous indignation, Henry makes Charles the aggressor rather than the aggrieved, and asks him

[52] Quicherat, *Procès* 5: 162–64 and *Procès* 5: 192–94. Joan is not named in the body of either edict.
[53] Quicherat, *Procès* 5: 136–37.
[54] Pernoud, *Retrial*, p. 165; Duparc, *Procès* 1: 394.
[55] *The Chronicles of Enguerrand de Monstrelet*, Thomas Johnes, trans. (London, 1840; repr. 1849) 1: 558.

to have compassion on the poor people "who have, on your account, been so long and grievously harassed."[56]

Joan is briefly alluded to twice in Bedford's letter, paired both times with the monk Frère Richard, as Charles's damnable allies, "the abandoned woman" and "the apostate monk." But her *Lettre* has an intermittent although fairly steady effect on the disposition of Bedford's letter. In addition to defending Henry's right to rule France, Bedford resumes the game of challenging titles, denying Charles's kingship by portraying him as someone "wont to style [him]self Dauphin of Vienne, but at present without cause call[ing] himself king."[57] In a contest himself for the ear of the people, Bedford may have the *Lettre* or even *Virgo puellares* in mind when he objects to the manner in which the French deceive simple people with impossible promises of peace and security and require perjury of the inhabitants, which is a reference to Joan's requirement of obedience, since the inhabitants of occupied France were sworn to England through the treaty of Troyes.

The immediate intention of Bedford's letter, however, is to arrange a time and place to meet Charles in person. Pointedly insisting on his duty to defend the English king's right, and "to repulse you from his territories, by the aid of the All-Powerful," Bedford makes a mockery of Joan's claims that "in whatever place we find you, we shall strike therein and make so great a *hahay* that none so great has been in France for a thousand years." Depicting Charles as an opponent impossible to draw into battle, Bedford's tactic is to plead with Charles to stop eluding him: "We . . . have taken the field in person, and . . . shall pursue you from place to place in the hope of meeting you, which we have never yet done."[58] But Bedford, no more than Charles, appears to savor the thought of tumultuous battle as envisioned in the *Lettre*. In a triple sequence of phrases with the same syntactic quality as the Deuteronomic "if . . . then" sequence in Joan's *Lettre*, Bedford states that the English will indeed "with our swords defend the cause of our quarrel before God, as our judge" (a reminiscence of Joan's "aux horions"), but only, "when no other means can accommodate [our] differences." Whether the haggard tone on which Bedford's letter concludes exhibits a general unraveling of the war effort on both sides, or only the lassitude and exasperation of Bedford himself, cannot be determined, yet if Bedford intended his letter to be the English answer to the *Lettre aux Anglais*, its ambivalence and general lack of grandeur permit only an unfavorable comparison.

From the condemnation trial we have Joan's verification of the text of the *Lettre* and her personal claim to its intellectual content. However, as is true throughout so much of the trial, in probing Joan about the *Lettre*, the judges

[56] Johnes, Monstrelet, *Chronicles* 1: 558.
[57] Johnes, Monstrelet, *Chronicles* 1: 558.
[58] Johnes, Monstrelet, *Chronicles* 1: 558.

touch only sporadically on key theological questions that might lead to true debate about discernment, dwelling instead on errant details which they seize upon in petty attempts to trap her. In focusing on the *Lettre*, they devote considerable energy to accusing her of inappropriately adding the superscription Jesus Maria to her letters, unnecessarily, it would seem, because Joan answered that this was not her doing but the habit of the clerks who wrote her letters. On one issue, however, they score a significant victory by establishing, on her testimony, that she spurned the idea of negotiation and was wedded solely to the *voie de fait* or the military route to peace. This fact comes out in the 3 March session, in a discussion set apart from the specific questioning about the *Lettre*. The text of the trial relates that in a conversation between Joan and Catherine de la Rochelle, herself a visionary, Joan took exception to a wish on Catherine's part to seek out the duke of Burgundy and make peace. According to the Latin transcript, Joan stated that "it seemed to her that peace would not be found, except at the lance's point."[59] When the prosecutor drew up the first set of seventy articles of accusation against the Maid, her disallowance of negotiation as a tool for peace was written into article 56. Having managed to raise an issue of substance, however, inexplicably, they eliminated it from the official final twelve articles.

Of the original articles of accusation, at least half a dozen take aim at the *Lettre*. It is article 18, however, that demonstrates how deceitfully the doctors went about establishing their case. Twisting Joan's reference to "the fairest deed ever done for Christianity," from a proposal for a crusade to the allegation that she delighted in killing other Christians, they stated as her opinion that, since the enemies would not yield, "to make war on [the king's enemies] was to her mind of the greatest benefit to all Christendom."[60] Only in the shortened articles of accusation do three significant theological points relating to the *Lettre*, contained in a single short paragraph, finally emerge. Without prior mention in the earlier articles, the new article 6 condemns the phrase "by the blows would the favor of the God of Heaven be seen," whose importance we have discussed. Next, it charges her with writing that those who disobeyed her warnings would be killed. And finally, although obliquely, it charges Joan with saying that she wrote her letter at the command of God. But there in article 6, diminishing the impact of the three arguments of consequence, are also two points which absorbed the judges but amount to little in theological terms: the affixed names Jesus Maria, and the charge that a cross on one of her letters meant not to trust its contents, evidence, along with the judges' failure to grasp a number of other theological arguments in the *Lettre*, that at Rouen the clergy did not always recognize the forest for the trees.

---

[59] Barrett, *Trial*, p. 85; Quicherat, *Procès* 1: 108.
[60] Barrett, *Trial*, p. 170; Quicherat, *Procès* 1: 233.

Henry VI's letter to the duke of Burgundy was written to demonstrate that putting Joan to death was the act of good Catholics, performed by them for the exaltation of the faith, and a step "which will tend . . . to the strengthening of the Catholic faith."[61] It is composed with a sense of greater remove from the war than Bedford's letter which was written from the field. Reversing the Joan of Arc narrative, in which the French suffered at the hands of the English, Henry's letter positions Joan in the role of oppressor – exercising "her inhuman cruelties by shedding Christian blood" – and himself as legitimate sovereign. In his version of events, divine mercy (in the form of Joan's capture) has been visited upon the people, because God would no longer tolerate the "great mischiefs, murders, and detestable cruelties she has committed against our sovereignty, and on a loyal obedient people."[62]

Not only has Henry struck a blow against heresy through Joan's death, but he has eliminated someone who was "always endeavouring to prevent the unity and safety of Christians."[63] Here is reference again to the myth of Christian unity inaugurated by the signing of the *Treaty of Troyes*. Inducing people to false beliefs and stirring up seditions are others of her crimes, but her crucial error ("But what was worse . . .") is her claim to independent supernatural inspiration, for, as Henry's letter states: "She refused to acknowledge any power on earth but God and his saints."[64] The letter charges her with presumption for claiming communication with saints, but as we know, from the English point of view her crime was worse than that, for as she told it, her connection was directly to God. Proud to have removed an agitator who trusted only in her own beliefs, someone who "greatly scandalized all Christendom," Henry's letter appears, nevertheless, to be trying in vain to prove that by ridding Christianity of Joan he has equaled or bettered her promise to do "the fairest deed ever done for Christianity." Despite the best efforts of the English, the two attempts to exalt the faith remain unequal.

While the English, for their part, were reacting to Joan and the challenges posed by her *Lettre aux Anglais*, the French were beginning to develop a response of their own. Through specific French efforts to disseminate the texts of the *Poitiers Conclusions*, the *Lettre aux Anglais*, and the Johannic prophecies, news of the Maid was spreading. It appears that although some clerks and chroniclers merely transcribed the documents in their histories and record books once obtained, others used the spirit and message of the documents to reinvigorate the French campaign. It might be noted that if Charles was indeed as hard to find as Bedford implied in his letter, those who

---

[61] Johnes, Monstrelet, *Chronicles* 1: 588.
[62] Johnes, Monstrelet, *Chronicles* 1: 589.
[63] Johnes, Monstrelet, *Chronicles* 1: 589.
[64] Johnes, Monstrelet, *Chronicles* 1: 588. Note that this letter, written after the trial, includes reference to her saints.

believed, as did Joan, that peace would be won by the sword, could feel there was good reason to revive the spirit of the *Lettre*. Two people with this conviction were Jacques Gelu and Christine de Pizan. Each uses the *Lettre* to defend the *voie de fait*. Their works, the *Dissertatio* of Gelu and the *Ditié* of Christine, are the subjects of the next two chapters.

6

The *Dissertatio* of Jacques Gelu

When we arrive at the next document, which is a discernment treatise by the archbishop of Embrun, Jacques Gelu, entitled *De puella aurelianensi dissertatio* (hereafter the *Dissertatio*),[1] it is clear that we are witness to a new phase in the Johannic debate. This treatise stands in unmistakable contrast to the early letters of suspicion that Gelu wrote to the king on the threshold of the theological debate. The archbishop has dramatically reversed himself on the Maid.

At first, the treatise Gelu writes seems to belong to the same early stage of investigation as DQP, because like that treatise the *Dissertatio* is structured around the identification and explanation of theological questions. The best argument that DQP did in fact circulate, but which is still not strong, comes from a vague affinity between DQP and certain parts of the *Dissertatio*. In any event, much time has elapsed since the period of first reactions to Joan and the time of the early deliberations. How much time has passed is open to speculation, for this is an undated treatise, but the outer limits for the composition of the *Dissertatio* place it after the victory at Orléans, an event whose occurrence is implied by Gelu, and before the coronation at Reims, to which he makes no reference. With the passage of time has come new information. Gelu, who sends the *Dissertatio* to the king, has undoubtedly continued to correspond with Charles. In fact, it is conceivable that not only DQP, but also the *Poitiers Conclusions* and the *Lettre aux Anglais*, all texts presumably written after Gelu's early letters, have been forwarded to him in full and that he has conquered his doubts and reversed his opinion of Joan under their favorable influence.

Of all our authors, Gelu is the one most ready to admit that he does not understand. But by the time of the *Dissertatio*, what he does not understand,

---

[1] The Latin text can be found in Pierre Lanéry d'Arc, *Mémoires et consultations en faveur de Jeanne d'Arc par les juges du procès de réhabilitation, d'après les manuscrits authentiques, publiés pour la première fois* (Paris, 1889). For an adequate French summary see Ayroles, *Jeanne d'Arc* 1: 39–52. The treatise has recently been titled *De adventu Johanne* by Olivier Bouzy, "Le Traité de Jacques Gelu, *De adventu Johanne*," *Bulletin de l'Association des Amis du Centre Jeanne d'Arc* 16 (1992): 29–39. Margolis, *Joan of Arc* lists it as *Tractatus de Puella* at no. 893.

he has at least come to believe. This trust in the veracity of Joan's mission has come at a price, and we can easily imagine the debate Gelu has conducted with himself in the passing months, to finally arrive at a stage of complete support for Joan. It is difficult to question his integrity, however, and imagine that he has bowed to Joan's popularity at this point in supporting her, because his insistence that the king follow her advice is not based on enthusiasm. He would likely have preferred an angel, or at the least a man, to do what Joan has been sent to accomplish. Moreover, based on the gathering of inferences from the treatise, we come to understand that the *Dissertatio* rests on a conflict. One scholar has seen in the treatise a reaffirmation of the *Poitiers Conclusions*, which is a convincing theory as far as it goes, provided that we do not imagine, as does the author of the theory, the existence of a written denunciation of the Poitiers decision which Gelu seeks, through the *Dissertatio*, to refute.[2] We should also include here that the archbishop's treatise is equally a reaffirmation of the *Lettre aux Anglais*. For the *Dissertatio* is ultimately about military strategy and military tactics, thus representing a departure from the narrow theology of our two previous discernment tracts, DQP and the *Conclusions*. Far from attempting to curry favor with the king by endorsing the Maid, Gelu and Charles appear to have entirely reversed positions. In the *Dissertatio*, a portrait emerges of Charles as a wavering or reluctant king, carelessly poised to trust in his own opinion or that of others, while Gelu struggles to force him to recognize and appreciate the hand of providence acting in his favor. The message that issues from the *Dissertatio* could be summed up as follows: pray for guidance, certainly, Gelu seems to say, but listen to the Maid.

In an unusually frank and intimate dedicatory letter which has survived with the *Dissertatio*, Gelu resumes the role that he held in the earlier correspondence of theological counselor to the king. It is our good fortune that this short dedicatory letter to Charles VII accompanying the *Dissertatio* has survived. Importantly, the letter confirms that the treatise was intended for Charles. It does not, however, demonstrate that the tract was commissioned by the king. The letter opens with a rather formulaic theatricality announcing "wonders" (*miranda*) marked by the presence of the Maid, which have recently occurred (*circa nuperrime*), and it offers the first evidence of a growing, but undatable, cult or popular commotion surrounding Joan (*omnium aures pulsare non cessant*). Yet an unevenness in tone also reveals moments of the studied indifference of a theologian, found already in DQP. We should not be mislead, however, by the archbishop's apparent effort to balance the two sides with the words "some assert" (*quibusdam asserentibus*) and "others believe" (*aliis opinantibus*). The debate is an uneven one. It takes place between those who see providence bestowing favor on Charles's person and his progeny for ages to come, and those who

---

[2] Liocourt, *Jeanne d'Arc* 2: 72.

believe that they see the cause of justice and find Joan in violation of this principle. But ultimately, as one scholar has stated, the story of Joan's victories, interpreted by Gelu's pen, is "an apologetic argument in favor of the dogma of providence."[3] Although, as Anatole France observes, it is only after Gelu has "followed [the arguments of] his adversary for a long time" that he gives his own reading of events, the tract abounds in clear statements that this treatise did not originate from a spirit of neutrality as did DQP.

Despite the prolix style of the *Dissertatio*, marked by redundancies and arguments which tend to migrate from one category to another, the structure of the treatise is readily discernible. In an introductory section, Gelu observes how the unusual nature of Joan's case required that he meditate on the possible causes of the present events. An incredibly compact biographical sketch of Joan takes only a single sentence to relate. More importantly, and alone among theologians writing on Joan, Gelu offers a detailed narrative of the historical backdrop against which he explains Joan's arrival. Five quickly treated reasons are given to justify divine intervention through the Maid. Since there are those who disagree, however, Gelu presents five numbered points (*quaestiunculas*) raised in objection to the case. The remainder of the treatise (over three-quarters) treats the five points of contest in order, each numbered point fully developing the objection before refuting it.

The *Dissertatio* opens with the acknowledgment that Gelu reacted with doubt (*dubiae rei eventum*) and astonishment (*re mirari*) to the first reports about the Maid, causing him to scrutinize divine mercy and justice for the possible causes of such an unusual circumstance. For Gelu the results of his meditation were very positive, although at this point he refers only indirectly to Joan's mission, looking at events from the broadest Christian standpoint, yet noting the effect for France: the faith is confirmed, there is cause for joy among Catholics, and a source of celebration for the "supreme excellence of the French lineage" (*praecelsae domus Franciae excellentiam*), its ruler and kingdom, and its "most Christian [*christianissimorum*] inhabitants." The argument that events owe not to divine providence but to fate has been overturned by Joan's arrival. For Gelu, the "unique" (*singulare*) and "marvellous" (*mirandum*) evidence of what he relates is before one's very eyes, in the form of aid extended by God "through the Maid" (*per Puellam*) for the restoration of the kingdom. Moreover, by writing, Gelu believes that he sets the record straight for posterity "in case future generations hesitate regarding this matter" (*ne posterae circa praedicta haesitent aetates*).

Gelu never mentions either prophecies glorifying the house of France (Second Charlemagne prophecy) or those denouncing it (Bridget's prophecies on France, or the Isabeau / Joan prophecy). Instead he tells in devastating detail the narrative of France's descent into desolation, although an echo of the Charlemagne prophecy can be heard as he recounts the Valois lineage

---

[3] Goyau, "Jacques Gelu," p. 312.

(*Karolus . . . habuit Karolum* and *Karolus . . . genuit Karolum*). As the archbishop begins his recital of France's afflictions, it is completely unclear what value he sees in forcing his royal ward to recall such an escalation of calamities. From problems of dynastic succession came sedition, assassination, and massacres. The English took advantage of a house divided, seizing part of French territory. Despite having earned the confidence of king and queen, Charles VII was unjustly disinherited (*contra jus . . . exhaeredari*). While some paid homage to the English, others extorted from Charles parts of the royal domain, as still others stripped him of his wealth, and rumors vilifying him circulated through the kingdom. Epitomizing the disorder, and highlighting the issue of obedience which DQP gave as the central point of Joan's mission, is Gelu's observation that "there was scarcely anyone left offering obedience to the king" (*vix reperiebatur qui domino regi obediret*). Princes and lords who had lost hope, renounced their loyalty and withdrew into their own domains. The rumor spread that whoever could obtain a part of the realm by force could keep it (*cuilibet licitum erat de regno sibi appropriare quae occupare poterat*).

On completing this devastating portrait of Charles and his realm, Gelu arrives at his purpose: the kingdom was destitute of human aid (*auxilio destitutus humano*), no longer able to help itself (*unde sibi succurrere posset, non habebat*). To a theologian the disastrous situation is not without a silver lining. Under such circumstances, it would not be a case of tempting God to ask for and expect divine aid, since all human solutions had failed. This, then, is the theological necessity with which the *Poitiers Conclusions* opened, and it is also Gelu's cue to begin describing Joan and her part in the story of redemption and restitution.

The biographical sketch of Joan is almost trivial in its brevity. Gelu offers only a few items of information. He depicts Joan as an adolescent maid (*adolescentulam puellam*) torn from her flocks for a divine mission. He adds emphatically that she has not been the subject of coaching,[4] and discloses that she wears men's clothes (*habitum virilem gestantem*). The final piece of information is a statement of her mission, more specific than we have seen previously, and more military. Her mission is to lead the king's army to conquer the rebels, expel his enemies from the kingdom, and restore him to his domain.[5] In every manner but one, this statement coincides with the essence of the *Lettre aux Anglais*; however, that letter naturally omitted reference to the Burgundian rebels because it was directed at the English.

Gelu justifies the selection of a young maid by recourse to 1 Corinthians 1:27, the verse already invoked by DQP: "And the weak things of the world

---

[4] Lanéry d'Arc, *Mémoires*, p. 571: "Non stola magistrali, non conversatione prudentium, non instructione doctorum."

[5] Lanéry d'Arc, *Mémoires*, p. 571: "quatinus princeps esset exercitus regii ad domandum rebelles et expellendum ipsius inimicos a regno, ac eum in dominiis suis restituendum."

hath God chosen, that he may confound the strong." He will return to this
same proof at intervals throughout the treatise. The discrepancy between
what she is (a young maid [*puellae et juveni*]) and what she does (lead the
army, outfit herself in armor, and conquer "strong, trained and bellicose
men" who are all in terror of her) induces Gelu to call her accomplishments
marvels (*mirabili*), things one cannot understand.[6] However, this leads the
archbishop to the paradox of wonder: such intervention is indeed marvelous,
as he already stated at the outset of his dedicatory letter. But hampered by the
need to prove plausibility, Gelu notes that "this ought to induce no wonder"
(*nullam admirationem inducere debent*) since "by few or by many, and even
through intervention by the female sex, God can conquer, as the exemplum
of Deborah illustrates."[7]

But even though we perceive these facts as if in a mirror, that is, appearing
clearly before us, Gelu continues, there are reasons to believe that God's
compassion was merited; and he lists five of them. First, he observes that the
king's cause is just (*justitia*) because he is now the only son (*filius, nunc
unicus*) of Charles VI; his parents were duly married (*constante matrimonio
genitus*) making him natural (*naturalis*) and legitimate (*legitimus*). His *de
facto* disinheritance (*exhaeredarunt*) is therefore untenable (*contra jus
naturale, divinum et humanum*).[8] Second, Gelu lists the merit of Charles's
ancestors. He notes that the French have never erred in the faith (*de Francia
dicatur quod sola monstro caruit*), alluding to St. Jerome's famed statement
that "only Gaul remained free of the monster of heresy" (*Sola Gallia monstra
non habuit*). In this he perpetuates a theme already found in the works of
contemporaries, namely Pierre d'Ailly, Nicolas de Clamanges, Alain Chartier,
and Christine de Pizan, which would reappear at the nullification trial.[9]
Third, Gelu mentions the prayers of the oppressed and the English disrespect
for human decency. He charges them with feeding grass to prisoners, leaving
the dead unburied, and massacring even ecclesiastics, virgins, the elderly, the
young, and pregnant women. Fourth, he insists that the English have no valid
title in France and have sinfully usurped what belongs to others. Fifth, he
notes that their "insatiable cruelty" has had an effect far beyond the
immediate conflict. Without suggesting that a crusade against the infidel
would be energy better spent, Gelu nonetheless proclaims that the English
have disturbed all of Christianity (*tota christianitas turbata*), in fact the whole

[6] Lanéry d'Arc, *Mémoires*, p. 571.
[7] Lanéry d'Arc, *Mémoires*, p. 572: "in paucis veluti in multis, victoriam etiam sexus
muliebris interventu aequaliter praestare potest, ut Debbora factum exstitit."
[8] Lanéry d'Arc, *Mémoires*, p. 572.
[9] Saint Jerome, *Contra Vigilantium*, I, PL, 23, col. 339. See Cecchetti, "Un'egloga," p. 56.
For the Chartier and Christine de Pizan references, see Pascale Bourgain-Hemeryck, *Les
oeuvres latines d'Alain Chartier* (Paris, 1977), p. 177 and p. 193, and Christine de Pizan,
'The *Livre de la cité des dames* of Christine de Pisan: A Critical Edition', unpublished
doctoral dissertation, Maureen Cheney Curnow, ed., 3 vols. (Ann Arbor, Mich., 1978–
79), p. 871, respectively.

universe (*imo orbis universus*).[10] And, he observes, just as the English found their opportunity in a divided France, so the infidel (*inimici . . . crucis Christi*) are reveling in the news of such ruin among Christians (*talia exitia inter christianos*).

However, Gelu admits that there is disagreement with such an account, and here he turns to Joan's detractors, whose challenges to the Maid's mission he has heard, and whose points he is now prepared to debate:

> It has been asserted to us that learned men [*viros . . . litteratos*] have constantly stated that the aforesaid Maid is not sent by God [*non a Deo missam*], but rather through the deception [*deceptam et illusam*] of diabolical arts [*arte diabolica*] [and] that her power comes not from God [*non in Dei*] but from the ministrations of the devil [*daemonum ministerio*].[11]

Two accusations are quickly outlined, both to receive fuller treatment in the five principal points of debate to follow. The first is the accusation that God acts in a single blow (*uno impetu aut momento*) and that Joan began her mission "already some time ago" (*jam diu*) but has not completed it. The second is the allegation that God is more likely to send an angel than, as Gelu puts it, a "simple young girl tending sheep, subject to every illusion and easily deceived through the nature of her sex, living in idleness and protracted isolation," the type of person, they charge, who is especially subject to deception by the devil (*daemon cautus . . . plerum . . . illudit*).[12]

These two attacks have plainly angered Gelu, causing him to address them outside the structure he has devised for their discussion, yet as he begins his five central arguments, he assumes the demeanor of the fair-minded prelate, a stance adopted in earnest in DQP, but scarcely accurate for the orientation of the *Dissertatio* as a whole. The present material, Gelu announces, he will merely elucidate (*materia praesens elucescat*), because truths are more splendid when stirred up in the light (*veritas agitata magis splendescit in lucem*). Whereas the counterclaims to his case will precede each part of his reply, the archbishop's answers to the five points constitute his general pleading for continued confidence in the Maid.

The first question asks: Is it suitable for God to involve himself in the affairs of an individual person or a nation? Also treated here is a point already raised: whether instances of divine intervention always occur in a single blow. We saw the first question treated in DQP in *propositio* three (pro) and *propositio* four (contra), although discussion in DQP is limited to

---

[10] Lanéry d'Arc, *Mémoires*, p. 573.

[11] Lanéry d'Arc, *Mémoires*, p. 573.

[12] Lanéry d'Arc, *Mémoires*, p. 573: "juvenculam simplicem cum ovibus nutritam, omni illusioni subjectam et de facili deceptibilem propter sexus naturam et vitae in otio peractae solitudinem."

nations, making no mention of individuals. Logically, DQP did not treat the second question, because at such an early date no one was objecting that her mission was taking too long. No time considerations at all are raised in DQP regarding the accomplishment of her mission.

Although DQP argued plainly against God's involvement with a specific people (*propositio* four contra), the author admitted one exception: "As long as the celebrated people were the servants of God, they had in exchange such temporal goods." This is the exemption invoked for France by Gelu. According to the archbishop, if a king, a people, or a kingdom serves God faithfully (*decenter et devote Deo famuletur*), their devotion will redound to God's glory so that he will involve himself specially (*singulariter se intromittere*) in their protection. In proof of this point Gelu cites from Scripture the examples of Moses, Jacob, David, and others. With the proof through human example that such things can indeed occur, Gelu resorts again to the "no wonder" rhetorical trope ("Therefore, we should not wonder that . . .") to establish the reasonableness of this ostensibly implausible event.

Fully prepared to admit the responsibility of Charles and his people for the desolation of the kingdom, as if in agreement with Bridget's allegations of French sin, Gelu argues that patience in enduring correction and the continued hope of the French people justify divine mercy. Then, raising a series of astonishing rhetorical questions, Gelu cites the life of Tobit and asks why God would not help Charles, who is his minister, if he helped a private individual? Citing the people of Israel, he asks why, once punished for their faults, the French people could not expect succor, since the Israelites remained God's elect after correction. In the final comparison, sure to strain the nerves of Joan's critics, Gelu equates Joan implicitly with Christ: if God sent his son for the salvation of the world, why would he not send Joan (*unam de suis creaturis*) to free a king and his people from the jaws of their enemies?

As to whether God needs time for such a victory, Gelu declares that, in contradiction to the claims that divine intervention occurs instantaneously (*unico momento aut instanti*), God can take as long as he wishes. The Bible bears witness to cases involving a lapse of time (*temporis lapsu*) or a long interval (*long intervallo*), such as the six days required for the creation. Although Gelu deeply respects the merits of meditating upon the cause of events, he sees the question under discussion as belonging to the realm of divine mysteries (*arcana Dei*). Thus he leaves this topic alluding to the message of Ecclesiastes 7:24 on the futility of trying to understand matters meant to be taken on faith.[13]

Question two asks: Would God employ men rather than angels to perform

---

[13] Ecclesiastes 7:24: "I have tried all things in wisdom. I have said: I will be wise: and it departed farther from me." Latin Vulg. "Cuncta temptavi in sapientia dixi sapiens efficiar et ipsa longius recessit a me."

his works? The brief answer to this question is that God chooses whatever instrument is suitable to a given case. Gelu explains that angels and archangels are fitting only for cases of high honor. Many men have been used as divine instruments, as the examples of Joshua, Judas Maccabaeus, David, and others confirm. Women too – and here Gelu cites only Judith and Esther – have been chosen. Even animals may serve this purpose, he affirms, such as the dove God sent to Noah. In the present case, Gelu continues, the pride of the enemy justifies the use not only of a woman, but of a young girl. The purpose is to demonstrate to English overconfidence that the numbers and strength of their armies are no match for the might of God. At this point, his patience tried, Gelu strives to demonstrate how the selection of Joan is perfectly matched to bring dishonor on the English. Gelu is willing (for the moment) to submit the Maid to denigration for the purpose of vilifying the English, so willing, in fact, that one pauses for a moment to wonder whether his tone is misogynistic or is ironic: the opponent of the English is nothing but a country girl (*juvenculam rusticanis*), of ignoble parentage (*parentibus infimis*), from a humble birthplace (*humillimis in sua regione ortam*), engaged in wretched labor (*vili ministerio traditam*), subject to illusions (*omni fragilitati subjectam*), untaught (*indoctam*), and simple beyond the imaginable (*ultra quod dici potest simplicem*). Regardless of where Gelu positions himself privately on God's use of a woman as a divine instrument, in his hands the theme of the humble overcoming the proud receives a novel and negative cast which recalls his original feelings toward the Maid in the early correspondence. This attitude is very different from the tribute paid to Joan's shepherdess simplicity by the author of DQP and far removed indeed from the source of feminine honor that Christine de Pizan will draw from the same theme in the *Ditié*.

Question three faces the problem of Joan's masculine role: Is it appropriate that divine wisdom commit to a woman tasks suited to men? Taking the scholastic approach by presenting the contrary argument first, Gelu answers that it would appear not. The order of the universe is upset (*ordo rerum confunderetur*), feminine decency and modesty (*verecundiam et pudicitiam*) are violated, and, crucially, Joan's male clothing is a transgression of Deuteronomy 22:5. Even men are confined to their appropriate roles, Gelu explains, and Saul among others was severely punished for usurping functions reserved for priests. On the other hand, Gelu explains, now beginning his defense of Joan, women have been given certain gifts of prophecy denied to men, as the case of the sibyls confirms. If the sibyls had such commissions, why could the Maid not have a commission greater than that of men? Since God does not err, whatever he does is good. If he desires to change the order of things, he can refashion the entire world (*totum ordinem naturae*) since he is omnipotent.

Building his argument toward a justification of the Maid's masculine clothes, Gelu notes that the freedom to change laws and interpret them according to circumstances is invested in both God and man. Gelu contrasts the written law with the living law (*lex animata*), drawing on points made by Aquinas, seconded by Gerson and others, that time, place and circumstances touch upon the validity of any legislation, and he notes that no law can envision the full gamut of possibilities.[14] "To know the law," writes Gelu, "is not to know the written law but the intention."[15] Basing himself now on the principle that the end justifies the means, Gelu argues the case for Joan's male dress given the needs of her mission, which he bases on the definition he offered earlier: to lead the king's army, subdue the rebels, expel the enemies, and restore the king to his dominion.[16]

Now in one of his occasional definitive statements, Gelu declares that

God can prescribe that the Maid preside over armed men [*armatis viris praeesset*] and even direct them [*eos regeret*], and that she can fight and conquer boldly in a practiced manner . . . in men's clothes [*in habitu virili*].[17]

Where no more justification is required, Gelu still adds several points: the English violate the Decalogue, they stripped the king of his inheritance, and they are therefore without just cause (*sine causa justa*). Then in a unique reflection, Gelu revisits his earlier debasement of Joan, elaborated previously to demonstrate how apt an instrument she was for the contemptible English, to now show additional contempt of the enemy by the fact of her wearing male clothes: to break the pride of the English, God has sent a small and simple maid (*parvulam puellam simplicem*), lowly (*status inferioris*), untaught (*indoctam*), and unskilled (*inexercitatam*) in men's clothing (*in habitu virili*).[18]

Before he adds his final points to the justification of Joan's dress, Gelu comments on the confirmation the present circumstances give to the ascendancy of providence over fate. In fact, Gelu comments, providential care in the form of divine mercy is most likely when human wisdom is of no avail, in other words, in a case of true necessity (*tunc enim convenit . . . interponere, quia desperata*), an assertion giving greater validity to a theological reading of the appeal to necessity in the opening of the *Poitiers Conclusions*. Finally, Gelu gives further answers to the charge of indecency leveled at Joan's male clothes. He judges that, given that her conversation is with men, this is the appropriate dress (*decentius enim est*). Furthermore, following Aquinas, he notes that similar lives require similar dress. In other words, if Joan fights as a man she must dress as one. The verdict of question three is that the general law declaring that only men may perform men's actions can be overturned.

---

[14] Lanéry d'Arc, *Mémoires*, p. 582.
[15] Lanéry d'Arc, *Mémoires*, p. 583.
[16] She was, of course, already in men's clothes when she came to the king to claim this mission, which Gelu noted in his biographical sketch.
[17] Lanéry d'Arc, *Mémoires*, p. 583.
[18] Lanéry d'Arc, *Mémoires*, p. 583.

With question four we arrive at the heart of *discretio spirituum*, for Gelu now asks: "Are we able to know, and by what means, when works come from God (*a Deo*) or are the product of diabolical arts (*arte diabolica*)?" This is the crucial question of supernatural inspiration, and hence of discernment, which becomes pertinent only now that the previous questions have been treated. For it has been established that Charles and France are not excluded from the possibility of divine providence, and that even an ignorant girl could be specially elected by God. Thus we arrive at the point where the archbishop can be expected to make a personal pronouncement on the Maid's case. Although question four proposes to examine the "works" (*opera*) rather than the girl, the discussion shows that a judgment on the latter presupposes an understanding of the former, since works are the only route we have to understanding the individual. In this way we will know if Joan is from God.

First Gelu presents the obstacles to a judgment: it would seem that there is no means by which we can know. Our intellect perceives things through the senses, but their unreliability is signaled by 2 Corinthians 11:14: "For satan himself transformeth himself into an angel of light."[19] DQP (*propositio* three contra) emphasized the difficulty of judging from external signs, pointing out that false prophets can simulate true prophets, and that any act a prophet can perform, a false prophet can counterfeit. Now Gelu reminds us again of the limits of men in making these distinctions; only God sees the heart of man (*solius enim Dei est cordium esse scrutatorem . . .*), while men are confined to judging by the external works (*opera exteriora*).[20] Gelu cites Matthew 7:16: "By their fruits you shall know them," the standard biblical verse focused on the dilemma. It was in fact this verse that was implicit in the permission granted Joan in the *Poitiers Conclusions* to advance to Orléans to prove herself.

But Gelu insists on a special emphasis: the element of time. Here the archbishop returns to an idea he expressed in his earlier correspondence with the king. Circumventing the difficulty of the impenetrable heart, Gelu alleges that where an internal evil is concerned, which he identifies here as hypocrisy (*hypocritae*), the malady cannot stay hidden (*Nam extreme laedentia non diu stare possunt*).[21] Eventually, such diseases erupt violently (*violenter erumpunt*) to the outside where humans perceive them for what they are. From this point, Gelu moves to the moment he has taken twenty-five pages of the treatise to reach, his personal judgment based on the arguments:

Applying this to our case, whether our Maid and her works be from God [*a Deo*], as far as human fragility can know [*quantam humana fragilitas*

[19] Lanéry d'Arc, *Mémoires*, p. 585.
[20] Lanéry d'Arc, *Mémoires*, p. 589.
[21] Lanéry d'Arc, *Mémoires*, p. 590.

noscere sinit], we can respond affirmatively [*affirmative respondere*], for it is clear that they are from God [*a Deo sint*].[22]

Then, referring to his sources (*velut nobis relatum est*),[23] Gelu lists Joan's orthodox practices and virtuous conduct, crucial evidence, as we have seen, in arriving at a positive finding in *discretio spirituum*: she is a "good and faithful Christian," who honors God, practices the sacraments frequently and devotedly; she is honest in her words and conversation, speaks little, thereby avoiding many sins, and eats sparingly. As for those vices which would disqualify her case, Gelu alleges that there is "nothing indecorous [*nihil indecorum*], no baseness [*nihil turpe*], nor anything unsuited to maidenly modesty [*nihil quod non deceat verecundiam puellarem*]"[24] to report.

We will recall that a list of virtues, similar to the one just recounted, accompanied Girard's first missive to Gelu in Joan's early days at Chinon, but that Girard's enumeration did nothing to assuage Gelu's doubts about the girl. Nor did that evidence settle the case for the author of DQP. There is little question, then, that the testimony to which he now gives confidence is not Girard's but that of the doctors at Poitiers, those "pious and learned men" whom he had earlier counseled the king to have "lay bare her spirit," before she was even allowed to stand near him. In his hands, no doubt, is the document of the *Poitiers Conclusions* itself. This alone is documentation that a theologian can trust, and should trust, for *discretio spirituum* would be useless if its results were not taken into account.

Even before this point Gelu seems to rely on the *Conclusions*, warning against frivolous belief, citing the need for a sign, and adducing the same examples of Gamaliel and Gideon already advanced by the *Conclusions*. And Gelu's concession that any endorsement of Joan carries certain limitations ("as far as human fragility can know") has its counterpart in the *Conclusions*, where it is stated that she has been probed "as far as possible [by the king]" (*en tant que luy est possible*). Yet Gelu stands at a vantage point where he can augment the findings of both Girard and the *Poitiers Conclusions*, satisfying himself with regard to the Maid's mission given the passage of even more time. For these are not the observations of a day, he declares, but of "several months" (*plurimum mensium*). Were there anything bad in her, it would have surfaced by now.

From one sentence to the next, Gelu turns from the evidence of the *Poitiers Conclusions* to the testimony of the *Lettre aux Anglais*, as if he had sat down to write his treatise with both these sources before him. In a sense, his two sources form an incongruous pair: one focused on the Maid's passive feminine virtues, the other on the warrior Joan, a duality which Gelu seems to acknowledge lends a certain vulnerability to his case. For he follows

[22] Lanéry d'Arc, *Mémoires*, p. 590.
[23] Lanéry d'Arc, *Mémoires*, p. 590.
[24] Lanéry d'Arc, *Mémoires*, p. 590.

with an effort to confront his most difficult challenge, countering the charge that the acts of war in which Joan engages are evidence of the devil, since goodness and peace rather than violence and the shedding of blood are associated with God. Although the aggressive tone of the *Lettre* is perhaps partly to blame for his problem, Gelu uses the *Lettre*, as the disseminators of the document must have wished, as a defense against the accusations, which he specifies: she is cruel; she quenches her thirst on human blood; she uses force; she wears men's clothing. He replies that although she engages in war, she is not cruel and shows mercy to those who appeal to the king, or to those enemies who leave voluntarily. Anyone departing for England could leave in peace, and those French rebels returning to obedience could expect indulgence from the king. It is true, Gelu admits, that Joan uses force, but it is justified by her mission, which common law (*juris communis*) and reason (*rationi*) authorize.[25] As for Joan's male dress, Gelu states that he has defended it enough already, but he adds one very important point, which is once again a result of the test of time, and a further proof of Joan's validity, coming to him from his sources (*ut nobis relatum est*).[26] Blending two images, the traditionally feminine and the military, which other authors are loath to combine, Gelu offers this proof:

> Even with this military life [*inter armatos*], she lives honestly [*honeste*], modestly [*pudice*], and decently [*decenter*], doing nothing . . . which does not fit a virginal young girl [*virginem puellam*].[27]

In recognition of the severity of the male-clothing charge, Gelu daringly endorses the testimony of his sources, saying that "taking this point under careful consideration [*bene ponderata*], we piously believe [*pie credimus*]," formally invoking the veneration allowed a belief not officially approved by the church.

The drama of Gelu's declaration of faith in the Maid, captured by the words "we piously believe," can be gauged by recalling his complete suspicion of Joan in the early correspondence. Based on time and the evidence, Gelu has reversed his personal opinion on Joan. But his flexibility only underscores the faults of Joan's detractors, who adhere rigidly to their first impressions. Enlisting the testimony of Proverbs 3:5 ("Lean not upon thy own prudence") and 3:7 ("Be not wise in thy own conceit"), he warns that we must not adhere so much to our own opinions that we exclude reason (*rationem*) and argument (*persuasionem*). But there remains a significant argument still to be mounted in question four, the evidence specifically of Joan's works, and once again the accusations involve the military aspect of her mission.

[25] Lanéry d'Arc, *Mémoires*, p. 591.
[26] Lanéry d'Arc, *Mémoires*, p. 591.
[27] Lanéry d'Arc, *Mémoires*, p. 591.

For those good works which Joan accomplishes the case is simple. Since God does not seek to harm, good actions cannot be diabolical. Bad actions, however, present a wholly different situation, which necessitates that Gelu engage in a startling piece of reasoning. Things considered in themselves to be evil (*de genere malorum*), like killing, plunder, inflicting injury, and creating terror, must be submitted to scrutiny for their end result (*finis*).[28] Taking refuge in the justice of preserving the state (*tuitione rei publicae*), Gelu announces that killing is not only licit but meritorious (*meritorium est*) when the war is just (*si . . . bellum sit justum*).[29] Drawing strength from the church fathers, he alleges that if the end of war is peace, the means to that end are justified. Then turning to the legality of the war, in terms of Joan's issuing summonses, Gelu refers to the *Lettre aux Anglais* and her other summonses: "She has warned and warns the enemy that it occupies France without title or valid cause" (*sine titulo et causa validis*). Those who return to their own country (*ad patriam propriam*) will not be harmed; but those who refuse to acquiesce to her warnings may justifiably be killed. From this evidence, Gelu draws an unusual conclusion. Going to the greatest length possible to thwart the claim that Joan's deeds arise from diabolical arts, he terms the bad actions good, owing to their good end, and consequently he can argue that they proceed from God (*sic a Deo debent dici facta*).[30] Thus Joan's case is carefully spared.

We arrive now at Gelu's final question: When an enterprise takes place on the order of God, should one add to it the actions of human prudence? In other words, here Gelu will address the following problem: when God entrusts a task to a divine envoy, does human action come into play or is God's power sufficient unto itself? In this *quaestiunculus*, Gelu is answering an unstated objection which takes approximately this form: If Joan has come to work miracles, she should work them, but if God is the executor why should men be involved? At Poitiers, Guillaume Aimeri had objected to Joan's request for soldiers in a similar vein: "You assert that a Voice told you, God willed to deliver the people of France . . . but, if God wills to deliver them, it is not necessary to have soldiers."[31] It is as if the question had never been put to rest.

By the time of the *Dissertatio*, however, the request for soldiers had long ago been resolved in Joan's favor; now the focus is on daily war preparation. Gelu answers the question from Scripture and from nature: the Bible states [Deuteronomy 6:16]: "Thou shalt not tempt the Lord thy God." This means that no one must require a miracle where human means suffice. But when God decides to intervene, Gelu explains, man must work with him in a partnership "for we are God's co-workers" (*Dei . . . coadjutores sumus*).

[28] Lanéry d'Arc, *Mémoires*, p. 591.
[29] Lanéry d'Arc, *Mémoires*, p. 592.
[30] Lanéry d'Arc, *Mémoires*, p. 593.
[31] Murray, *Jeanne d'Arc*, p. 306; Duparc, *Procès* 1: 472.

Work is in our nature, he continues, and we possess industry and free will in order to execute our tasks; the Israelites, for example, sent out explorers before conquering the land of Canaan.[32]

To underscore the importance of action over empty pleas, in a statement reminiscent of Alain Chartier's call for French action to replace prayer, Gelu makes a curious contrast – given what he is about to say about Joan – between the ineffective method used by most women to court divine favor and the mechanisms, by contrast, which work. "It is neither by women's wishes (*votis*) nor supplications (*suppliciis*)," he asserts, "that one obtains divine aid; a good outcome owes to action (*agendo*) and advisement (*consulendo*)."[33] It is especially the present endeavor that requires human preparation, Gelu continues, because it is a protracted affair (*tractu temporis indiget*), and it is impossible to be everywhere at once.

As Gelu reaches the final paragraphs of the *Dissertatio*, the personal relationship that was apparent between the prelate and his royal advisee in the dedicatory letter reappears, but now it is part of the fabric of the treatise itself. The unspecified detractors, those unbelievers or skeptics with whom Gelu has debated throughout most of his treatise, recede for a moment into the background. The archbishop wishes to urge strong, private counsel on the king, advice toward which the entire treatise now appears to have been building, and in so doing he proves the relationship between divine intervention and human action to be increasingly complex.

When God assigns a mission to someone, Gelu advises, we must welcome it with piety, conforming to it without resistance of any kind (*nullomodo resisteretur*). Consequently, the will of the divine messenger (*nuntii divini*) Joan, should be "totally obeyed" (*totaliter obediretur*), especially in things bearing on the essential parts of the mission.

Then, making a sometimes misunderstood reference to the *Poitiers Conclusions*, composed a month or more before, the archbishop reminds the king of the cautions inherent in discernment, as outlined in that document. Before accepting the individual as sent by God (*a Deo missa*), the spirit is probed as to whether it be from God (*a Deo*) or the devil (*parte adversa*), and faith is not applied lightly (*non . . . leviter . . . fides . . . adhibenda*) or without great thought and deliberation (*sine magno pondere et advisamento*).[34] But, he declaims, offering telltale signs of the *Poitiers Conclusions* but broadening its verdict (since the *Conclusions* endorsed only Joan's advancement to Orléans): when the case has been examined and is known, as much as human fragility permits, the affair is received as if ordered and undertaken by God (*tanquam a Deo ordinatum et commissum*). Since Joan has been so examined, Gelu seems to say, it follows that belief in her mission is patent.

---

[32] Lanéry d'Arc, *Mémoires*, p. 593.
[33] Lanéry d'Arc, *Mémoires*, p. 593.
[34] Lanéry d'Arc, *Mémoires*, p. 598.

Then he adds a warning, in case Charles should wrongly decide to trust himself or someone other than Joan and cause her mission to miscarry in his folly:

> Thus the king should fear lest, if he not follow the Maid's advice, thinking he does well, or counting on human wisdom [*prudentia humana*], he be abandoned by God [*a Domino relinqueretur*], his aims frustrated.[35]

Announcing a second "pious belief" (*pie credimus*), Gelu labels Joan the angel of the God of armies (*angelum . . . Dei exercituum*), as if to reply to the criticism made by others that angels were better suited for her mission. But, he admits, "angel is a name, not her nature" (*angelus enim nomen officii est, non naturae*).[36]

The king is thus faced with a choice between following divine wisdom (*sapientiae divinae*) or human wisdom (*humanae prudentiae*); and the decision he should make, of course, is obvious. Gelu advises the king to seek out the wishes of the Maid "first and foremost" (*primo et principaliter*) telling the king he must follow her "as if from God" (*tanquam a Deo*)[37] and the execution of her wishes is to be seen as part of the mission conferred upon her. His curious recommendation is that the king follow Joan's advice even "if it seems doubtful to us" (*quamvis esset dubium nobis*) or "unlikely to come about" (*non magnam apparentiam quoad non habens*).[38] He urges Charles to provide war machines, bridges, ladders, rations, and finances – the preparations of human wisdom – all things without which a miracle would be required. However, he intones, as if from the pulpit: "When through divine wisdom something greater is to be done, human prudence ought to yield, humbling itself and attempting nothing."[39] In these instances the Maid's counsel should be followed. In fact, Gelu states in closure, that the king should consult the Maid seeking with her each day an act to perform pleasing to God, so as to prevent being abandoned by him. Thus ends the *Dissertatio* on the same note of warning as the *Poitiers Conclusions*.

The change in Gelu's position about Joan's mission by the time of the *Dissertatio* should be evident from the foregoing discussion. The prelate has not only come to accept that a young village girl with no training can rightfully lead the king's army, but he believes her opinion should prevail "even if it seems doubtful to us" or "unlikely to come about." Gelu's acceptance of Joan's military role in the *Dissertatio* stands in unmistakable

---

[35] Lanéry d'Arc, *Mémoires*, p. 598.
[36] Lanéry d'Arc, *Mémoires*, p. 599.
[37] Lanéry d'Arc, *Mémoires*, p. 599.
[38] Lanéry d'Arc, *Mémoires*, p. 599.
[39] Lanéry d'Arc, *Mémoires*, p. 599: "Sed ubi per divinam sapientiam aliquid est magis quam alias faciendum, succumbere debet et humiliare se prudentia humana et nihil debet attentare."

contrast to the two descriptions in the treatise of the Maid's abject origins and simplicity, which Gelu utilized to show how fitting an instrument she was for the despised enemy. That these views once coincided with Gelu's own impression of Joan he never tells us in the *Dissertatio*.

The next work in the debate is the *Ditié* of Christine de Pizan. The possibility of her having obtained a copy of the *Dissertatio* is plausible. It would seem that her poem could not have mounted such an insightful theological argument without the benefit of some theological source; the similarities between the *Dissertatio* and the *Ditié* make a case for Christine's having known the archbishop's treatise. What Gelu composed in the debate over Joan's supernatural origins as a male prelate, however, Christine will recast as a female poet. It is our only occasion (for centuries) to hear a woman's voice speak about the Maid.

7

Christine de Pizan's *Ditié de Jehanne d'Arc*

The next document in the Johannic debate was in all likelihood composed in a cloister at the abbey of Poissy, outside Paris, but it was not composed by a prelate. The new voice in the debate is that of Christine de Pizan, a common citizen, but a scholar and writer with strong ties to the French court. With the composition of Christine's sixty-one stanza poem, entitled *Le Ditié de Jehanne d'Arc*, we see the theological debate at a more advanced stage and, importantly, we see it from the special perspective of a woman and a poet.[1]

The *Ditié* is unusual in that it is clearly dated and attributed. It was completed by Christine on 31 July 1429, as she herself says in the final stanza. Therefore, we can assume that the poem was written after Gelu's *Dissertatio*, perhaps by a month or more, and consequently that the *Ditié* represents the latest stage in the theological debate thus far. Similarly to the *Dissertatio*, Christine's poem was written in favor of Joan, but unlike that treatise and all the documents and texts that precede it, the *Ditié* was not written in land under Charles VII's dominion, but in Anglo-Burgundian or "enemy" territory, a circumstance which may never have been adequately emphasized in the reading of Christine's poem. The *Ditié* has generally been understood as a celebratory poem, yet its immediate purpose is to create support in Burgundian-held Paris for Charles VII, whose triumphant reentry into Paris Christine anticipated shortly, and its long-term goal is the achievement of a still-elusive peace. Never does she mention a single negative argument about Joan, but in the background there are scattered references to detractors and uncertainties. It is this crosscurrent of unease which should be considered the key factor in the poem's tone, and Christine's efforts to overcome that unease the main energy of the *Ditié*. In this context, the *Ditié* appears to be primarily polemical in nature.

It is the aim of this chapter to show that the *Ditié* can best be understood as a series of proofs, rendered poetically, to provide assurance that God sent Joan for the recovery of France. This places the French poet Christine in the unlikely context of the debate over the divinity of Joan's mission. It has sometimes been thought that Christine was living in isolation at Poissy,

---

[1] All citations are from the Kennedy and Varty edition of the *Ditié*, except as noted.

entirely out of touch, and that it is a wonder that she ever heard of the Maid at all. But an examination of the *Ditié* for evidence of her sources suggests that Christine was very well informed, and that she must have been supplied in writing with theological information as well as the royalist propaganda documents which were in wider circulation. To explain this circumstance, we can look to the princess Marie de France, the king's sister, who was in residence at that time in the abbey, or to the contact Christine may have maintained with the Valois chancellery after the death of her son, Jean de Castel, who had followed Charles into exile and who served as a royal secretary until his death around 1425.[2]

In order to facilitate understanding of the discussion of the poem, a brief summary of the *Ditié*, outlining its structure and themes, is now provided. The *Ditié* divides naturally into separate sections by rhetorical apostrophes. Stanzas 1–12, comprising the only section that is not an apostrophe, concern the poet (*Je, Christine*). Stanzas 13–20 focus on Charles (*Et tu, Charles*); stanzas 21–36, on Joan (*Et toy, Pucelle beneurée*); stanzas 37–61 announce in different ways, to different constituencies, the message Christine bears of Joan's divine intervention and its meaning for France.

Within these broad categories further subdivisions are possible. The first four stanzas describe the personal joy of the poet Christine at the prospect of the reversal of France's fate in the Hundred Years War (1–4). Christine anticipates the termination of the English occupation of Paris, now that Charles VII, miraculously crowned king, is approaching Paris (5); in order that Charles be restored to power in Paris she calls on the populace to welcome him back from exile as their king (6). The next stanzas (7–12) announce the poet's main objective, to explain how divine intervention has been brought about (7), with emphasis on the justice of the French cause and the evidence of divine approbation. In the eight stanzas addressed to Charles (13–20), Christine asks him to recognize the role of providence in the present events and to prove himself worthy of heavenly election. The last stanza is a prayer of thanks to God for aiding Charles (20). In the principal segment on Joan (21–36), the first eight stanzas (21–28) establish the miracle of Joan by reference to the miracles of Old Testament heroes and heroines, to which Joan's are superior. Eight narrative stanzas on the Maid herself (29–36), describe her examination by the theologians at Poitiers, the prophecies associated with her mission, Joan's exemplary life (29–32), her miraculous victory at Orléans, and the marvel of her later military accomplishments (33–36), attributing everything to God. In the remaining stanzas (37–61), in apostrophes to different war parties, Christine counsels through praise or threats, the French men-at-arms (*Et vous, gens d'armes*) (37–38), the English enemy (*Si rabaissez, Anglois*) (39–45), the Burgundians (*Et vous, rebelles*

---

[2] Charity Cannon Willard, *Christine de Pizan: Her Life and Works* (New York, 1984), p. 202.

Le Ditié de Jehanne d'Arc

rouppieux) (46–56), the Parisians (*O Paris*) (55–56), and finally the rebellious French towns (*Et vous, toutes villes rebelles*) (57–59). Stanza 60 sketches the anticipated reign of peace heralded by the end of the war, and the last stanza gives closure to the poem and records its date.

The *Ditié* opens with a joyful announcement: "In 1429 the sun began to shine again."[3] The wondrous turn of events in France, which will be the subject of Christine's poem, has brought about a metamorphosis in Charles VII, who has been transformed from "rejected child" to "crowned King in might and majesty" (lines 38–39). Stanza seven makes it known that the story the poet tells of France's restoration is sacred history, for the burden on Christine, as she describes it, is to recount "how God . . . accomplished all this through His grace" (lines 49–50).

Christine chooses the conventional metaphor of the change of seasons to describe the new situation in France but adds several new touches. The tears of frustration and grief that she has shed up to now seem to have watered the new spring season and "brought greenness out of barren winter." Also, drawing on the dual meaning of "vers" as both "green" and "verse" to create a *double entendre* at line 25 (*le vers retourné*), Christine speaks not only of the new hope ("re-greening") brought by the recently crowned king, but of the return of her own poetic inspiration as well.

The immediate event that has provoked her to take up her pen is revealed in stanza five: the king's return to Paris. His departure from the capital, described in the first stanza, occurred in ignominious circumstances. Therefore, without wishing to emphasize his flight, yet needing to mark that moment as the beginning of Christine's confinement and suffering in a walled abbey, the poet merely alludes to eleven years in a "dreary cage," thus allowing the reader only indirect access to a date the poet judges to be best forgotten, the year 1418, the time of the massacres in Paris.

The opening words of the *Ditié*, "I Christine," may seem a curious beginning for a poem honoring Joan of Arc, but the logic of this choice becomes understandable as the theological framework of the poem begins to unfold. In fact, Christine writes to bear witness. The tears and complaints of the early stanzas are more than self-indulgence, for she uses herself to stand as a representative of the voice of the people. One of Christine's earlier compositions, the *Epistre à la reine*, a letter to Isabeau de Bavière, dated 5 October 1405, explains more clearly how she speaks for the collective suffering of the common people, when she tells the queen: "You, seated on your royal throne surrounded with honors, cannot know, except by someone's report, the common problems . . . which prevail upon your subjects."[4] There she wrote to prod the queen to recognize the "affliction,"

---

[3] Kennedy and Varty, *Ditié*, p. 41.
[4] *The* Epistle of the Prison of Human Life *with* An Epistle to the Queen of France *and* Lament on the Evils of the Civil War, Josette A. Wisman, ed. and trans., Garland Library of Medieval Literature, 21, ser. A. (New York, 1984), p. 73.

"sadness," "desolation," and "misery" of the French people, and to use the power of her royal position to seek a peace treaty in the civil war, for "if it happens that pity, charity, clemency and love can not be found in a high princess, where then shall it be found?"[5] By the time the *Ditié* is written in 1429 the tide has turned, and as Christine depicts the situation, peace for the realm is at hand, although certainly not through the intervention of the queen, as Christine had once thought possible.

If we recall the similarly unflinching portrayal of the desolation of the kingdom by Gelu in the *Dissertatio*, and think also of the appeal to "necessity" so prominently placed in the opening line of the *Poitiers Conclusions*, we will be able to recognize that Christine's early stanzas demonstrate through the individual life, the collective necessity that would induce God to offer a remedy for France. Several other themes found in the *Dissertatio* are also present in Christine's early stanzas: the legitimacy of Charles's claim to the throne as son of the king, with its implied reference to the disinheritance of the treaty of Troyes; the reward that God delivers to those who maintain patience and hope; and the proof to unbelievers that providence is still operative. One theme finds expansion in the *Ditié*, however, well beyond its expression in Gelu's treatise. It is the obligation of the poet Christine to record the miracle of France's restoration for posterity. With a voice part archangelic and part prophetic, Christine proclaims: "Now hear, throughout the whole world, of something which is more wonderful than anything else!" (lines 57–58).

It is in declaring the right of this miracle to be remembered and written down "in many a chronicle and history-book," however, that Christine first alludes in stanza seven to the element of debate in the poem, for she judges her narrative worthy of being remembered and recorded "no matter whom it may displease" (line 55). Now a second look at the preceding stanzas shows an element of daring where previously only a joyful welcome to the approaching king seemed intended. For Christine is in fact making a boldly political plea to the inhabitants of Paris. By advising that they "now . . . greet *our* king" (emphasis mine), she asks that the rule of the English occupiers be overturned and that Parisians grant Charles a vote of confidence by coming out to greet him. This is the return of the true monarch to the capital from which he was driven out eleven years before. Now the words of her appeal take on the complexion of propaganda, and the meaning of the phrase "let no one hold back" (line 45), which at first seemed only rhetorical, conveys a literal impact. Here lies Christine's recognition of the intertwined fates of the monarch and his people, expressed so clearly a decade earlier by Robert Blondel in the *Complanctus bonorum Gallicorum*, translated into French by a Norman cleric named Robinet:

---

[5] Wisman, *Epistle*, p. 75.

Le Ditié de Jehanne d'Arc

O people! Recognize as your lord
The Dauphin noble and wise,
For his prosperity is our own
And his ruin is our undoing.[6]

As the *Ditié* continues, the polemical nature of the poem can no longer go unrecognized. Christine highlights the divine agency responsible for the recovery of France – which we now know that some people will dispute – by means of her insistent repetition of the word "through" (*par*). Slowly working up to the Maid's part in the affairs of France, from stanzas ten to fourteen, yet still reluctant to call Joan by name, Christine refers to the recovery of the kingdom "through divine command," "through such a miracle," "through a tender virgin," through divine intervention," "through God's blessing," "through the Maid," and finally "through the intelligence of the Maid." This awkward repetition, which may have struck previous critics as a sign of the haste and careless spirit in which Christine composed the *Ditié*, might better be read as Christine's strenuous effort to prove that Joan, and the mission she conducts, are from God.

In addition to the virtues of patience and hope, whose importance Christine indicated earlier as mechanisms by which divine aid has been elicited, in stanza twelve she furnishes the conventional explanation, already seen in DQP and Gelu, of France's unblemished Christian past. Making one of three fleeting references in the *Ditié* to her sources, an unusual circumstance for an author previously given to naming Aristotle or Boethius as readily as Vincent of Beauvais or Matheolus, the poet states: "I read . . . that the Lilies of France never erred in matters of faith" (lines 94–96). This is an allusion, through the conventional symbolism of the lily as representation of the monarchy, to the previously encountered claim of St. Jerome that only Gaul was free of the monster of heresy. Christine depicts the honor conferred on the crown as God's demonstration of "how much He favours it" (line 92), making it clear that if "He finds more faith in the Royal House than anywhere else" no one should be surprised for "there is nothing new in this" (line 95). In other words, the Maid's mission fits easily into the long-standing tradition of divine solicitude for France.

Stanza thirteen marks a change in approach which Christine will adopt for the remainder of the *Ditié*, a deliberate posture which reveals her turning to one constituency after another, trying to fight battles and effect outcomes on a number of different fronts. Here Christine is clearly playing the role of propagandist, but how consciously she saw herself as following Joan's lead and imitating her energy is difficult to assess. As if she encloses a letter in the *Ditié* for everyone involved in the war, each identifiable by the opening

---

[6] Robert Blondel, *Oeuvres de Robert Blondel, historien normand du XVe siècle*, A. Héron, ed., 2 vols. (Rouen, 1891–93) 1: 82. Cited by P. S. Lewis, *Essays in Later Medieval French History* (London, 1985), p. 186.

apostrophe, Christine speaks to Charles VII, the Maid, the French men-at-arms, the English, the Burgundian rebels, the city of Paris, and other rebellious cities.

To the end of the poem, as she delivers her various messages, Christine never falters in her belief that Joan has been sent by God. Increasingly demonstrating her understanding of the theological requirements of *discretio spirituum*, Christine dispenses throughout the remainder of the *Ditié* proofs which guarantee the matter of Joan's supernatural mission. To have obtained such pertinent information about the theological issues raised by the Maid's mission, Christine appears to have had access, as stated above, to at least one actual discernment treatise, the *Dissertatio* of Gelu.[7] Although an argument could be made for the presence of several reminiscences of DQP as well,[8] it is the tract sent by the archbishop, bearing a covering letter to the king, that lies, in all likelihood, at the bottom of Christine's skilled reasoning of Joan's case. In order to account for this knowledge, we must assume that the *Dissertatio* came into Christine's hands after being dispatched to Charles's sister Marie de France at the convent of Poissy. A French version of the *Dissertatio*, alluded to in the literature but no longer extant, might have been Christine's point of access to Gelu's ideas, although her own knowledge of Latin is confirmed by Martin Le Franc.[9]

Yet the poet's reliance on the work of Gelu does not diminish an almost indisputable fact. Christine was, to all appearances, the recipient of the "full" dossier of propaganda documents – the *Poitiers Conclusions*, the *Lettre aux Anglais*, and a small collection of prophecies – from which she drew further arguments in favor of Joan and deepened her own understanding of the profound changes brought about by the Maid. Verbal traces are most conspicuous from the *Lettre aux Anglais*, whose spirit we will see Christine adopt in the *Ditié*, thus initiating a considerable departure from her previous writing, and a departure as well from all her earlier notions of the role of women in the affairs of war and peace.[10] However, Christine's clear understanding of the tentativeness of the approval granted in the *Poitiers Conclusions* is the cause, on numerous occasions in the *Ditié*, of Christine's important need to bear witness to miracles performed and prophecies fulfilled, thus reminding us of her opening words "I, Christine." The

---

[7] The logic of this dependence was noted by Anatole France, who saw similarities between the two works which he failed to develop. See France, *Jeanne d'Arc* 2: 34.

[8] This possibility is raised in my article "The Literary Image of Joan of Arc: Prior Influences," *Speculum* 56 (1981): 815.

[9] See Gaston Paris, "Un poème inédit de Martin Le Franc," *Romania* 16 (1887): 415. Martin speaks of Christine "whose virtue is manifest in letters and in the Latin language."

[10] See Thelma S. Fenster and Mary Carpenter Erler, eds., *Poems of Cupid, God of Love: Christine de Pizan's* Epistre au dieu d'Amours *and* Dit de la Rose, *Thomas Hoccleve's* The Letter of Cupid (Leiden, 1990), lines 668–76, p. 66.

collected prophecies, including the prophecy of the Flying Stag, which we have not seen before, offer Christine verification from the past of Joan's mission and new promises about her mission for the future. They also allow Christine to find her own voice as a prophet through which she announces these future events to her reader.

None of the poet's efforts to bolster Joan's cause occur because Christine might herself doubt that the Maid is divinely sent. Joan's special election is so secure in Christine's mind that she consciously ignores her heroine for large stretches of the poem. In fact, we will see this neglect of the Maid sometimes become a reverse mechanism of praise in the *Ditié*, because Joan's superiority and merit are so obvious to Christine that they do not require that attention be constantly drawn to her. The problem, as Christine sees it, is other people. It is not that God's presence is in doubt, but that humans, unable or unwilling to recognize it, have the potential to ruin the gains attained thus far, by not doing the right thing. This is, in essence, the threat of the stiff-necked, whose crime Gerson characterized when he wrote in *De probatione spirituum* regarding those who repulsed visions from the Holy Spirit: "What is it but to resist the Holy Spirit and to stifle His vivifying grace?"[11] It also seems to be a fear that drives the *Ditié*. As we look at Christine's first exhortation, seven stanzas directed at Charles VII, we will begin to recognize that behind her outward show of confidence and her encouragement of her monarch and his special destiny, Christine harbors doubts regarding him. Then, as the uncertainty mounts during the course of the poem, it will become increasingly evident that Christine uses her poem to teach, encourage, reason with, or threaten all those people whose behavior could jeopardize divine favor, and as a consequence, peace. From this perspective, the *Ditié* looks more like a curb against disaster than a simple hymn of praise.

A first point to bear in mind on approaching Christine's seven stanzas to the king is the difference in the ages of the speaker and the addressee. Christine had grown up at the court of Charles VII's grandfather, Charles V, and at the time of the *Ditié* was approaching the age of sixty-five. The *Ditié* is her last work and her silence from then on signals the fact of her death – but whether she lived long enough to see her hopes confounded is not known. By contrast, Charles VII was a youth of twenty-six, only a handful of years older than the Maid, whom everyone characterized as being very young. Thus the tone is not too different from that of the mature archbishop Gelu offering guidance to his royal charge, in the dedicatory letter that accompanied the *Dissertatio*.

Similarly to the archbishop's letter, Christine wants only the good of the realm and the preservation of Charles's dominion. Gelu had told the king in his letter that the candor of his remarks were caused by love and he hoped that they would be taken as such. The same could be said about Christine.

---

[11] Boland, *Concept*, p. 34.

But Christine's remarks camouflage a similar but even harsher message than the basic theme of Gelu's letter: that Charles must treat those returning to his obedience with the same gentleness that God has shown him. Careful attention to Christine's words demonstrates a particular undercutting of the king. This mostly arises from the inauspicious beginnings of Charles's rule. It is as if the two salient facts of his reign thus far, which Christine has alluded to early in the poem – the king's flight from the capital and his repudiation by his mother – are a negative legacy that Charles must now learn to overcome. Rather than praise her king, Christine impresses him with the special role to which he has acceded through recent episodes of divine intervention. Not Charles, but the name, is what Christine calls noble (*VIIe d'icellui hault nom,* line 98).

By truly becoming "Charles, King of France," Christine lets the king know that he will have to accept the mantle of a special destiny. This is the force of her discourse on the solemn deeds God wishes him to achieve, and on Christine's allusion to the Second Charlemagne prophecy ("Charles son of Charles") and the Flying Stag prophecy. It is not a desire to flatter and compliment. She even extends the idea of Charles's sacred mission to include divine election, stating, with affinities both to DQP (*populus israel populus regni Francie*) and to the *Dissertatio,* where Charles is God's minister (*domino regi ministerio*), that "God . . . elected you as His servant" (lines 142–43).

We must assume from the manner in which Christine frames her argument that she saw the title and role of monarch existing somehow separately and independently of the holder of that title until the arrival of Joan of Arc. The war that Charles waged and the country he was on the point of losing were signs that he might not be God's designee for the continuation of the glorious French line. Recent events, Christine explains, have given the "first manifestation" (*si com premisse en an,* line 143) that God has elected him. However, the poet makes it evident that the turn of events owes nothing to the actions of Charles 'himself. Clearly not a victor, he has nevertheless won victories, but only through the agency of Joan: "See your honour exalted by the Maid who has laid low your enemies beneath your standard (and this *is* new!)" (lines 101–104).

A measure of sympathy could be in order for Charles. His fate might seem inordinately dictated by the forces of women: a disinheriting mother, a preachy and moralizing poet, a youthful maid who outdoes him at war. But Joan's strength is seen as emanating from God. And the single most important message Christine imparts to Charles is that the power to fulfill his newly granted special destiny lies within himself. Here Christine expresses a theme we have already encountered. In acknowledgment of a show of providence from heaven, human beings must do their part; as Christine remarks in stanza eighteen, Charles is elected, "on condition that [he] do [his] duty" (*mais que faces ton deu*) (line 144). The requirements are stated: serve God; be good, upright, and a lover of justice; avoid pride; be gentle and well disposed towards your people; love God, thank God and fear God. Her hope, of course, is that Charles will rise to meet the requirements of the role: "I pray to God that you may be the person I have described" (line 130). But in the very notion of hope lies the implication of a state not yet achieved.

There are two steps dictating what Charles must do: recognition and gratitude. Therefore, Christine tries first to impress on Charles the incredible distance he has recently come, through the juxtaposition of words showing defeat, ruin and loss contrasted with those of elevation and recovery. Then she invokes the impossibility topos ("for it was believed quite impossible," lines 105–106), as she notes the unlikely speed with which everything has happened ("in a short time"), thus underscoring by these means the miraculous, and consequently the hand of providence. These are by now familiar theological proofs, albeit unexpected from the hand of a poet.

But Christine, the propagandist, is willing to go even further, exaggerating the claims of victory to make Charles take notice. With the outcome of the Paris campaign hardly predetermined (Paris would in fact not be retaken until 1437), she exclaims in stanzas thirteen and fourteen that his enemies have been "laid low beneath [his] standard" (*soubzmis soubz [son] penon*), that the country is "manifestly [his]" (*visiblement tien*), and that he has recovered it (*tu l'as recouvré*). This has taken place despite those who wish him harm. Expressing her personal feelings to him with the words "I firmly believe," "I pray that," and "I hope that," Christine also repeats conventional moral instruction as was commonly found in a genre called Mirrors for Princes. Through a mixture of tactics she wishes to mold him at least to the image of his grandfather Charles V, known as "the wise," whose virtues and kingship she detailed in her biography *Le livre des fais et bonnes meurs du Sage Roy Charles V*, and if the prophecies are brought to bear, even beyond. Finally, as if to model for Charles the devotion he owes God for honors which she states, similarly to Gelu, lie beyond his ability to acknowledge with complete gratitude, Christine writes stanza twenty as a prayer of thanks to God.

When we reach the next section of the *Ditié*, at last we find stanzas directly focusing on Joan (stanzas 21–36), more than twice as many as Christine allotted to Charles. The delay in arriving at Joan has been a conscious tactic and the claim that the Maid has been forgotten a rhetorical ploy. By postponement, a certain victory is scored for feminine patience and humility, Christine's as well as Joan's, and a proof seems to be established that virtue can subsist without the requirement of glory. However, the attention when it comes will be the sweeter for the delay. Similarly indirect is Christine's employment of the topos of forgetting, which is in fact a convention of the rhetoric of praise. The very words "Are you to be forgotten?" are a standard signal in collections of illustrious biography throughout the centuries for a life that merits inclusion.

In the stanzas on the Maid, Christine blends a set of proofs with intermittent outbursts of joy. Here the *Ditié* can truly be called celebratory. The prime reason for happiness, of course, is the evidence in Joan of providence. But Christine, who also finds in Joan much to vindicate positions she had adopted in the past with regard to women, cannot help but revive two of her earlier literary roles, that of participant in the *Querelle du Roman de la Rose* and of biographer of illustrious women in the *Cité des dames*. It is also in this group of stanzas that Christine's recourse to the *Poitiers Conclusions*, the *Lettre aux Anglais*, and several prophecies first appears.

It is in the first eight stanzas (21–28) of this section that Christine both establishes the supernatural quality of Joan and simultaneously begins to grapple with the artistic expression of praise. Since she works in a poetic medium, Christine has more latitude than do the theologians to play with the verbal accents of her themes, and she is never as cautious as their office requires them to be, but she still treats the same issues with which we have seen them concerned. Thus we at last find in these stanzas, at line 171, as we also found it deep within the *Dissertatio* of Gelu, Christine's explicit pronouncement that Joan is a "Maiden sent from God" (*Pucelle de Dieu ordonné*).

As if this were also Christine's answer to the first question raised in DQP ("should one go to the extent of believing that she is a true young girl of human nature?"), but with an answer quite different from his, she manipulates the different valences of human and divine existence to prove that, in fact, Joan's life represents something greater than human existence. Already destined for sainthood in Christine's poem, the Maid is termed "blessed" (*beneurée*), and in wordplay in stanza 22 she is the object of the *double entendre* "born at a propitious hour" and "born of blessedness" (*de bonne heure [bonheur] née*). Christine considers Joan the recipient of an infusion of grace through the Holy Spirit and the recipient not only formerly but now as well (*en qui ot et a*) of "an abundance of noble gifts" (*toute largesse de hault don*, line 174).[12] If we consider the possibility, which we will see specifically introduced in DMV, that people may have been beginning to challenge the Maid's ascendancy based on the fact of her diminishing miracles, Christine's use of both the past and the present tenses becomes an argument that Joan's divine mission did not terminate with the coronation at Reims.

Christine's preoccupation with the exact nature of the Maid, which she as poet makes resistant to a definite answer in her verse, continues even in the less directly theological stanzas of this section (23–28). Here the poet, who is (in contrast to Joan) a mere mortal, tries to find a way within her means to honor a being who has already received the ultimate honor of divine selection. Several times Christine attempts to come to terms with the contradictions, using the topos of inexpressibility – "Could one ever praise

---

[12] Kennedy and Varty, *Ditié*, p. 44, admitting the ambiguity by a bracketed explanation in their translation: "[i.e. the Holy Spirit]," attribute the "gifts" to the Holy Spirit rather than Joan.

you enough?" (line 166) and "Who can ever begin to repay you?" (line 176) – to exhibit her own inadequacy as a writer. Despite her inadequacy she still has a need to express her gratitude, although she recognizes at the same time the superfluity of praise where a supernatural being is concerned.

To solve the dilemma of how to pay tribute to Joan, Christine casts the Maid as one of the worthies of antiquity. The topos of the Nine Worthies (*neuf preux*) and the female pendant (*neuf preuses*) constituted a respected and popular format in the late Middle Ages for expressing honor. Usually composed of three pagans, three Jews and three Christians, the topos undergoes an important transformation in Christine's hands. Echoing the same Old Testament emphasis which both DQP and the *Dissertatio* placed on the French, as similar or equal to the people of God, the *Ditié* recasts the conventional triadic structure into a canon of only Hebrew prophets. In narrating the accomplishments of Moses, Joshua, and Gideon, Christine compares them to Joan, declaring her right to be included among them, as part of God's elect (*Pucelle eslite*, line 184). Audaciously, given the high qualities of the prophets, Christine enlists yet another topos, the theme of surpassing, and announces that Joan's accomplishments exceed those of the biblical prophets.

Turning to the biblical proof, which appears so many times in writings on Joan, to justify her declaration, Christine summons the argument of 1 Corinthians 1:27 of the weak overcoming the strong, although she does not cite the verse directly as the theologians do. It is in stanzas 24 and 25 that she works through this theme. By means of this biblical verse, the paradox of the young virgin and the simple shepherdess, who is also the champion who drives out the enemy, is explained because, as Christine states: "God gives the strength and power" (. . . *Dieu force et povoir donne*) (line 187). Coming to terms with the dilemma of the human need to marvel at God's creation of Joan, despite the superfluity of the praise and the inherent impossibility of its adequacy, Christine separates the two realms: "As far as God is concerned, this was easily accomplished. But as for us, we never heard tell of such an extraordinary marvel" (lines 200–202).

It must be noted that Christine has little to say about Joan's accomplishments as a member of her sex. One rather stiff stanza cites Esther, Judith, and Deborah, aptly selecting the characterization of the three women, from among the many that the Middle Ages conferred on them, that best links the French to the Hebrew elect: their role as restorers of the people of God (*Par lesqueles Dieu restora / Son pueple*) (lines 219–20). The full canon of female worthies appears to be of no interest to Christine, particularly, it would appear, because the group of nine, unlike the men, most often consisted exclusively of pagans, specifically, nine Amazons. And all the illustrious biographies from her *Cité des dames* are swept away in one phrase: "And I have heard of many other worthy women as well" (lines 221–22).

Whether because Joan functions in the role of a man or because, if men stand higher in the social hierarchy, any woman who surpasses a man attains greater glory than by surpassing a woman, Christine honors Joan primarily among the men. Still, in a manner reminiscent of Gelu (yet wholly without the misogynistic resonances of the archbishop), she underscores not only that Joan is a woman, but a young girl, so that the signs of her low status will reveal even more effectively the extent of her accomplishment. But before we leave the praise sequence of stanzas 21 through 28, we must look at a hidden battle that Christine wages for Joan and the cause of women in the form of "feminist" *double entendres.*

If we return to the question raised in DQP as to Joan's physical nature, we can identify words and themes from the *Querelle du Roman de la Rose* which Christine reissues with a new theological meaning, to simultaneously answer the old misogynistic insults and to assert Joan's supernatural nature. Thus in stanza 24, Christine exclaims about all Joan's attainments: "Here indeed is something quite extraordinary!" (*oultre nature*). The term she employs literally means "beyond nature," but the implications are multiple. First, Christine takes exception to the term used for dissolute women or women who go against their sex (*contra naturam*); second, because military feats are deemed possible only for men, this makes Joan "beyond nature;" finally, and most importantly, because it is a proof that Joan was sent by God, Joan is "beyond nature" or "other worldly" (*oultre nature*) because of her heavenly or angelic nature. (This usage might even seem designed to contradict Gelu, who insisted that although she was the angel of the army, it was her name not her nature.) Another instance of the same technique appears in the concluding phrase of stanza 25, where God's creation of the Maid is called "easily accomplished" (*chose legiere*); yet the term can also mean "a frivolous thing," which in the context of the *Querelle* was a misogynistic insult. Given the theological infrastructure of the *Ditié*, however, "lightness" again seems to symbolize Joan's angelic being. A third and final example is located in the last line of stanza 26. There Christine asserts that in Joan "a heart greater than that of any man" has been placed. Similarly to the other instances, the word "man" can be read two ways: Joan is braver than men (*omme*), and Joan has a heart greater than human beings, or mankind (*omme*). Having established the implication of Joan's own lightness of being, achieved by the instances of verbal flexibility in three successive stanzas (24–26), Christine now declares Joan to be "miraculously sent by divine command" (*Par miracle fut envoiée / Et divine amonition*, lines 225–26) to the king.[13] With this crucial claim now plainly stated, Christine, perhaps with her written sources lined up beside her on her writing desk, begins to narrate the Chinon–Poitiers period of Joan's story.

---

[13] Christine also mentions that Joan was "conducted by the angel of the Lord to the king" (lines 227–28), an unusual exception to the poet's insistence elsewhere in the *Ditié* of Joan's direct and unmediated relationship with God.

114

In Stanza 29 Christine begins to treat the matter of Poitiers and the theological examination of Joan. From stanza seven, in which the poet urged Parisians to support Charles, until now, the *Ditié* has been suspended in time and space. Now a flashback to Poitiers seems to promise the historical and biographical "tale" of the *Ditié* of which we have so far seen very little. But Christine, no more than the theologians, writes a chronicle; nor is this a biography suitable for entry in the *Cité des dames*. There is no reference here to Joan's background (although an allusion to Joan as shepherdess was made earlier), no details of the early days at Chinon (Charles disguised among the courtiers, the Maid's secret), no request for armor, no mention of her male clothes, no promise of restoration, no reference to either Orléans or Reims as initial objectives in Joan's mission.

The interest of Poitiers for Christine is in fact the same interest placed on it by the theologians: to determine whether or not Joan had been sent by God. That is why Christine's opening line in stanza 29 ("She was miraculously sent . . .") strikes one as a curious introduction to such a probe, for Christine already states the conclusion in advance of the very proposition the doctors have gathered to determine. In the earlier stanzas directed at Joan, Christine had also affirmed in multiple ways, especially through the suppleness of her language, that the Maid was not from this world. It is as if Christine were now capitalizing on the lack of a geographical anchor in the phrase "sent by God," to imply that Joan was heaven sent, not sent from Domrémy. Thus Christine appears prophetic herself, knowing as she does the outcome of Joan's test well before the doctors who tested her.

Still, Christine fully respects the testing procedure that was carried on by the "clerks and wise men" (*clers et sages*) at Poitiers, and thoroughly understands the care that was required. Her two stanzas on Poitiers (29 and 30) are as deliberate and plodding as the *Poitiers Conclusions* themselves, and should answer those who deny that an exacting theological examination took place. This was a test to see if they could believe Joan's words, a theological point which Christine recognizes when she states their aim: ". . . so that they could find out if she was telling the truth" (*Pour ensercher se chose voire / Disoit*) (lines 236–37). More surprising, however, is Christine's clear understanding of the two requirements needed to meet St. Paul's injunction in 1 John 4:1 (*Probate spiritus, si ex Deo sunt*): an examination of the life and the demonstration of a miracle. Although stanzas 32 and 33 might not seem related to Poitiers, there, consecutively, in these stanzas, are the proofs of the two requirements: stanza 32 describes "the beauty of her life" (*sa belle vie*), and stanza 33 the miracle at Orléans.

However, the two proofs are not equally important and we can better understand Christine's function as witness in the *Ditié* if we appreciate the difference. The proof of Joan's good life had already been attested at Poitiers, but the miracle had not. Therefore, Christine, at the end of July, is a signatory to the verification that Joan completed the second requirement. Of course there is joy in Christine's exclamation about the victory at Orléans, but it is the nature of the victory as theological proof that needs to be underscored: "Oh, how clear this was at the siege of Orléans. . . . It is my belief that no miracle was ever more evident" (. . . *onc miracle . . . Ne fut plus cler*) (lines 260–61).

The evidence of the *Poitiers Conclusions* serves Christine well in anchoring Joan's case in reality. The fact that she was "carefully put to the test" by the doctors and "well examined" allows Christine to declare that "her achievement is no illusion" (line 229). But, where possible, Christine collects evidence from other sources as well. In a second, shorter group of stanzas honoring Joan (34–36), Christine uses the unbelievability of the Maid's accomplishments as a mechanism of praise. The famous stanza 34, beginning "Oh! What honour for the female sex!" (line 265–66), opposes the power of Joan to the fruitless effort of "5000 men." "Before the event," writes Christine, "they would scarcely have believed this possible" (line 272). She substantiates this, however, by recourse in the next stanza to the proof of the eyewitness, stating that Joan does this "in full view of everyone" (*mains yeulx voiant*, line 280).

Christine may not always be equally discriminating in her evaluation of different forms of evidence. Her handling of prophecy, which we have previously treated, is a case in point. After so cogently summing up the task and requirements of the Poitiers commission, it is odd to find her argue in stanza 30 that "it was found in history-records that [Joan] was destined to accomplish her mission," and follow this with the claim that "Merlin, the Sibyl and Bede foresaw her coming [and] entered her in their writings" (lines 242–44), when our previous examination of the prophecies' claims to foretell Joan's mission demonstrated them to be either irrelevant to Joan or contrived. Perhaps Christine plays the role of conscious propagandist here; perhaps she truly believes that the prophecies announced Joan. In any case, the seductiveness to a writer and scholar of proof in the form of the written word may account for Christine's trust.

From her copies of the *Poitiers Conclusions* and the prophecies, Christine seems to turn to the *Lettre aux Anglais*, beginning with the mention of Orléans at stanza 33, the siege for which the *Lettre* was written. The earlier stanzas devoted to Joan (21–28) were not devoid of the rhetoric of war and violence that Christine now begins to use more freely, as she approaches the moment when she will address the enemies of the monarchy. But those stanzas were tempered with qualifications that preserved a traditional view of women's nature and were moderated by frequent signs of the poet's gentle affection towards her female subject. Thus in Christine's rendering Joan did not engage in actions leading to killing, she merely untied a bond binding France (lines 164–65), blessed the land with peace (line 168), and led the French out of evil (lines 183–84). Although Christine calls Joan the champion "who casts the rebels down" (line 191), the effect is mitigated two lines earlier by the counter-image of Joan as female nurturer, offering "the sweet, nourishing milk of peace" from her virgin breast. When the time comes to assert that the Maid cast down enemies at a greater rate than Joshua, Christine chooses not to insist, as she has elsewhere, on the possibility of this skill, but on its impossibility. And in stanza 26, when Joan's military prowess has reached the level of "an extraordinary marvel" (*si grant merveille*), Christine states simply: "This is God's doing" (*Mais ce fait Dieu*, line 207).

However, now at roughly the midpoint in the *Ditié*, Christine seems willing to change once again the language she already changed in stanza two "from tears to song," this time, as it appears, adopting the war rhetoric of Joan's *Lettre* for purposes of intimidation, persuasion, and proof. Looked at from one perspective, there is nothing new about writing in a genre which tries to gain psychological ascendancy over an opponent in war. Propagandistic war poetry for the period of the Hundred Years War is well attested.[14] The main difference, however, is that Christine, without Joan's influence, would doubtless never have agreed to speak this new language of war. In her previous *Epistre à la reine* (1405) and *Lamentacion sur les maux de la France* (1410), Christine modeled herself after female prototypes in the Bible and in classical antiquity, whose main weapon to end wars was their tears, and whose principle functions in attaining peace were as intercessors, mediators, appeasers of male anger, and advocates of the helpless. The Sabine women, whose example Christine plainly admired when she composed the *Lamentacion*, arrived on the battlefield but not to fight. "You threw yourselves with hair disheveled into the battlefield," she wrote, "your children in your arms, and . . . shouted: 'Have pity on our dear loved ones! Make peace.'"[15] The physicality of the women as obstacles and their presence at the scene of battle represents a rigor which holds more appeal than mere women's weeping, but in fact the Sabines were little more than conventional peaceweavers.

Naturally, Christine's application of the *Lettre aux Anglais* to new addressees in the *Ditié* requires some adjustment. Now focused on the arena of war, her remaining commentary is directed at the French men-at-arms, the English, the turncoat Burgundians, the inhabitants of Paris, and those other cities which rebelled against Charles's rule. The English, for whom the *Lettre* was drafted, figure only in a minor way in the second half of the *Ditié*. Only three stanzas (39–41) are unequivocally directed at them; the ensuing stanzas on the idea of a crusade hold information for the English, which Joan alluded to in the *Lettre*, but information also pertinent to all concerned. Continuing the emphasis of earlier in her literary career on the

---

[14] Especially pertinent for the *Ditié* are the "Ballade du sacre de Reims (17 juillet 1429)," Pierre Champion, ed. *Le Moyen Age* 22, 2nd ser., 13 (1909): 370–77 and the verse "Ariere, Englois," known as the "Ballade contre les Anglais," previously cited.

[15] Wisman, *Epistle*, p. 89.

damage resulting from civil war, one of Christine's main preoccupations in the *Ditié* is the fissure between the two parties. It is unlikely that she intended her poem to be read by the English, nor is there any evidence that the poem ever reached England in medieval times, despite the popularity of some of her writing there. Already in her *Epistre à la reine* she had cited Luke 11:17: "Every kingdom divided against itself, shall be brought to desolation,"[16] and now national unity is still her primary concern.

The basis for centering her efforts on the rebels is threefold. First, she saw the unascertained convictions of the Parisians as the decisive factor in the prospect of Charles's return to Paris. Second, as she had previously clarified in the *Epistre à la reine*, well before Gelu made the same point in the *Dissertatio*,[17] civil war was a cause for rejoicing among one's enemies and a signal to invade,[18] whereas a reverse momentum could drive the enemy away. Finally, having lived in an era when the "sweet natural blood" (*doulz sang naturel*) of the royal house served humanity (*le droit comble de la benignité du monde*),[19] as she stated it in the *Lamentacion*, Christine was devastated to see dissension among men whom she described in the same document as "loved ones by nature, and enemies by accident."[20] The Parisian citizens to whom she especially addresses the *Ditié* might never have heard of the Maid, and still less the *Lettre*, although first knowledge of the former often came through the latter. Joan's summons was, after all, initially intended only for the English. But the recognition – first by Charles's publicists, and secondly by Christine, who herself takes up the cause of royalist publicity in the *Ditié* – that the *Lettre* bore an announcement as fitting for the French as for the English, placed a considerable tool for the tactics of sacred propaganda at Christine's disposal.[21] That a writer of Christine's caliber saw the *Lettre* as worthy of inscribing her own poetry merits our attention; the poet was willing to embrace a document which a contemporary chronicler and acquaintance saw as composed "in poorly disposed rough and heavy language" (*en gros et lourd language et mal ordonné*).[22]

Christine opens her final sequence of apostrophes with two stanzas to the loyal French military forces (37 and 38), meting out praise, promising honor

---

[16] Wisman, *Epistle*, p. 73; I have used the Douay translation.

[17] Gelu's fifth reason as to why God might aid the French notes that "even the enemies of the cross of Jesus are supremely joyful to hear of such wars between Christians," Lanéry d'Arc, *Mémoires*, p. 573.

[18] Wisman, *Epistle*, p. 79: "There is no doubt that the enemies of the kingdom, rejoicing at this turn of events, would come along with a great army to dishonor all."

[19] Wisman, *Epistle*, p. 84.

[20] Wisman, *Epistle*, p. 95.

[21] On Christine's strategic propaganda see Liliane Dulac, "Un écrit militant de Christine de Pizan: *Le Ditié de Jeanne d'Arc*," in *Aspects of Female Existence: Proceedings from The St. Gertrude Symposium, Copenhagen, September, 1978*, Birte Carlé et al., eds. (Gyldendal, 1980), pp. 115–34.

[22] Thomassin, *Registre* in Quicherat, *Procès* 4: 306.

and reward, and offering encouragement to her own side before she distributes blame to the enemy. The harsh lesson which she herself has learned, that loyalty to the monarchy brings suffering and risk, Christine recognizes as being magnified many times in their case, since in service to a principle ("in defence of what is right," line 298) they "expose life and limb . . . confronting every danger" (lines 297 and 299). The principle is the crucial notion of a just war, a concept we have seen treated in depth by theologians writing on Joan, which she also argued herself in the *Lettre*, and which is vigorously contradicted on multiple grounds by the English.

As we have seen, not the least of the justifying principles of the French campaign is the Deuteronomic warning contained in the *Lettre* itself, with its offer of peace. Christine understands this and before the Maid (who is not yet at Paris) can summon the citizens of Paris, the *Ditié* serves them advance notice. "Now as loyal Frenchmen," she exhorts, "prepare [*ordonner*] your hearts and give yourselves to him" (line 470),[23] permitting the equivocality of "him" (*lui*), to refer either to Charles (line 465) or God (line 468), the pronoun's more immediate antecedent. The greatest validation of the French offensive, however, comes from the prospect of a crusade and the attainment of universal peace. In the *Lettre*, the promise that Paris will be retaken is presented as the will of God, occurring in order that the French proceed to the more grandiose responsibility of preserving the faith. For Christine, this casts even the reconquest of Paris as part of the crusade phenomenon, since Christian unity is a prerequisite for confronting the Saracens.

As we saw Gelu insist, however, and Joan herself acknowledge when she told the prelate Guillaume Aimeri at Poitiers that "the soldiers will fight, and God will give the victory,"[24] God extends mercy but men must fight the battles. That one must not expect the whole victory to come from God is explained in the warning of Deuteronomy 6:16: "Thou shalt not tempt the Lord thy God." Thus Christine makes the daring promise (*dire l'os*, line 304) to the men-at-arms that: "Whoever fights for justice wins a place in Paradise" (lines 303–304). By contrast, she had made it clear in the *Lamentacion* that soldiers walking off the battlefield victorious in a civil war won no honor.[25]

Inserted between stanzas to the loyal French soldiers and the turncoat French, Christine deigns to address the English. The English segment (39–45) appears longer than it in fact is, because in stanzas 42 to 44 Christine also elucidates to her audience the meaning of the final lines of the *Lettre*, where Joan alludes to "the fairest deed ever done for Christianity." Taking her cue

---

[23] I have preferred to translate "ordonner" as "prepare" rather than "submit" to take into account the extra time Christine's *Ditié* gives them to contemplate their decision before Joan arrives.
[24] Murray, *Jeanne d'Arc*, p. 306; Duparc, *Procès* 1: 472.
[25] "Oh, you, knight who comes from such a battle, tell me, I pray you, what honor did you win there?" Wisman, *Epistle*, p. 87. The answer to this rhetorical question is none.

once again from the *Lettre*, Christine envisions Joan exercising the same uncompromising spirit towards heretics and unbelievers that the Maid first directed towards the enemy at Orléans, and where respect for Christianity is wanting there will be no mercy (*ne point n'aura misericorde*, line 335). Charles and Joan will conquer, their fates intermingled. The purpose of describing the French plans for a crusade becomes clear in the last stanza of the segment, where Christine disparages the war between France and England, arguing that Joan has better things to do, namely to preserve the Christian faith: "And yet destroying the [worthless] English [*Englecherie*] is not her main concern for her aspirations lie more elsewhere . . . to ensure the survival of the Faith" (lines 353–56). In this, Christine goes farther than Gelu, who never exploits the *Lettre's* promise of a crusade, and fails to adduce the evidence of the Second Charlemagne prophecy, a source which may never have reached the archbishop in Dauphiné.

Christine's lines to the English contrast with St. Bridget's prophecies, where both England and France were depicted as animals intent on destroying each other. In the *Ditié*, the only animals (except for the wolves who devour the dead, [lines 318–20]) are English. The thrust of her message to them, which draws certainty from the assurances of the *Lettre*, is that the tables have been turned. There will be no more meat for these horned English carnivores; all that awaits them in France is certain death. From Christine's pen comes the declaration that English ideas of permanence (in France) have proven to be no more than an illusion. Woven into the texture of the stanzas to the English are key messages from the *Lettre*, which now, as the *Lettre* did earlier at Orléans, provide the basis for a declaration of change. Christine acknowledges that a stalemate and a static situation has been allowed to endure. But drawing on the *Lettre*, she warns: "And know that she will cast down the English for good, for this is God's will" (lines 321–23). Here she signals the turning point in the deadlock, accounting for the delays by stating: "You were not yet treading the path upon which God casts down the proud" (lines 311–12), a juncture which has now been reached, for as Christine declares (and Henry VI proclaims about Joan herself in his letter of 1431): "God will tolerate this no longer" (lines 326–27). The promise of change, ready for Christine to draw upon again, was already unmistakable in the *Lettre*, for Joan had declared: "in whatever place I meet your people in France, I shall make them leave. . . . And be not of another opinion." In Christine's view all this comes about because God has abruptly decided to separate the good from the bad, listening to the prayers of the former and punishing the latter (stanza 41).

Before leaving the stanzas to the English, an isolated stanza about Joan (44) deserves brief mention. Growing out of the promise in the preceding stanzas that Joan will participate in a final glorious crusade, the stanza states in praise of Joan that she "should wear the crown" (of honor, and perhaps sainthood). Two important theological points are made in this stanza. First, in answer to any detractor who might still try to argue that Joan had failed to turn her words into deeds – recalling the words of Matthew 7:16: "By their fruits you shall know them" – Christine presents the divinity of Joan's mission as assured "for her deeds show [it] clearly enough already" (*Car ses faiz ja monstrent assez,* line 347). Second, embedded unobtrusively in this stanza is Christine's pronouncement on a very controversial topic of major concern to contemporaries, the extent and duration of Joan's mission: "And she has not yet accomplished her whole mission" (*Et n'a pas encor tout parfait!*) (line 350). This statement answers anyone who saw Joan's mission as completed after the coronation at Reims, or felt that she was losing her ability to perform miracles.

From stanza 46 to the end of the poem, Christine addresses three final groups, all Burgundians who swore the oath of loyalty to the English required by the treaty of Troyes: the "base rebels" (46–52), Paris (53–56), and the "rebel towns" (57). Drawing on the non-specific threats that are so plentiful in the *Lettre*, Christine redirects Joan's portentous tone toward the French. "Beware that more does not befall you" (line 366) and "remember what the outcome will be" (line 368), she cautions, just as the *Lettre* warned "expect tidings from the Maid [*attendez les nouvelles de la Pucelle*], who will come to see you shortly, to your very great harm." The main theological point Christine directs at the Burgundians is to argue the miracle of Joan through the impossibility of her deeds. Once again, the proof is a corollary to the biblical precept in 1 Corinthians 1:27 of the weak confounding the strong. For as the poet states, if this were not God's doing "how else could the Maid who strikes you all down dead have been sent [*tramise*] to us?" (lines 372–74). To answer Christine, they will be obliged to say that Joan was "sent by God." Christine also presents the coronation itself as a proof ("Has she not led the king to his coronation?") (line 377), not only because of the magnitude of the deed, but because her opponents were left powerless, and "there were certainly plenty" (*y ot tout plain,* line 381). By analogy, the rebels Christine addresses will receive a similar fate.

The *Lettre* promised that God would imbue the Maid with superhuman strength: "Know well that the King of Heaven will send greater strength to the Maid and her good men-at-arms than you in all your assaults can overwhelm." It is this point that allows Christine to scorn the blindness of the rebels in a rhetorical question, well worthy of having been pronounced by Joan herself: "You don't have sufficient strength! Do you want to fight against God?" (lines 375–76). As Joan wished the English to understand, and now Christine repeats to the Burgundians, whoever wages battle with Joan fights against God.

At stanza 50, as the flashbacks, exhortations, and meditations that filled the central portion of the *Ditié* give way to the present again, and thus to the prospect of the imminent arrival of the French, the armor of confidence which Christine has worn so well up to now starts to show chinks. It is not that she abandons the clamorous tone of the *Lettre*; in fact, the most direct reminiscences of the *Lettre* occur here, such as the phrase at line 406 denoting inevitability "whether they will it or not" (*vueillent ou non*) and the promise to take Paris (*Car ens entrera . . . La Pucelle lui a promis*) (lines 425–26). She states that the spilling of blood grieves Charles (*de sang espandre se deult*, line 460) and emphasizes Charles's promise of pardon. She even supports the assertion of the Burgundian *Chronique des cordeliers* that through awe and fear towns were surrendering without a blow struck (*pou sont envahis*, line 399).[26] But borrowing from the *Lettre's* Deuteronomic justification of killing, she argues (just as astonishingly as it was when we saw Gelu state the same claim) that bloodletting in a just war against recalcitrant opponents is meritorious: "But, in the end, if someone does not want to hand over . . . what is rightly his, he is perfectly justified [*il fait bien*] if he does recover it by force and bloodshed" (lines 461–64).

What is different at the end of July is the large number of uncertainties: whether Paris will look on Charles with favor, whether the duke of Burgundy will mount an offensive against Charles or cease to view him as an enemy, if a truce (Christine never uses the word herself) will delay the Maid's arrival, and finally, whether the "good inhabitants" ([les] *bons*) of Paris will dare to speak out, as Christine herself has dared to do in the *Ditié*. Of these factors, only the behavior of the Parisians is potentially in her power to change. As evidence of opponents (*les contrediz*) mounts in the concluding stanzas, Christine appears more and more helpless, despite her every best effort. Stanzas which were once self-assured now become mixed with doubts ("I don't know if") and prayers ("And I pray to God that"). In the end, all she can do is represent for the hesitant the image of that powerful relationship to which the French hold so persistently in their writings on Joan: the cooperative peace between God and his special people. In stanza 60, moving away from Charles, whom Christine had increasingly tried to put at the center of the picture as she spoke of his advancing campaign,[27] the poet Christine introduces a "triple entendre" on the word "chief" (leader, ruler, or author), which parallels testimony suggesting the same practice, on occasion, in Joan's speech.[28] She exhorts all concerned to be loyal to God, their "greater ruler" (*chief greigneur*, line 478).[29] Here the comparison is clear: Charles may be destined to be the leader (or author) of great deeds

---

[26] Quicherat, *Chronique des cordeliers*, p. 73.

[27] At line 393, Joan is no more than "the little Maid" (*la Pucellette*). See Nadia Margolis, "Elegant Closures: The Use of the Diminutive in Christine de Pizan and Jean de Meun," in *Reinterpreting Christine de Pizan*, Earl Jeffrey Richards, ed., with Joan Williamson, Nadia Margolis, and Christine Reno (Athens, Ga., 1992), pp. 111–23.

[28] For instance, see her comment regarding the higher allegiance she owed God (*suo supremo domino*) as compared to Charles (*rex suus*), Barrett, *Trial*, p. 79 and p. 80, respectively; Quicherat, *Procès* 1: 95, 96.

[29] Kennedy and Varty, *Ditié*, p. 50, opt for "supreme" although their glossary acknowledges that "greigneur" is a comparative form.

(*chief,* line 120), and Joan "supreme captain" (*chevetaine,* line 286), but this power is outweighed by that of God, the "greater ruler." This is Christine's final expression to the Burgundians of her belief that Joan, the *Lettre aux Anglais,* and the *Ditié* all serve as reminders of something more substantial, the requirement of obedience to God.

We have important information about the dissemination of the *Ditié* and the manner in which it was understood by contemporaries through the three manuscripts which have survived. Manuscript 390 of the Bibliothèque Inguimbertine at Carpentras is of interest to us only insofar as it dates from the fifteenth century and demonstrates that the *Ditié* (transcribed in full) was prized for its poetic value, apparently irrespectively of the theological, propagandistic, or Johannic content. The *Ditié* occupies the final position in a leather-bound paper manuscript of poetry, which also includes a *pastourelle,* debate love poetry and Alain Chartier's celebrated poem *La Belle Dame sans Mercy* (1424).[30]

The manuscript presumed earliest, Berne 205, allows us to date rather precisely the recording of the *Ditié* in its pages. Nicolas du Pleissy, one of the compilers of the ample and diverse entries which constitute Berne 205, precedes his transcription of Christine's text with a notice of his nomination to an administrative position in Sens on 17 January 1430, which was "no doubt as a reward for his loyalty to Charles VII," state Kennedy and Varty.[31] Exactly ten days before du Pleissy's nomination, on 7 January 1430, the town of Sens had returned to the obedience of Charles VII. Until that time, Sens fit the description of Christine's "rebel towns" (line 449). Overcome by Anglo-Burgundian forces in 1420, the citizens of this border town, had refused, on several occasions, to return to French rule. A faction of inhabitants, however, among whom must have been du Pleissy, used their influence (and perhaps the influence of the *Ditié?*) to open talks with the royal party in December 1429, and a month later Sens offered its submission to Charles.

Du Pleissy's codex, which demonstrates his preference for political literature, includes, in addition to the *Ditié* (fol. 62), several other Johannic texts, along with such political pieces as a French verse chronogram on the siege of Montereau of 1437 (fol. 82b), two poems in celebration of the peace at Arras (fols. 132b and 190a), a *complainte* of France,[32] a theatrical piece based on the council of Basel (fols. 551a – 570b),[33] and French verse (fol. 153b), strongly resembling stanzas 53–56 of the *Ditié,* admonishing Paris to surrender to Charles.[34] Remarkably, the other documents on the Maid, which

[30] Kennedy and Varty, *Ditié,* p. 4.
[31] Kennedy and Varty, *Ditié,* p. 3.
[32] Jonathan Beck, *Le concil de Basle (1434): Les origines du théâtre réformiste et partisan en France,* Studies in the History of Christian Thought, 18 (Leiden, 1979), p. 11, n. 5.
[33] Beck, *Le concil,* p. 11.
[34] De Roche and Wissler, "Documents," pp. 370–71.

either follow the *Ditié* directly or appear later in the manuscript, are the *Lettre aux Anglais* (fol. 68), the *Poitiers Conclusions* (fol. 69), the two- and three-verse Merlin prophecies (fols. 133a and 133b), and *Virgo puellares* with a French translation (fol. 133a).

Although the early editors de Roche and Wissler find the position of Christine's *Ditié* in Berne 205, where it is flanked on one side by du Pleissy's license and on the other by the *Lettre* and *Poitiers Conclusions*, "in those surroundings . . . curious,"[35] if the latter two documents served as Christine's sources, a plausible linkage already exists. Furthermore, if the intention of disseminating the original propaganda documents (*Lettre, Conclusions,* and prophecies) during the summer of 1429 was to rejuvenate a stalled campaign, the value of the *Ditié* in this regard must have been quickly recognized. For judging from the evidence of Berne 205, it appears that the *Ditié* was pressed into service as royalist propaganda, as a supplement to the sources which provided its inspiration, within six months of its composition. The verses admonishing Paris to surrender, if in fact based on the *Ditié*, form yet another link in the chain of French propaganda.

The logic of dispatching propaganda to towns like Sens, where geographical position dictated strong Anglo-Burgundian influence, but where pockets of loyalist support also existed, is obvious. This is in fact very nearly the pattern for the dissemination of the original three propaganda documents.[36] Although the *Lettre* was routed to La Rochelle, a town loyal to France, *Virgo puellares* appears in the Kaerrymel manuscript in Anglo-Burgundian Brittany,[37] and the *Lettre* and *Conclusions* were received in Tournai, a loyal French town surrounded by enemy-held territory, where they were transcribed in the *Chronique de Tournai*.[38] And the substance of the *Lettre* and *Conclusions*, if not the texts themselves, traveled a sympathetic route from Bruges to Venice, as evidenced by allusions in the *Morosini* chronicle. Christine's access to the texts at the loyal French convent of Poissy, in land otherwise sworn to England, yields one further example.

The third surviving copy of the *Ditié* exists only as a fragment, reduced in length to include "only that which particularly deals with the Maid," according to Mathieu Thomassin in his *Registre delphinal*.[39] Thomassin was commissioned in 1456 to write the *Registre* for the future Louis XI, then dauphin.[40] He is struck by the phenomenon of a female poet of his

[35] De Roche and Wissler, "Documents," p. 332.
[36] For a full description of the propagation of these texts, see Lefèvre-Pontalis, *Sources;* Cordier, *Jeanne d'Arc*, chapter 7 "La propagande et la légende," pp. 171–77; Bouzy, "Prediction," especially pp. 40–43.
[37] Paulin Paris, *Les manuscrits françois de la bibliothèque du roi*, vol. 7 (Paris, 1848), manuscript 7301, pp. 377–84.
[38] *Chronique de Tournai* in *Corpus chronicorum Flandriae*, J.-J. de Smet, ed., Collection de chroniques belges inédites (Brussels, 1856) 3: 406–409.
[39] Quicherat, *Procès* 4: 310.
[40] Quicherat, *Procès* 4: 303.

acquaintance ("I often saw her in Paris") writing on a female restorer of the realm, and so he observes: "And I preferred to place here the treatise of the said Christine rather than another, so as to always honor the female sex."[41] Strictly speaking, he oversteps the boundaries of his history of Dauphiné in devoting space to Joan, but he justifies the excursus by the Maid's connection to the reign of the dauphin Charles, and by the reliance of Dauphiné on the kingdom: "Dauphiné [was] inseparably . . . joined to the said kingdom, and if the kingdom had been lost, [Dauphiné would have been equally lost]."[42] Although Thomassin offers personal information about the Maid, the accumulation of Johannic documents at his disposal – whether documents gathered by Thomassin after 1456, or, since 1429, already deposited together in Dauphiné archives, we do not know – must have influenced his decision to devote more than a half-dozen pages to Joan. For in his possession were the Merlin prophecy (*Descendet virgo*), *Virgo puellares*, the *Poitiers Conclusions*, the *Lettre aux Anglais*, and excerpts from the *Ditié*, a nearly complete collection. A parallel he draws between "the maid Virgin Mary," responsible for the "reparation and restoration of the human lineage" and "the said Maid Joan," responsible for the "reparation and restoration of the kingdom of France," indicates his familiarity with the EVA / AVE prophecy as well.[43] Here again, under a single umbrella, we find the *Ditié* coupled with its sources, through an avenue which is virtually certain to have been official, telling the story of Joan's divine mission. From early in his passage on the Maid, Thomassin has seen the meaning of her mission. The kingdom was under such siege that it would have been reduced to English obedience "if God had not had pity, and sent aid by means of a poor little shepherdess named Joan."[44] Even the chronicler Thomassin, although rather formulaically and twenty-seven years after the fact, has made a pronouncement in favor of Joan's divine mission.

---

[41] Quicherat, *Procès* 4: 310: "Et j'ay plus tost désiré de mettre icy le traictié de laditte Christine que des autres, afin de tousjours honnorer le sexe féminin." Interestingly, he refers to Christine's poem as a "traictié" rather than a "ditié."

[42] Thomassin fails to complete his thought, as observed by Quicherat, *Procès* 4: 311, n. 1.

[43] Quicherat, *Procès* 4: 310. Thomassin refers to Mary as "la pucelle Vierge Marie" and Joan as "laditte Pucelle Jehanne."

[44] Quicherat, *Procès* 4: 304.

8

De mirabili victoria

As we begin the discussion of *De mirabili victoria*, it should be explained that DMV was the most popular among contemporary treatises written on Joan of Arc, and that it also exerted the widest contemporary influence. Because of multiple problems raised by this tract, which will be elucidated in these pages, it is with reluctance that DMV will be referred to here as an actual theological treatise, although it is certain that the author wished his work to be understood in this manner and that contemporaries perceived it as such. The author mounted such a vigorous and impassioned defense of the Maid (and quite possibly oversaw the treatise's distribution with the same energy), that within a few months of its composition, DMV was known in Paris, Bruges, Venice, and Rome. Later it would also appear broadly excerpted in manuscripts at two locations in Spain, undergo transcription at the council of Basel, and to some extent, against the odds, find a prominent place among the extra-judicial treatises adduced at the nullification trial nearly a quarter of a century after the date of DMV's composition.

While the words "about a marvelous victory" (*de mirabili victoria*), found in the heading of several manuscripts,[1] suggest that the author of DMV wishes to report the victory at Orléans, either as chronicle, or as sacred history in the manner of Christine's *Ditié* ("how God . . . accomplished all this through His grace"), neither Orléans nor its great victory is ever mentioned in the body of the text. A single allusion to "a first miracle" (*primum miraculum*)[2] no doubt refers to Joan's first triumph at Orléans, proving the author's awareness at least of the victory vaunted in the heading, but the heading is a false introduction to the treatise, for DMV is certainly not about Orléans nor is it a historical narrative, either secular or sacred.

The tract is best described as a pro-Joan polemic, which proclaims its enthusiasm for the Maid in response to the accusations of detractors. An obviously vexed author seeks to counter Joan's opponents with his own arguments. This circumstance justifies our interpreting his work as a text

[1] Manuscript information and a French translation of DMV can be found in J.-B. Monnoyeur, *Traité de Jean Gerson sur la Pucelle* (Paris, 1930).
[2] Wayman, "The Chancellor," p. 300.

belonging to the Johannic debate. In fact, if we consider the texts described up to now as the first phase of this debate, DMV and the activity it generates become the second (and final) phase of the debate in the fifteenth century. Under the rubric of second-phase texts, in addition to DMV itself, we will discuss the *Collectarium* of Jean Dupuy, the anonymous *Reply of a Parisian Cleric*, and Martin Le Franc's passage on Joan in the *Champion des dames*, each the subject of a separate chapter, as well as make brief mention of the *Morosini* chronicle and the introduction of DMV by Guillaume Bouillé into the nullification trial. Taken collectively, these texts replace or create a parallel history to the early discussions of *discretio spirituum* as reflected in DQP, the three propaganda documents, the *Dissertatio*, and the *Ditié*.

It is unclear why DMV, a treatise generally attributed to the royalist theologian Jean Gerson, and its satellite texts would not simply have joined the growing body of Johannic texts, those addressed in our previous chapters, as new accretions in a single tradition, but such is not the case. When we turn to DMV, to a considerable degree we leave behind the affiliations among texts such as DQP, the three propaganda documents, the *Dissertatio*, and the *Ditié*, in exchange for a new set of affiliated, but different texts. With the exception of the *Morosini* chronicle, which is by any measure an oddly unique text, no medieval witness to DMV knows any of the three propaganda documents. While the author of DMV has himself heard of the painstaking investigation of Joan's case, which he describes as having been "submitted to research and thorough investigations . . . by numerous investigators" (*interrogate sunt et cognitae diu et multum et per multos*), he does not mention Chinon or Poitiers, cannot be said to make a reliable allusion to the *Poitiers Conclusions*, and leaves not a trace in his text of the *Lettre aux Anglais* or makes any reference to the Johannic prophecies. The one possible exception is *Virgo puellares*, the least tractable of all the prophecies to a theological reading.

Although the three propaganda documents seem to have circulated only quasi-officially, since they lacked the king's seal, their presence is attested at numerous sites to which royal information was regularly dispatched – Tournai, La Rochelle, Sens, Dauphiné, and undoubtedly the convent of Poissy – so that the flow of official and marginally official documents to the king's favorite locations, in return for the inhabitants' loyalty, is fairly seamless. This suggests that, if DMV had royalist connections, those allies to whom the king regularly dispensed royal circulars and to whom he had sent numerous Johannic documents should have received the most important piece of all, a treatise defending the Maid, by Gerson, the most celebrated theologian of Charles's party. But there is no sign that this ever happened. Tournai and La Rochelle can be used as test cases. Although those cities received numerous royal communiqués, among which the *Conclusions* and *Lettre* are attested in Tournai and the *Lettre* in La Rochelle, DMV cannot be linked to either location. More surprising is the case of Sens and Dauphiné, because copies of the *Ditié* reached those locations along with the propaganda texts, even though Christine's poem was written long after the *Conclusions* and the *Lettre*. This fact suggests that Charles continued to send new pieces of propaganda as they were written. If the *Ditié*, which was not composed until after the coronation, was disseminated to locations in direct contact with the crown, DMV should logically have experienced the same fate. That tract had been available longer and bore the stamp of a theologian not a poet. We also know that DMV was indeed in circulation, just not in royal circulation apparently.

Presently, we will raise the issue of how we can measure the authenticity of different Johannic texts, in order to apply those standards to DMV, because there are unresolved problems about the treatise which imperil its authenticity. For the moment, however, it is enough to introduce a summary of DMV, which by itself will signal the work's relative isolation from the tradition described thus far, making us wonder why its author had not been better informed by the monarchy, especially if this author was Gerson.

On the basis of the manuscript evidence, DMV is a two-part treatise, although differences between two distinct sections in the first part suggest an additional division. The opening passage (section one of part one) contains an intricate scholastic discussion about truth and probability. The distinction is drawn between two kinds of faith, necessities of faith (*necessitate fidei*), that is, required beliefs imposed on all members of the church, and voluntary pious beliefs (*pietate . . . fidei*), allowed by the church to the laity as a concession to local cults in cases which have not received permanent status.[3] In essence, this is the difference between faith and devotion.[4] Since at the time of writing Joan's case had received no official decision by church "superiors" (e.g. referral to Rome, a canonization process, a heresy trial), the author of DMV claims that arguments containing a reasonable degree of probability could be generated both for and against her. This, the author allowed, was normal, for whereas ultimately two contradictory things cannot both be true, until the truth is known they can both be probable. He then listed three conditions required of a case for pious belief: first, it must intensify devotion to God; second, be based on probable arguments or be supported by the testimony of witnesses; third, have been examined by the proper theologians to rule out evidence of any error of faith. In the text, the optional nature of pious belief is reinforced by the vernacular proverb: "He who does not believe this is not damned" and examples of pious belief reflecting a Parisian context – the Immaculate Conception and the veneration of the head of St. Denis – are offered. Nothing in the segment demonstrates convincingly that it was composed for Joan's case and there

[3] Wayman, "The Chancellor," p. 297; Monnoyeur, *Traité*, p. 21 and p. 22.
[4] Lucien Fabre, *Joan of Arc*, Gerard Hopkins, trans. (New York, 1954), p. 348.

is no reference at all to the Maid. An important translation of DMV, in fact, chooses to ignore this discussion completely, and begins translating the tract only midway through part one (section two of part one) where Joan enters the picture.[5]

Although the two sections of part I are markedly dissimilar, the first paragraph of the second section purports to base a declaration of faith in the Maid on the preceding argumentation: "In conformity with these premises [*concludendum . . . ex praemissis*], and the circumstances being considered with their good result . . . it is pious, salutary, of true and devout belief to approve the Maid's case." Then the author adds two now familiar reasons: the justice of restoring a king to his kingdom and the fairness of expelling and defeating his enemies.

Next, instead of offering the list of Joan's virtues and Catholic practices customarily used to defend her case, the author denies four errors that would disqualify her case. They have the ring of actual accusations he has heard leveled against her: the use of spells, superstition, and fraud, and the charge that self-interest drives her actions. Claiming by reference to a line from Cato ("We do not have to judge what everyone says"), and a more appropriate biblical reminder from 2 Timothy 2:24 that "the servant of the Lord must not wrangle," he confronts Joan's detractors ("talkative, light-minded or malicious people") and insists that pious belief in Joan should be tolerated, more so than a cult propagated without canonization. He then turns to four justifications of his cause (*causam nostram*): first, the belief of the king's council (a reference to the *Poitiers Conclusions*?) and the military in her words and their willingness to obey her, especially considering the derision they risked if they had been vanquished; second, a pious enthusiasm among the French balanced by confusion in the enemy; third, a languor and cowardice in the enemy accomplished by invoking the hymn to Mary followed by the words of Exodus: "Let fear and dread fall upon them";[6] fourth, the familiar argument that the Maid employs the means of human prudence and avoids tempting God, always remaining within the limits of her mission. There follow the exempla of Deborah, St. Catherine of Alexandria, Judith, and Judas Maccabaeus as proof that Joan's case conforms to "natural order" (*aliquid naturale*).[7]

At the close of part I, the author responds to an accusation from an unknown quarter that Joan has not been able to produce continuous miracles and he insists that frustration about the case should not lead to the conclusion that her deeds are the work of the evil spirit instead of God. Afterwards, he refers to "four civil and theological documents" by the Maid.

[5] Francq, "Gerson," p. 61. Francq's translation is reproduced as Appendix IV.
[6] Wayman, "The Chancellor," p. 300; Monnoyeur, *Traité*, p. 27: The text is from Exodus 15:16.
[7] Wayman, "The Chancellor," p. 300.

They pertain to the king and princes, the militia, the ecclesiastics and people, and, especially, the Maid herself, but the documents are not explained except inasmuch as they pertain to righteous living, piety, justice, and sobriety.[8] For the Maid, the author continues, God's grace must not be misused for "vain curiosity" (*vanitates curiosas*), "social profits" (*mundanos questus*), "hatred of parties" (*odia partialia*), "seditious quarrels" (*seditiones contentiosas*), "vengeance for the past" (*vindictas de preteritis*), or "inept bragging" (*gloriationes ineptas*).[9] The last lines of part I call for the generous contribution of financial support to bring the return of peace. There is the echo in these words of the request of *Virgo puellares* for recruits, that plea also made in anticipation of achieving peace.[10] The section concludes with the claim: "This is the Lord's doing" (*A Domino factum est istud*).

Part II of DMV is set off by the heading: "Three truths follow" (*sequitur triplex veritas*), in capital letters in some manuscripts, suggesting a supplement or appendix to the treatise. Except in continuing the defense of Joan, part II is not connected to the previous part. In particular, it bears no relation to the treatise's opening passage (section one of part one). Part II gives three arguments in defense of the Maid's male clothes: first, that the judicial obligation of the ancient law (a reference to the prohibition against transvestism in Deuteronomy 22:5) is lifted; second, that the moral aspect of the law remains intact, thus decency of dress is required, but "time, necessity, purpose, manner and other similar conditions" (*quando oportet, cur oportet, qualiter oportet et ita de reliquis*) must be taken into account in making a judgment (the argument of necessity is found in Aquinas);[11] third, that the law does not condemn "the wearing of manly and warrior-like clothes by the Maid who is a warrior and acts in a manly manner" (*usum vestis virilis et militaris in puella nostra virili et militari*).[12] The "three truths" take up less than half of part II, although the annex is primarily known for these three explanations.

After the third justification a shift of focus occurs. The author makes a second pronouncement of faith in the Maid, this one stated in definitive terms. He declares that "unquestionable signs prove that she has been chosen by the King of Heaven as His standard-bearer" (*quam ex certis signis eligit Rex coelestis omnium tamquam vexilliferam*) and alludes to the power of women to overthrow iniquity. Because of her virginity, he continues, the Maid, like St. Cecilia, is surrounded by helpful angels (*auxiliantibus angelis*).

---

[8] Wayman, "The Chancellor," pp. 300–301.

[9] Wayman, "The Chancellor," p. 301.

[10] See the Kaerrymel manuscript in Paris, *Les manuscrits* 7: 379–80: "And if men have enough courage to join the battle. . . . Then it will be the end of the war."

[11] Aquinas, *Summa* 44: 239 [2a2ae. 169, 2]: "The wearing of the clothes of the opposite sex is wrong. . . . It is expressly forbidden in the Law. . . . However, it may be done without sin in case of necessity."

[12] Wayman, "The Chancellor," p. 302.

His last point argues that Joan may cut her hair, despite the seeming prohibition of the Apostle (1 Corinthians 11:5–6).

In conclusion, the author makes an astonishing assertion given the force and finality with which it is uttered:

> May the tongues of iniquity be stopped. . . . For, when divine power operates . . . it becomes dangerous, presumptuous and foolhardy to blame and to criticize things which have been instituted by God.[13]

Next, he refers to the existence of additional validation from "sacred and secular history," but adduces as additional examples only the further examples of Camilla and the Amazons. Finally, he ends with the warning that disbelief, ingratitude, and lies could cause God to withdraw his hand, a fear we have seen expressed several times before now:

> Ah! henceforth, may the party which has justice [*pars habens justam causam*] on its side take care not to stop in its course and render useless, by disbelief, ingratitude and other prevarications [*per incredulitatem et ingratitudinem vel alias injusticias*], the divine help [*divinum . . . auxilium*] whose commencement manifested itself in such an evident and marvelous [*tam patenter et mirabiliter*] manner.[14]

This warning brings DMV to a conclusion.

Although a number of points made in the preceding synopsis of DMV will be recognizable from the discussion in the preceding chapters, there is reason to believe that this treatise should have less right to our trust – not only as a treatise on *discretio spirituum*, but as a work written by Jean Gerson, completed on 14 May 1429 – than the texts previously examined. Whether by the unity of their themes, the orthodox nature of their contents, the presence of date of composition and name of author (Gerson's *De probatione*, Christine's *Ditié*) embedded in the texts themselves, the names of the addressees and authors stated in the letters, or similar factors, there was no reason to challenge any previous text on the grounds of its authenticity. Although not all texts were written with knowledge of the others, the overlapping themes, at times even on very small points, allow us to trust in them as representations of an agreed-upon French reality.

For DMV the problems begin with the rubric. As already mentioned, the "marvelous victory" is not the subject of the treatise. The promise of the opening words of the title of DMV in certain manuscripts: "about the Maid and the faith she is due" (*super facto Puellae et credulitate ei praestanda*),[15] are only partially realized in the body of the text. A comparison of the author's treatment of *discretio spirituum*, implied by the words "the faith she is due,"

---

13 Wayman, "The Chancellor," p. 302.
14 Wayman, "The Chancellor," pp. 302–303.
15 Monnoyeur, *Traité*, p. 41.

with either Gerson's *De probatione*, the *Poitiers Conclusions*, or Gelu's *Dissertatio* demonstrates a number of differences. Moreover, the title under scrutiny here may not be the authentic title. Monnoyeur notes its absence in Du Pin's early edition of DMV and describes a line scratched out in B.N. manuscript 14904 (fol. 201) which he believes held the true title.[16] In addition, for the 14 May date of composition to be possible, a date which has been generally accepted, news of the victory at Orléans (8 May) would have necessarily traveled to Lyon, where Gerson had taken up residence, at uncharacteristic speeds, especially if time is also allowed for the composition of the treatise.

It becomes more obvious that the 14 May date of composition must be rejected when we look at internal clues in DMV as a means of dating the treatise. First, the author's unbridled enthusiasm for the divinity of Joan's mission cannot be squared with the early stages of *discretio spirituum*, when caution is called for. Since the author knows about the investigation of Joan and describes it as already having been conducted, he is clearly writing after Poitiers. Therefore, his treatise is not being written to participate in that procedure, nor does his opinion appear to have been solicited at that time. He definitely writes at a pivotal and contentious moment in the Maid's career, identifiable as a period of waiting and possible frustration (*si frustraretur ab omne expectatione sua et nostra*), during which our author may fear that Joan's detractors are gaining the upper hand. These circumstances seem entirely incompatible with a date just six days after a joyous victory. Also, if we recognize that both written criticisms and defenses of Joan's male dress increased in the late summer and fall of 1429, our author's defense of her masculine attire may point to a date of composition for DMV in that time frame, or somewhat earlier. Since Gerson died on 12 July of the same year, linking DMV's composition to the growing debate over her male clothes makes Gerson less likely to be the treatise's author.

Before coming to the two most decisive factors against the claim that DMV is Gerson's discernment treatise on Joan – the difference in themes and the uncharacteristic approach to discernment, as compared to genuine works of *discretio spirituum* – there is a pair of smaller points to be made. First, the author of DMV, as we have mentioned, seems to be very out of touch. This is manifested by his failure to demonstrate any knowledge of the information disseminated by Girard and l'Hermite, which, in turn, suggests that he was overlooked for consultation during the outreach for early opinions on the Maid. Differently from the case of Gelu, there is no evidence of any royal correspondence between the author of DMV and Charles, nor has the king sent him the three propaganda texts. Moreover, DMV is oddly constructed. The treatise consists of a collection of disparate passages, linked by choppy transitions or no transition at all. The scholastic section and the conclusion

[16] Monnoyeur, *Traité*, p. 40.

of the treatise are particularly jarring, even contradictory, as if they are not cut from the same cloth. These relatively minor issues, which become more serious if we wish to attribute the treatise to the talent of Gerson (Vallet de Viriville, for instance, notes in DMV Gerson's "sagging intellect"),[17] add to the generally problematic nature of DMV, which arises particularly in the two central difficulties to now come under discussion.

There is nothing at first that makes DMV seem very different from our other texts. After all, the author comprehends that ceasing to believe in the Maid may jeopardize God's aid and hence peace. He acknowledges detractors, defends belief in Joan, and lists points for his cause. Moreover, he adduces exempla, alludes to moral requirements (the four official warnings), and carefully justifies the male dress challenged in DQP. Beyond that, the author refers to "signs" that prove Joan has been chosen by God, alludes to the ability of youth and femininity to overthrow the enemy, makes reference to Joan's virginity, proclaims the just cause of his party, and occasionally alludes to Scripture. On the surface, there is consonance rather than dissonance.

But let us begin with the author's depiction of the king as a starting point for evaluating the differences. In DMV the pivotal position of Charles in the narrative of the Maid and in the crucial perpetuation of the Valois line is dismissed with a single remark, that it is "most just" (*justissima*) to "restore the king to his kingdom" (*restitutio regis ad regnum suum*). There is no reference to the king's legitimacy either as direct descendent of Charles VI (*Karolus filius Karoli*), legitimate offspring of his mother, or as the blood heir whose case outweighs the merely verbal claim of Henry VI established in the *Treaty of Troyes*. The words "true heir" or "legitimate heir" are conspicuously absent. Nor is there any concrete sense of the English usurpation and occupation of French lands, no notion of France's inalienable right to the fatherland, no duplication, for instance, of Gelu's or any other contemporary's use of the word "patria."

Absent also is the idea of France's noble Christian past, often expressed through recourse to St. Jerome's statement that only France was free of heresy, or the commonplace notion of the need to sustain the royal lineage, whose protective myth centers on the idea that Charles has been "preserved," both to foster great deeds and to see his lineage grow. The sentiment that Joan's arrival is a signal to Charles of the weighty destiny placed by God on his shoulders is entirely disregarded in DMV. As portrayed in DMV, France has no special role in Christianity for which peace between French and English is a prerequisite. Until the concluding section of the tract, war for the author of DMV is primarily a narrow, legal, and military affair.

To all concerned, the victory of Orléans symbolized the idea of a turnaround, the moment when the respective fates of the French and English

---

[17] Auguste Vallet de Viriville, *Histoire de Charles VII, roi de France et de son époque (1403–1461)*, 3 vols., Société de l'Histoire de France (Paris, 1862–65) 2: 94.

changed places. Our author demonstrates that he knows this only five lines from the end of the treatise when he refers to "the divine help whose commencement manifested itself in such an evident and marvelous manner." He acknowledges the renewal of French spirit but does not connect the psychological assault that has contributed to France's triumph over the enemy to the influence of the *Lettre* or the Maid's summonses. Instead he oddly attributes the enemy's growing fear to the recitation of the biblical hymn to Mary, of which there is no similar mention anywhere. The fact that, given France's unexpected reversal of fortune, the call for surrender is now coming from a different side, and that French promises of pardon and mercy are in the air for those who were so recently devastating France, are of little interest to our author. In yet another difference, the Maid's gentle, feminine side (except for a passing allusion to her friendship with angels) never appears in DMV, either as proof of her character or as an antidote to her provocative warrior image. Thus the author omits the accustomed division in Joan's behavior, seen as early as DQP, that she was fierce at war but conventionally feminine when removed from the arena of battle.

Although the subjects of the four points adduced early in the treatise by our author "in favor of our cause" do indeed focus on the war and the English, the relative lack of interest in political and military issues shown in the remainder of the treatise can be accounted for by the author's one overriding concern: to counter the undermining of Joan's cause by detractors. We never discover anything precise about these detractors except their faults. They are "talkative" (*garrulitate*), "light-minded" (*levitate*), and "malicious" (*dolositate*),[18] in addition to being ungrateful (*ingratitudinem*) and blasphemous (*blasphemias*).[19] These are men whom the author labels "the tongues of iniquity" (*os loquentium iniqua*).[20] They are not, it must be recognized, formal enemies of Charles VII, but members of the author's own party ("the party which has justice on its side" [*pars habens justam causam*]),[21] yet we never learn whether they are Burgundians, sympathizers of the English at the University of Paris, doubters within the king's immediate circle, or prelates preparing to abandon the Maid's cause.after first supporting it.

The accusations which the author refutes, that Joan resorts to spells, superstitions, frauds, and tries to secure her own interest, are generally Burgundian allegations. Would a member of the French party, in a gesture of unity, include the Burgundians under the rubric "the party which has justice on it side?" No clear answers emerge. The context is arguably ecclesiastical, the setting perhaps abbatial, where rumors might fly from monastery to monastery; and, if the opening section of the treatise, with its allusions to

---

[18] Wayman, "The Chancellor," p. 299.
[19] Wayman, "The Chancellor," p. 300.
[20] Wayman, "The Chancellor," p. 302.
[21] Wayman, "The Chancellor," p. 302.

university controversies, is authentic, the author's location could conceivably be not Lyon, but Paris. That would mean, of course, that Gerson, residing in Lyon, did not compose the treatise. None of this, however, is more than conjecture. What is certain, however, is that the author takes a parochial view of the Christian world, for he never claims that all of Christendom is scandalized or harmed, improved or exalted, or even affected. This is quite atypical of the rhetoric of the Hundred Years War in which Christians were sensitive to the issues of fighting other Christians. Each side wished to demonstrate that by the sins of the opponent the Christian world was on the point of collapse.

In DMV the author exhibits an atypical response to Joan herself. It is perfectly within the norm for him to refuse to dwell on her biography; we have seen this in virtually every author. But he is not concerned with the ambiguities of her physical nature or her role, although he grants her the metaphorical role of divine standard-bearer (*eligit Rex coelestis omnium tamquam vexilliferam*).[22] Also, the lengths to which Gelu went to argue that it was Joan's divine mission that obliged her to wear men's clothes is an argument our author overlooks. In fact, the very important notion of mission, its length and scope, and the way those two factors determined the nature of the Maid's influence, never seem to penetrate the author's consciousness. As far as he is concerned, Joan is predominantly a warrior figure who acts in a manly manner (*puella nostra virili et militari*),[23] although he acknowledges too that she is "a woman, a young girl [and] a virgin" (*femine puellaris et virginis*).[24] He never specifically states that she is war chief – perhaps because that was knowledge generally known through the *Lettre aux Anglais* – but he describes the army as fighting "under her" (*sub ea*).[25]

Since most writers feel compelled to define the Maid's role relative to angels, DMV makes its own pronouncement. As we have seen, for Christine, Joan was sent by God, making the journey to the king "accompanied by the angel of God"; for Gelu, she was the "angel of God of the armies" (in title not in nature); for the English she was tantamount to the "angel of darkness." However, DMV veers from this norm on two accounts. Instead of making the novel but popular connection common among Johannic writers, which is first found in the Merlin prophecy and perpetuated in the *Lettre aux Anglais*, that the status of *pucelle* was linked to the possibility of Joan's presence on the battlefield, the author of DMV makes only the usual and expected connection, that her virginity was a sign of relationship to heavenly things. Thus her virginity in DMV "forms a link of friendship and relationship" with angels but does not authorize her warrior role as we would expect, based on other Johannic texts. The other point of difference is more considerable. The

---

[22] Wayman, "The Chancellor," p. 302.
[23] Wayman, "The Chancellor," p. 302.
[24] Wayman, "The Chancellor," p. 302.
[25] Wayman, "The Chancellor," p. 299.

author of DMV is the only prelate who denies the direct, unmediated nature of Joan's inspiration, which Gerson in *De probatione* referred to as "direction not merely from angels, but from God himself."[26] This undermining of Joan as possessor of the highest form of inspiration is recorded in the short but potent phrase claiming that the Maid is "surrounded by helpful angels" (*auxiliantibus angelis*). The degradation of her divine mission by this hasty but sympathetic remark, however, does not seem to be an intentional comment on her status as a prophet by the author. It would, on the other hand, become the crux of the matter at Rouen.

A final mark of difference from other authors manifests itself in the DMV author's curious use of validating exempla. In the texts we discussed prior to DMV, several points were clear. There was a preference for Old Testament models. Esther, Judith, and, often but not obligatorily, Deborah formed a triad, whose linkage dates back at least as far as St. Jerome. On the other hand, the Amazons, except for the allusion to the feminine Mars in *Virgo puellares*, were not considered acceptable prototypes. This was because the emphasis in selecting exempla for Joan was on prophets and saviors of the people of God. The Amazons, moreover, were pagans, and did not enjoy the special status of the sibyls, occasional models for Joan, as prophets of Christ. Christine de Pizan, among others, had rehabilitated the image of the Amazons in the *Cité des dames*, as had Benoit de Sainte-Maure before her in the *Roman de Troie*, but for Christine the Amazons' warrior valor remained strictly in the realm of fiction. Although the popularity of the Amazons, depicted in late-medieval painting, tapestry, sculpture, and pageantry, as the *neuf preuses*, or Nine Worthy Women, granted the likes of Semiramis and Thomyris a new respectability, to a theologian the more-deeply ingrained image would be the feverishly hostile portrayal of the Amazons in Dares or Dictys, or in the medieval encyclopedic tradition, where they appear as unquestionable monsters. For our author, then, to profess additional support for his case in "sacred and secular history" (*historiis sacris et gentilium*)[27] and follow this with the single exemplum of Camilla and the Amazons remains odd and unexplainable.

As we advance now to the most serious charge against DMV – its curious, unorthodox, and sometimes erroneous handling of *discretio spirituum* – we need first to give the author his due by listing each allusion he makes to Joan's divine mission. The line number will be included to illustrate how slowly he arrives at the crux of discernment, discussion of whether the Maid was sent by God.[28] Since the scholastic section of DMV is not about the Maid, the first allusion occurs only at line 128 of the treatise, a surprising

---

[26] Boland, *Concept*, p. 33; Glorieux, *Oeuvres* 9: 181.

[27] Wayman, "The Chancellor," p. 302.

[28] Lines are listed according to Monnoyeur's Latin text because Francq's translation omits the opening passage of the text. Monnoyeur does not number the lines but only the relative position of the phrases in the text is important.

fifty-seven lines into the section where Joan is introduced (second section of part I), and the reference is no more than Joan's own claim: "the orders and inspirations she is convinced she received from God" (*reputet a deo se habere monitiones seu instinctus*).[29] This is not because the author of DMV is 'saving the best for last,' as Christine did when she held off honoring the Maid until line 161 of the *Ditié*, for our author makes multiple references to Joan early in the treatise; he simply neglects four opportunities prior to this point to mention the supernatural factor involved in Joan's case when he speaks of her. The mere addition of the adjective "divine" to any of these phrases would have made their secular cast instantly theological, but instead the author speaks in a strangely non-spiritual manner of "approving the Maid's case" (*sustineri factum illius puellae*),[30] "the word of the Maid" (*ad vocem . . .*),[31] "under her command" (*sub ea*)[32] and "under her leadership" (*sub una muliercula militantes*).[33]

Finally, more than two-thirds of the way through the treatise, at lines 138 and 143, respectively, the author alludes to "a first miracle" (*primum miraculum*) and "God's achievement" (*a deo facta*), in preparation for his first direct statement of Joan's divine mission at line 155: "God's grace manifested in the Maid" (*gratia dei ostensa in hac puella*). From here on he freely states six more times, either by reference to God's favor (*deo propitio*, line 163), Joan's "election" (*electe puellae de postfetantes*, line 167, and *eligit Rex coelestis*, line 190), divine power (*divina virtus*, line 201), divine help (*divinum . . . auxilium*, line 205) or "things instituted by God" (*ea . . . a deo ordinata*, line 204), that the mission under examination is supernatural in origin. Unlike Gelu, who proceeds by rational theological argument to a point late in his treatise when he can in good conscious endorse the Maid, this author speaks of "unquestionable signs" (*certis signis*) proving she has been chosen by God,[34] but it is scarcely on the evidence of his treatise that such a deduction can be based. We must review the superior evidence and coherent argumentation of our previous texts to measure the difference.

One of the most noticeable absences in the DMV author's discussion is his silence regarding the concept with which the *Poitiers Conclusions* open, the fundamental idea of necessity. Without reference to the necessity of the king and his realm, the need for a redeemer or intercessor never arises. Earlier we saw Pierre de Versailles hold out hope that Charles himself would redeem France, Christine looked first to Isabeau de Bavière and later to the duke of Berry, and the prophecies foretold of intercession from a virgin (*puella*). The idea was commonplace. But in a case of true necessity, which was almost

29 Wayman, "The Chancellor," p. 300; Monnoyeur, *Traité*, p. 47.
30 Wayman, "The Chancellor," p. 298; Monnoyeur, *Traité*, p. 44.
31 Wayman, "The Chancellor," p. 299; Monnoyeur, *Traité*, p. 46.
32 Wayman, "The Chancellor," p. 299; Monnoyeur, *Traité*, p. 46.
33 Wayman, "The Chancellor," p. 299; Monnoyeur, *Traité*, p. 46.
34 Wayman, "The Chancellor," p. 302; Monnoyeur, *Traité*, p. 50.

universally acknowledged to be the situation in France (often termed the "desolation" or "pity" of France), there is justification for God's aid, precisely because, as so many contemporaries attested, France's affliction outstripped the capacity for human correction, and thus there was "no hope but from God." To the author of DMV, for reasons we cannot explain, this basic idea – part personal conviction, part literary trope – is either unaffecting, not understood, or unknown.

Let us also examine other concepts from the *Conclusions* omitted or misunderstood in DMV, primarily the theology of discernment. The *Conclusions* in complete orthodoxy listed two requirements for testing prophets: the character of the life and the production of a sign or miracle. That document listed Joan's virtues as proof of the first requirement. Through the combined influence of the *Conclusions* and, no doubt, Girard's letter before that, the idea of the list became *de rigueur* in writing about Joan. Atypically for a discernment tract, the author of DMV denies accusations leveled at her character, but mentions only a single virtue pertaining to her person: her virginity (*virginitas*).[35] He does not refer once to her attention to Catholic practices, such as communion and confession.

If we are willing to accept that the reference in the title of DMV to a "miraculous victory" is proof of the author's understanding that Orléans was to be the sign of Joan's supernatural calling – a not incontestable assumption – it would appear that he should also have fully understood the nature of the second requirement of discernment, the need to offer a miracle or sign. But, inexplicably, he fails to appreciate that Joan's actions must be above the capability of human actions in order to be deemed supernatural. The objection in the *Conclusions* that she had only made human promises up to that point (*non obstant que ces promesses soient seules oeuvres humaines*) demonstrates that the commissioners considered natural actions to be no proof at all. Yet the author of DMV uses his first set of validating exempla not to reinforce the Maid's case by reference to Old Testament figures[36] who were infused with the spirit of God – which would serve as an appropriate parallel – but, on the contrary, to prove that "included in all these cases, there is constantly an aspect of natural order [*semper aliquid naturale*]." Of course, he wishes to deflect charges that what Joan does is impossible, but if the action is not deemed impossible for humans to perform, then it is not a miracle. At this point he could have used help from Christine, who worked her way around this impasse when she wrote: "As far as God is concerned, this was easily accomplished. But for us, we never heard tell of such an extraordinary marvel" (lines 200–202).

When we look generally at the various lacunae in our author's knowledge

---

[35] Wayman, "The Chancellor," p. 302; Monnoyeur, *Traité*, p. 50.
[36] The example of Saint Catherine does not seem to be appropriately cited in this grouping.

of the theology which was commonly applied to the Maid's case, we can only wonder how it happens that he is ignorant of so much of the sacred narrative which had surrounded the Valois monarchy for years. The sentiment, first expressed in a Johannic text in DQP, that the French could "without impropriety" be called the "People of Israel," seems wholly unknown to the author of DMV, although he twice refers to Joan herself as "elected." Without the aid of that analogy, he fails to recognize that she is being judged as a prophet, so that he never mentions either what promises or prophecies she makes or whether she fulfills them. Therefore, unlike Christine, Gelu, and their sources, he is not in the business of bearing witness, testifying, as Christine stated, that "a thing is proven by its effect" or, in the words of Matthew 7:16: "By their fruits you shall know them." When he evokes the peace to follow the end of the war with the English, he turns to the canticle of Zechariah in Luke 1:71 and 75. Without the notion of the Old Testament prophet sent "not for our annihilation but for our correction," to recall the words of Gelu, one description of peace might seem equal to another. But DMV loses the drama that the analogy with the Old Testament makes possible, whereby a sinning people is reunited with God and receives, as DQP stated it, "happiness in the present time." Here again DMV is out of step with the grand narrative that sustained Joan's case theologically.

In DMV the question of why God would help an individual nation – an issue first treated by DQP in *propositio* four (contra) – is never raised. It is adequate to our author that France's enemies have been "so obstinate" (*pertinacissimorum*). Since he shows no recognition of the conflict between war in which Christians fight against Christians or for the improvement of the faith, he never uses the key superlative which had for a long time alluded to France's larger Christian mission, the word "most Christian" (*christianissimus*). In a discussion of just cause, it is this superlative that one might most expect to find. Presumably because the *Lettre aux Anglais* is not among the author's sources, in DMV France receives its Maid, but the mystically ambiguous expression "sent by God" (*envoyée de par Dieu* in French, or *missa a deo* in Latin) does not appear once. By contrast, DQP uses the phrase six times.

Not only might we wonder where the author of DMV has been (to be so out of touch), but we should be just as curious about who he is. Before comparing DMV textually to the genuine discernment treatise by Gerson, *De probatione*, we would do well to study our author first through the internal evidence in the treatise. He implies his own religious calling when he vows to remain aloof from controversy, since "a servant of the Lord should not contest" (2 Timothy 2:24).[37] But when he alludes to the testing of the Maid, he never demonstrates that he knows that prelates were involved (if this is Gerson, they were his colleagues and former students) or that *discretio*

[37] Wayman, "The Chancellor," p. 299.

spirituum dictated the procedure. Not a single biblical reference pertinent to *discretio* appears in his tract. Early in the treatise he refers only to the "king's council and the men at arms" as having been led to believe in her words.[38] Clearly he was not invited to participate in the probe of Joan, which seems evident not only from all the difficulties with his text, but also from his references to "superiors" who make the determinations. It is difficult not to imagine that Gerson himself would be one of those superiors.

Furthermore, the precise reason for writing the treatise is unclear. Of course, the author is defending belief in the Maid. But is he actually establishing grounds for Joan's divine mission, or is he only defending his individual right to pious belief in the Maid against detractors, at a time when belief in her mission was facing greater skepticism? The distinction is fine. Towards the end of the treatise it is plain that DMV was also written to change minds. There is an intransigence evident toward those who choose not to believe in Joan, which sets a different tone from the freedom of belief expressed in the proverb cited earlier ("he who does not believe is not damned"). The minds to be changed, however, are not members of his flock; he is not interpreting Joan's case to provide guidance for those who turn to him for his opinion. What he tells us is that he is replying to anti-Joan rumormongers. This will make his tract popular but it leaves a number of questions unanswered.

Here we might pause briefly to judge the claim of the Gersonian authorship of DMV based on comparison with his authentic work about St. Bridget, *De probatione*. Once a judgment is established as to how well DMV corresponds to Gerson's authentic work, we will look at what others thought of the treatise by examining the contemporary impact and influence of DMV through the evidence of medieval sources. It must be said in beginning a comparison of *De probatione* and DMV that, if we wish to attribute both works to Gerson, we need to admit that the fourteen years' interval between the two tracts has seen a marked breakdown and decay in the chancellor's ability to write a reasoned and cohesive argument in a comprehensible and precise manner. In the composition of *De probatione* these very qualities are Gerson's strengths. To start with an overview, noticeable areas of discrepancy can be divided into the following areas: the use of key arguments employed in *discretio spirituum*, the application of biblical citation and the recourse to authority, the sense of the lower ecclesiastical stature of the author of DMV, authorial reference to the notions of ecclesiastical caution, theological proof, and the testimony of time.

De probatione begins with the two fundamental biblical citations for *discretio spirituum*: 1 John 4:1: "Try the spirits if they be of God" and 2 Corinthians 11:14: "For satan himself transformeth himself into an angel of light." This is where discernment begins, with the idea of perception and the

---

[38] Wayman, "The Chancellor," p. 299.

problems of illusion and reality. Its special concerns are the limits of temporal knowledge as compared to the completeness (but inaccessibility) of divine truth, and, concerning the testing of individuals, the extreme difficulty of judging the inner man by external manifestations. Although Gerson would wish no one to think that, because perfect certainty in *discretio* was unattainable, venerable theologians should not come together to scrutinize cases and issue verdicts – his own involvement in the canonization procedure for St. Bridget disproves this – in *De probatione* we find a tract imbued with a sense of the extreme caution and heavy responsibility that rested on the shoulders of ecclesiastics in this regard. If we make a comparison here with DMV, it seems inconceivable that the words "unquestionable signs prove that she has been chosen by the King of Heaven" would issue from the same pen. This is particularly true based on the sixth reflection of *De probatione*, where Gerson grapples with the twin dangers of declaring false revelations true and true revelations false, concluding that "to try to discover some middle course between these two extremes [*medium . . . inter haec extrema*] is well worth while."[39]

For the period in which DMV was composed, an era we can safely call post-Poitiers, the author makes a psychologically understandable, but theologically unwarrantable, assumption about the nature of divine gifts: he fails to appreciate the continuous nature of discernment evaluation. It is undoubtedly around this concept that the most important theological developments of the later stages of Joan's mission occurred. To all appearances, Gelu's purpose in the *Dissertatio* was to counteract the king's credence in voices arguing that the Maid's inspiration had failed her, and that other courses of action were called for. Christine's ability to overcome doubt was based on trust in the promises of the *Lettre* and in the conviction that Joan's mission was not complete. But doubt was insinuating itself even within the king's party.

We must look to *De probatione* to learn the standard of proof for continuing to believe in a prophet after the initial approval. As if addressing the very situation of France in 1429, Gerson wrote that genuine prophets had to receive direction from God "not only once in a while when in extreme necessity, but almost constantly, or by daily communication."[40] What a potent concept for the Rouen judges to use against Joan, what a temptation for Joan to answer their challenge with the testimony of saints, and what a difficult standard of proof for her to meet for those of her own party: to continue to receive people's confidence, the miracles would need to keep coming. For Gerson, every principle might admit an exception, and it is easy to sympathize with the author of DMV that a bit of "waiting" should not warrant a pendulum swing from believing Joan's deeds "from God" (*a deo*)

[39] Boland, *Concept*, p. 29; Glorieux, *Oeuvres* 9: 179.
[40] Boland, *Concept*, p. 33; Glorieux, *Oeuvres* 9: 181.

to instantly adopting the opposite view, that they came "from the evil spirit" (*a maligno spiritu*). We might grant him, therefore, the excuse he makes for Joan when he states that "a first miracle does not always produce [*neque sequitur semper*] all the effect men expect of it."[41] But nowhere in his treatise does the author demonstrate what others seemed to recognize, that to believe in Joan one had to constantly have proof, and that the obligation to produce it was never lifted.

One stubborn problem remains when we juxtapose *De probatione* and DMV. It involves where the author of DMV stands within the church hierarchy. In *De probatione*, Gerson draws distinctions between those fit to conduct *discretio spirituum* and those who are not. Gerson is obviously among the former. Once those prelates with the charism make a judgment, pious belief among the general population may ensue. The point is amply made in the scholastic portion of DMV and reinforced in Gelu's declaration of his own pious belief in the Maid. The problem, which was broached earlier but bears repeating, is that DMV's author acts as if the right to believe in Joan has been granted him by others, the exalted prelates in charge of such decisions. In a way that is difficult to pinpoint, except in his deferral to "superiors," he seems to be saying that others have permitted him to believe in Joan, and he will continue to believe until that permission is taken away. Surely Gerson would have worried more generally about the devotion of the faithful, as he does in *De probatione*, than about the right to his own personal belief in the Maid.

Based on the standards of evidence of Joan of Arc documents in the fifteenth century, the diffusion of DMV must be considered quite remarkable. With the exception of the three propaganda documents, none of the sources discussed in earlier chapters is extant in any more than three exemplars. By contrast, DMV leaves traces in France, Belgium, Italy, Spain, and Switzerland. Since the *Ditié* reached two locations which were repositories of official or semi-official Johannic knowledge – Sens and Dauphiné – and because Gelu's *Dissertatio* appears to have been known at Poissy, another repository, it would seem that even with presumed royal endorsement, diffusion of Johannic material was quite limited. Since it is not to Chinon or Poitiers that one looks to find the preservation of documents on the Maid, but to the towns to which they were sent, if DMV had been disseminated through royal channels we would expect to find it in any of the following places: Poissy, Dauphiné, Tournai, La Rochelle, Sens, Brittany, Pas-de-Calais, Strasbourg, Mayence, Lübeck, or, after their capitulation, Reims or Troyes. All these sites received either informational bulletins from the king, one or all of the propaganda documents, or letters from Joan herself later in the campaign.[42]

---

[41] Wayman, "The Chancellor," p. 300.
[42] See Cordier, *Jeanne d'Arc*, pp. 171–77.

Instead, evidence of DMV is tied to Bruges, Venice, Paris, Rome, two locations in Spain, Basel, and Rouen. It appears that Charles VII had nothing to do with the dissemination of DMV, and still it prospered.

The exception to these separate routes of transmission occurs in a reference to DMV contained in the *Morosini* chronicle, specifically a letter of 20 November 1429, sent by the Italian merchant Justiniani in Bruges to his father in Venice. Assiduous in his efforts to collect each fragment of knowledge about Joan as it became available, this merchant managed a feat which no other contemporary appears to have duplicated: he not only learned of the contents of the three propaganda documents (although he does not transcribe them as some writers do) but also obtained a copy of DMV. For the latter he describes the circumstances leading to composition, which cannot, however, be credited. Based on information gathered by talking to "some prelates," Justiniani states that DMV is Gerson's intervention on behalf of the Maid, provoked by a decision at the University of Paris to register with the pope in Rome an accusation of heresy against Joan. Not only is there no evidence of such an action in papal archives, but our second witness to DMV, a French prelate actually residing in Rome, knows nothing of this accusation, nor does Aeneas Silvius, the future Pope Pius II, who wrote authoritatively and comprehensively about Joan. From a chronological viewpoint, it is absurd to think that by 14 May the University could have known enough about Joan to delate her to Rome on the grounds of heresy and for Gerson to have responded to such an accusation. Moreover, the author of DMV himself claims to be responding to malicious rumors, not a denunciation to the pope in Rome. The claim is but one of many bits of misinformation in the *Morosini* chronicle.

Less easily dismissed is Justiniani's claim to possession of a copy of DMV. He repeats in Italian roughly the same proverb that occurs so oddly and unexpectedly in the vernacular in DMV: "To believe is not wrong, and he who does not believe does not sin against the faith,"[43] and although the treatise did not survive with the correspondence, it is difficult to argue that some other work than DMV was in his possession. We need not, however, necessarily accept Justiniani's judgment that the treatise is "a very beautiful work" – better that the declaration come from a theologian – although we can sympathize with the emotion of a common citizen who learns that this "very renowned doctor of theology" has written in Joan's defense.

In fact, our second witness to DMV is a theologian, Jean Dupuy, author of the *Collectarium*, a universal history which he had just completed when he heard about the Maid. In the same time-frame as Justiniani's letter, but with no apparent connection to the copy of DMV sent by Justiniani to his father

---

[43] Dorez and Lefèvre-Pontalis, *Morosini* 3: 232: "Credere non è male, e chi non crede, non fa però contra la fede." Compare with the French: "Qui ne le croit, il n'est pas dampné," Wayman, "The Chancellor," p. 297. (Contained in section one of part one, therefore not in Francq's translation in Appendix IV.)

on 23 December 1429, Dupuy returned to his manuscript to include an addendum of several pages on the Maid. A small mystery surrounds the question of his direct receipt of DMV. He intended to include two excerpts that are clearly from the treatise, one "about the faith one can place in her" (*super credulitate ei prestanda*) and the other containing "three truths" (*triplex veritas*) in defense of her male clothes. The blanks he left in the Rome manuscript were never filled. It was not until well into the twentieth century that light was shed on DMV's relationship to the *Collectarium*, with the discovery of manuscripts in Madrid and Salamanca, each containing the addendum on Joan and excerpts from DMV, which are discussed in the next chapter.

Dupuy does not explain how much more information about Joan's mission he could have provided, announcing that he "will report only the beginning" (*solum exordium tangam*),[44] but it is unlikely that he would have omitted mention of the coronation had the news reached him. Thus Dupuy's tract can be deemed earlier in date than either the *Morosini* chronicle letter or our next witness, an anonymous canon lawyer from the law school of the University of Paris, whose treatise was written after the 8 September 1429 attack on Paris, to which he refers.[45] After two highly favorable witnesses to DMV we now have word from the other side. The notion of debate becomes more complex, since the Anglo-Burgundian Parisian cleric is responding to the royalist author of DMV, who was himself responding to accusations against the Maid. The nature of the cleric's attack is to focus on the parameters of justifiable behavior for a divine envoy, but DMV's firm defense of Joan's male clothes especially elicits the author's ire. Our evidence that the Parisian cleric is in fact replying to DMV, and not a different although similar treatise, is twofold. The single surviving manuscript, copied at Basel during the council in 1435, transcribes a large segment of DMV with the words "against which the following replies" (*contra quem replicantur sequentia*) prior to offering a rebuttal.[46] Moreover, although the canon lawyer answers DMV with a broader range of arguments than those contained in DMV, he mocks his opponent by turning his citations against him with quotations of his own. There seems no doubt that the two tracts are correctly joined in the Basel manuscript. Less certain is the general assumption that the Parisian cleric believed he was refuting Gerson. Although the tract's editor claims of the cleric that "without naming Gerson, he indicates him, nevertheless, in the clearest fashion,"[47] no details in the treatise actually support this assertion.

Since the Parisian cleric's reply is yoked to DMV in the Basel manuscript, it seems evident that in this instance, DMV reached the council through a

[44] Delisle, "Nouveau témoignage," p. 664.
[45] Valois, "Réponse d'un clerc parisien," p. 164.
[46] Valois, "Réponse d'un clerc parisien," p. 163.
[47] Valois, "Réponse d'un clerc parisien," p. 163.

hostile route. Many of Joan's judges attended the council and the author himself may have represented the University of Paris at Basel. Although the connection is vague, Justiniani seems to have acquired DMV through Parisian channels, given the reference, albeit untrustworthy, to the University of Paris's accusations against Joan as prompting the composition of DMV. Yet another Paris connection can be made, although equally tenuous. This connection is favorable to Joan, as were Justiniani's and Dupuy's, but little else can be said with certainty. What we know is that two manuscripts of DMV were preserved at the abbey of St. Victor in Paris,[48] which in itself is not odd since there were vigorous supporters of Gerson at the abbey, and they appear to have ascribed DMV to the chancellor. The one singular detail about the St. Victor connection, however, is that a quotation found in the scholastic section of DMV (*non patitur ludum, fama, fides, oculus*) was inscribed as the third line of a verse dictum located near the tombs of Victorines buried at the abbey.[49] The significance of this detail, if any, is not easy to assess. At the least, however, it tends to draw St. Victor into the story of DMV, thus strengthening further the bond between DMV and the city of Paris.

Just as there were hostile and friendly contexts in which DMV appeared in Paris, the same seems to be true about the council of Basel. This fact emerges from a significant witness to DMV, the prelate and poet Martin Le Franc, author of a sizable passage on Joan in his *Champion des dames* written between 1440 and 1442, seemingly during Le Franc's residence at the council as papal secretary to Felix V. Le Franc's circumstances make it possible for him to have had access to DMV either from the Anglo-Burgundian participants of the council or from Charles's supporters. Educated at Paris under the notorious Rouen judge Thomas de Courcelles, Le Franc would have had ample opportunity to discover the *Reply* of the Parisian cleric and with it DMV among the writings available at Basel. That this is not the case, however, becomes evident when we consider that Le Franc's discussion of the Maid is mounted as a debate, in conformity with the rest of his poem: thus the Champion defends Joan, while the Adversary attacks her. But there is no trace in the Adversary's arguments that Le Franc has read the Parisian cleric's tract. At this vast council, where manuscripts circulated in large numbers,[50] there must have been more than one way to obtain a copy of DMV. If true, this in itself is quite astonishing.

For the last two witnesses to DMV we must return to Paris, no longer for evidence of new sources of DMV, it seems, but for a second stage of activity

---

[48] Monnoyeur, *Traité*, p. 19, n. 1.
[49] Fourier Bonnard, *Histoire de l'abbaye royale et de l'ordre des chanoines réguliers de St.-Victor de Paris, première période (1113–1500)*, 2 vols. (Paris, 1904–1908) 1: 415.
[50] See Frederich Awalde Kremple, "Cultural Aspects of the Councils of Constance and Basel," unpublished doctoral dissertation (Ann Arbor, Mich., 1954), on the book trade at the councils.

in which DMV was exploited both as evidence for the nullification trial of 1456 and for use in the second complete printed edition of Gerson's works in 1514. Guillaume Bouillé is the name of the man responsible for the role played by DMV at the nullification trial. It was he whom Charles VII designated in 1452 to be the earliest architect of the trial which would in 1456 officially clear the Maid's name of all accusations leveled against her at Rouen. Somewhere in Paris,[51] this young prelate from Noyon, too young to have known anything at first hand of what we have called "the early debate," located DMV. To Bouillé, the acquisition of DMV must have seemed a pure stroke of good fortune. We cannot judge whether Bouillé also came upon any of the documents which together form the Valois "dossier" on Joan, that is, the three propaganda documents, DQP, the *Dissertatio,* or the *Ditié.* But given Bouillé's failure to enlist them as evidence, it would appear that he knew nothing of these texts, and came upon DMV because it was independently available.

But DMV was enough to serve Bouillé's purposes well. No matter that the tract was tied to a specific time and chapter of the debate which had long since passed, or that it was the only extra-judicial treatise, including Bouillé's own, that was not composed specifically for the new trial. Whatever else Bouillé knew about the treatise, he understood that he had the great Gerson's name on a document which claimed incontrovertibly ("unquestionable signs prove") that Joan had been divinely elected, and that in this same document, the "abomination" of her male clothes, for which she had died, was thoroughly defended, already in 1429. Imbued with the enthusiasm of DMV, Bouillé even permitted himself to take sentences directly from DMV for use in his own treatise. Thus, from where it had lain for more than two decades, DMV was redeployed in one final round of debate, just as Gelu and Christine had marshaled the propaganda documents for a second volley.

To follow DMV one final step further into the print tradition of Gerson's works takes us slightly beyond our fifteenth-century time frame, but it is a necessary extension to be able to observe the enigma of DMV, transposed essentially as a literary debate, a contest between two texts. It is this literary debate, however, which has determined opinions in the present day. The conflict is that of the respective claims of DQP and DMV, based heavily on questions of style, for the right to the title of Gerson's treatise on the Maid.

No one knows how the Cologne editor Johann Koelhoff made the necessary determinations of authenticity for the first edition of Gerson's complete works in 1484. We know, however, that DQP, which had been consigned to virtual oblivion for the intervening years, was printed in this edition as a work by Gerson. It is the opinion of one observer that this treatise had

---

[51] As far as I am aware, no copy of the treatise DMV can be linked to Rouen or to the condemnation trial.

perhaps lain with the chancellor's papers, since the time of Gerson's death.[52] If so, this finding has no absolute bearing on the true status of DQP.

Be that as it may, a second edition of Gerson's works appeared either in 1501 or the following year, the combined effort of Peter Schott, and his successor Jacob Wimpheling, under the direction of a new printer-editor, the Strasbourg humanist and Gerson-admirer, Geiler von Kaysersberg.[53] Wimpheling's fourth volume announced the addition of some unedited Gersonian texts which had been discovered in Paris and elsewhere,[54] one of them being DMV. It is entirely logical that a search in Paris turned up DMV; we have seen how pervasive the text had become, its profile especially heightened after 1456 when manuscripts of the nullification trial further increased its availability. In fact, it is not clear how Koelhoff, the first editor, overlooked DMV.[55]

At this point, the new editors took a strange step. Now faced with two contenders for the title of Gerson's treatise on the Maid, instead of eliminating DQP they reprinted it, accompanied by the disclaimer that it was ascribed to Jean Gerson "but seems rather to be the style of Heinrich von Gorckum."[56] Then, directly following, they printed DMV as the real treatise by the chancellor. Perhaps through their indecision the new editors set a trend, for the two distinct works were sometimes copied end-to-end as if they constituted a single treatise,[57] although they may also have been viewed as early and late Gersonian opinions. Nevertheless, DMV had won the day and it looked as if the treatise would prevail from then on without major contest.

In 1957 a complaint was raised from an unexpected sector. A scholar named Dorothy Wayman, who had read, start to finish, all four volumes of the Koelhoff edition of Gerson's *Opera*,[58] made an impassioned plea for

[52] Wayman, "The Chancellor," p. 283.
[53] L. Dacheux, *Un réformateur catholique à la fin du XVe siècle: Jean Geiler de Kaysersberg, prédicateur à la cathédrale de Strasbourg (1478–1510); étude sur sa vie et son temps* (Paris, 1876), pp. 431–32; *The Works of Peter Schott (1460–1490)*, Murray A. and Marian L. Cowie, eds., vol. 2 (Chapel Hill, N.C., 1971), p. 413.
[54] Dacheux, *Geiler*, p. 337, n. 2; Cowie and Cowie, *Schott*, p. 413.
[55] Cowie and Cowie, *Schott*, p. 413, describe the Schott-Wimpheling-Geiler edition as an "independent effort" due to its lack of resemblance to the 1483–84 Koelhoff edition at Cologne.
[56] Wayman, "The Chancellor," p. 284: "Cuius editio Joanni de Gerson ascribi sed magis apparet stilus Henrici de Gorckhem."
[57] I have not seen a manuscript of the anonymous *La legede des Flames artisiens et harynnuyers: ou autremet leur cronique abregee en laquelle sont contenues plusieurs hystoires de Frace* [sic] (1522), but the author reads Gerson's treatise as "confuting" Joan's enemies (as if describing DMV), although he lists the tract as beginning with the words: "Tulit me Deus . . ." which are the first words of DQP. See Lanéry d'Arc, *Livre d'Or*, p. 54. Lille MS 539, one of the extant manuscripts of DQP and DMV, was presumably copied from the Geiler-Schott printed edition of Gerson's works, not the other way around, since it postdates the printed edition.
[58] Wayman, "The Chancellor," p. 285.

restoration of DQP to Gersonian authorship, calling the stylistic ascription of DQP to Gorckum an "unfortified judgment,"[59] and referring to the treatise DMV as "barren" of description, "jerky" as to composition and polemic, and "careless" in its "few Scriptural citations."[60] In an argument parallel in terms of style to the kinds of objections raised in these pages with regard to DMV on discernment, Wayman launched an attack on DMV. Particularly undermining, she felt, was DMV's "mixed-up peroration, combining bits of the psalms with snatches from the breviary, all without chapter or verse." "Gerson," she remarked, "would never have been so inept."[61] Less convincing than Wayman's arguments based on style was her shaky hypothesis that a Burgundian agent, sent to Lyon by Cauchon to learn the chancellor's thoughts on the Maid, created DMV after hearing or briefly seeing Gerson's *real* treatise, misconstruing ideas and inserting anachronisms of his own.[62]

For a time, Wayman was nonetheless recognized as having brought a challenge to the authenticity of DMV,[63] and, especially among anglophones, she still is.[64] However, there was a greater need to preserve: that France's greatest contemporary theologian be on record as having refuted the Anglo-Burgundian arguments against Joan's male dress, and – as it was possible to argue because of DMV – well before the judges at Rouen officially accused her. The point is best made in reflections by two eminent scholars of the Maid, J.-B. Monnoyeur and Régine Pernoud. In 1930, Monnoyeur hypothesized:

> If Saint Joan of Arc had had before her, not a court of political adversaries but of real ecclesiastical judges, the very topical memoir by Gerson on the Maid would certainly have been entered into the condemnation trial, as it was at the rehabilitation trial,[65]

with the implication that Joan would have been exonerated. Pernoud rendered the implication of Monnoyeur's judgment explicit: "That someone from the University could support her and justify the wearing of men's clothes shows that if she had appeared before a true ecclesiastical court and

---

[59] Wayman, "The Chancellor," p. 285.

[60] Wayman, "The Chancellor," p. 285.

[61] Wayman, "The Chancellor," p. 291.

[62] Wayman, "The Chancellor," p. 291; See also Francq, "Gerson," pp. 71–72.

[63] See, for instance, Pernoud, *Joan of Arc*, p. 67, where Wayman's article challenging the authenticity of DMV is cited. But cf. Pernoud and Clin, *Jeanne d'Arc* where Wayman is no longer mentioned.

[64] Frances Gies, *Joan of Arc: The Legend and the Reality* (New York, 1981) cites Wayman's article (which implies agreement) but appears to draw accidentally from both DQP and DMV in describing "Gerson's" opinion (p. 57 and p. 167). Barstow, *Joan of Arc*, p. 134, accepts Wayman, but believes DMV might also be by Gerson. Warner, *Joan of Arc*, p. 146, enumerates arguments against DMV's authenticity but fails to draw a solid conclusion.

[65] Monnoyeur, *Traité*, p. 17.

not before a political court, she would certainly have been saved or at least this question would have been resolved differently."[66] Later, in the pages of the *Bulletin de l'Association des Amis du Centre Jeanne d'Arc*, Pernoud refused to countenance the view that DMV had prepared the way for the act of accusation at Rouen, transferring the blame instead onto DQP.[67] In the final analysis, it appears that the popularity of DMV was due not only to its vigorous endorsement of the Maid, found especially toward the end of the treatise, but also to the following circumstance: of all the documents we have examined, only DMV argues the point that most needed arguing, the defense of Joan's male clothes. For all its shortcomings, however they are argued, DMV offers the most pertinent argument in the debate in the light of the charges leveled against Joan at Rouen, and it seems certain that it will continue to be remembered for this reason.

---

[66] Pernoud and Clin, *Jeanne d'Arc*, pp. 308–309.
[67] Régine Pernoud, [Bibliography section] *Bulletin de l'Association des Amis du Centre Jeanne d'Arc* 16 (1992): 65.

9

Collectarium historiarum

An addendum about Joan of Arc to the *Collectarium historiarum*, a universal chronicle written by the Dominican theologian and Inquisitor of Toulouse, Jean Dupuy,[1] while living in Rome, is pertinent to DMV because of its presumed use of that treatise as a source. (One must say "presumed use" because of the rather remote possibility that the two treatises are independent tracts which only share a common source.) Dupuy says that he makes his addition because Joan's story is an event "so great, so considerable, and so unheard of that nothing similar seems to have happened since the world began."[2] This hyperbolic opening exceeds in intensity (while paralleling in sentiment) even the enthusiasm of the author of DMV, but is not atypical of other Italian sources on Joan.[3] The odd circumstance about Vatican lat. 3757, which until 1968 was the only manuscript of those containing the addendum on Joan of Arc to have been studied, is that the author leaves two blank spaces in his manuscript where he intends to cite material in confirmation of his favorable judgment of the Maid. The first blank (where eleven blank lines have been allotted), purporting to explain the ways by which one can have confidence in her, appears to await the transcription of the *Poitiers Conclusions*. The second nine-line blank is evidently designed for DMV's *Triplex veritas*, the three-point justification of Joan's male clothes, although the space allotted is also inadequate for that passage, as judged by the text of DMV.

But when Antoine Dondaine examined two Spanish manuscripts of the *Collectarium* containing the passage on Joan, he found that in those manuscripts where there were blanks in Vatican lat. 3757, they had been replaced

---

[1] Jean Dupuy's title to author of the *Collectarium* is convincingly argued by Antoine Dondaine in "Le Frère Prêcheur Jean Dupuy, évêque de Cahors, et son témoignage sur Jeanne d'Arc," *Archivum Fratrum Praedicatorum* 12 (1942): 118–84. This attribution supercedes Léopold Delisle's assertion that the author was Jean de la Colonne. See Delisle, "Nouveau témoignage," pp. 649–68.

[2] Delisle, "Nouveau témoignage," p. 663.

[3] See, for instance, the letter of the Franciscan friar Cosma Raimondi in Mercati, "Una lettera," also in Dorez and Lefèvre-Pontalis, *Morosini* 4: 368. See also the *Morosini* chronicle, especially the letter of Jean de Molins dated 30 June 1429 and that of Pancracio Justiniani on 9 July 1429.

by two large sections of DMV, in essence, the entire two-part treatise.[4] For the first blank contains the full text of DMV up to the *Triplex veritas*, except for two omissions. These are one sentence about the veneration of the relics of Saint-Denis, and the controversial declaration that concludes that section: "This is the work of the Lord" (*A domino factum est istud*). Since in both Spanish copies the arguments of DMV rather than the more logical *Poitiers Conclusions* were transcribed, at the point of the Vatican manuscript's first blank, this proves that even at some distance from France DMV was accepted as legitimizing belief in the divinity of Joan's mission. DMV's three points justifying male dress take the place in the Spanish codices of the second blank in the Vatican manuscript. Although only one-third of the section of DMV titled *Triplex veritas* actually pertains to the three points, the scribe of the Spanish manuscripts copies the entire section with no omissions. Since the Spanish manuscripts were written with the text of DMV at hand, they do not exhibit the space problem (inadequate blank lines) that would have faced the Vatican manuscript scribe or author had he tried to include such long excerpts. Since the Vatican manuscript is the logical original, given that Dupuy was living in Rome when he added his comments about the Maid, the relationship among the three manuscripts, and what material was in fact meant to fill the blanks in the Vatican manuscript, remains unclear.[5] It is doubtful that Dupuy intended DMV to be transcribed virtually intact in the body of his additional chapter as the Spanish manuscripts suggest.

The resemblance at certain moments between the *Collectarium* and DMV argues that DMV may have inspired Dupuy's writing of the treatise, apart from the two large excerpts. For instance, the peculiar emphasis in both texts on denying Joan's use of spells (*sortilega*) and superstitions (*superstitiosa*) is atypical of Valois or pro-Joan tracts, since all negative traits are generally omitted from French sources.[6] But on some points of overlap between the *Collectarium* and DMV, the two texts differ in detail. For example, whereas each author cites an Amazon, which is unusual among Valois writers and thus draws these tracts together, Dupuy mentions Penthesilea and DMV names Camilla. On balance, the evidence of textual reminiscences in the *Collectarium* from DMV is inconclusive.

The Spanish manuscripts seem to all but prove that Dupuy knew DMV.

---

[4] See the sequel to Dondaine's article: "Le témoignage de Jean Dupuy O.P. sur Jeanne d'Arc, note additionnelle à AFP XII (1942) 167–184," *Archivum Fratrum Praedicatorum* 38 (1968): 31–41.

[5] Georges Peyronnet, "Gerson, Charles VII et Jeanne d'Arc: La propagande au service de la guerre," *Revue d'histoire ecclésiastique* 84 (1989): 353, has hypothesized that the blanks in the Vatican manuscript owe to the removal from Rome of the original, either one of the Spanish manuscripts.

[6] Wayman, "The Chancellor," DMV, p. 298: "non reperitur uti sortilegiis . . . neque superstitionibus"; Delisle, "Nouveau témoignage," p. 664, "in nullo superstitiosa nec sortilega."

But the complicated way in which this might not be true is under the following circumstances: if, as Dondaine suggests, the *Triplex veritas* were not an exclusive part of DMV, but a justification of Joan's dress which circulated separately, perhaps drawn up at Poitiers and added to DMV after that tract was finished,[7] and if the first blank in Vatican lat. 3757 was indeed designed for evidence from the Poitiers investigation, which was not readily available in Rome or in Spain, that could mean that the incorporation of DMV in the two Spanish manuscripts represents action taken independently by the scribe of the Spanish manuscripts. Since DMV was available to the Spanish scribe, and the *Triplex veritas*, intended for inclusion in the *Collectarium*, were thus at hand, the scribe might have plunged into the transcription, regardless of the lack of a perfect fit overall. However, since the *Collectarium* uses the words found in the heading of several manuscripts of DMV (*super credulitate ei praestanda*) – even if, as we have seen, those headings are not necessarily authentic – the most straightforward conclusion, although not one with which we can be entirely satisfied, is that the Spanish manuscripts, in reproducing passages from DMV, do indeed carry out Dupuy's intention for Vatican lat. 3757.

Since most of Dupuy's knowledge of Joan came from sources other than DMV, editor Dondaine has hypothesized that the information in the *Collectarium* seeming to predate the victory at Orléans probably comes from the acts of the Poitiers investigation, an assertion which, if true, is not confirmable. As for Dupuy's source after Orléans, Dondaine favors an official communication received at the court of Rome, a document whose existence is equally unconfirmable. It seems most unlikely that Dupuy was asked by Charles's party for a theological consultation on the Maid. If this had been the case, this additional chapter to the *Collectarium* would undoubtedly contain distinct traces linking it to a document like Jean Girard's letter, written on behalf of the king, to introduce the Maid and ask for a judgment. Dupuy does indeed conclude with a distinct pronouncement in favor of Joan's supernatural mission, which might seem like a judgment written for Charles VII, but Dupuy's support of her case throughout the treatise dates from after the victory at Orléans, and is therefore too late for the Poitiers investigation. However, some person of less importance than the king, another Dominican, for instance, might have sent Dupuy the material on Joan and prevailed upon him to make a theological response. In any case, the air of spontaneity in Dupuy's first lines, implying that marvel alone induced him to write, need not be taken too literally. He, and many others, including the author of DMV, were in fact engaged in the conscious, and much less spontaneous, effort of evaluating whether one should place faith in the Maid.

In point of fact, it must be acknowledged that sometimes Dupuy's passage

---

[7] Dondaine, "Dupuy" [pt. 1] (1942), p. 177.

seems to follow Girard's Johannic information more closely than it does DMV. The *Collectarium* agrees with Girard's information in its confirmation of the tragic state of affairs in France on the eve of Joan's arrival; in emphasizing the unheard-of nature of the turn of events; in associating her with the care of sheep (no mention in DMV, except as the rubric to the *Triplex veritas*); in alluding to the frequency of her confession and communion (again silence in DMV); and in knowing that "pucelle" and "Jeanne" were the terms commonly used to refer to the Maid (Girard: "Jeanne, pucelle"; Dupuy: "pucelle, nommée Jeanne"). DMV, while it uses "puella" throughout, does so apparently as the designation for a young girl, rather than as a name bearing special significance; and DMV shows no knowledge that her name was "Jeanne."

But Girard and Dupuy diverge on other points. Girard cites Deborah, Judith, and the sibyls as validating examples, without offering details (at least in Fornier's summary), whereas Dupuy offers complete biographical sketches, in six or seven lines each, of Deborah, Judith, Esther, and Penthesilea. He apparently researched this information himself since he gives the most detailed information of any theologian writing on Joan of Arc. The two writers also offer somewhat different lists of Joan's virtues. While both agree on her basic attributes (irreproachable conduct and sobriety), only Girard specifically calls her "devout" and "chaste"; and in a minor difference, Girard says that Joan confesses and takes communion once a week, whereas Dupuy claims she confesses daily and takes communion weekly.[8] Further differences make it less likely that Dupuy received Girard's information: Girard gives Joan's age as sixteen and Dupuy as seventeen; Dupuy omits any mention of Vaucouleurs, any reference to Joan's presages and prophecies or to her brief theological examination at Chinon. Whereas Dupuy's generally restrained tone seems closer to Girard than to DMV, the combative cast to DMV being all but absent in the *Collectarium*, this seems greater proof of DMV's uniqueness than of Dupuy's possession of a letter from Girard.

Dupuy's roughly three-page discussion of Joan, appended to his *Collectarium* primarily for its presumed interest for posterity, is framed as a presentation of proofs that Joan is from God. The discussion touches on many arguments we have seen before; there is similitude, as just discussed, between the *Collectarium* and Girard's letter, but also with the *Poitiers Conclusions*, the *Ditié*, and the *Dissertatio*. On strictly theological points, the *Collectarium* follows the contours of most French treatises, sometimes demonstrating its theological superiority to DMV. This logically raises additional questions about the relationship between the two treatises. On two topics, however, the *Collectarium* has distinct affinities with DMV: in the celebration rather than the rationalization of Joan's military role, and in the

---

[8] Delisle, "Nouveau témoignage," pp. 651–52.

sketching of the negative possibilities inherent in Joan's case, in particular, the objections one commonly associates with the Inquisition.

Although the chapter on Joan is structured as a discernment investigation, the arguments are interspersed with fragments of narrative, many of which also serve as proofs. For purposes of discussion, the tract can be broken down into the following divisions: an introduction; the excerpts from DMV (missing in the Vatican manuscript); four exempla of female conquerors; the battle of Orléans presented as a miracle; an evaluation of Joan's person according to principles of *discretio spirituum*; Dupuy's declaration of belief in the Maid's divine mission; and the curious incident of the "investiture" of the kingdom of France, already seen in a previous chapter. In discussing this work, we must also consider several points pertinent to our discussion in a description of the English invasion which directly precedes the chapter about the Maid.

The historical extract which precedes the discussion of Joan achieves roughly the same purpose as the picture of France's desolation painted by Gelu at the start of the *Dissertatio*. The themes are familiar: the military occupation of France by the English, the treachery, scandal, and confusion in the fatherland "once so glorious" (*olim gloriosissimo*), the king's disinheritance ([*ex*]*heredationem regis*), the "most Christian" (*christianissimo*) status of Charles, king of France, and the divine aid sent to the people of Israel in the form of an angel.

The opening lines of the chapter give the conventional declaration of the novelty (*novitates*) and unheard of (*invisa*) nature of the Maid's arrival. The imminent ruin of France, thought by so many to be inevitable, is acknowledged (*regnum ruine totali*), and Dupuy adds that the scepter was to pass to a stranger (*sceptrum . . . liberari debebat exteris*). As if in answer to the challenge of the *Poitiers Conclusions* that Joan's deeds had not yet attained the level of a miracle, Dupuy claims that her acts "seem more divine than human" (*potius censenda sunt divina quam humana*).[9]

If we pass over the part of the treatise which follows, that containing the two excerpts from DMV, the next topic Dupuy turns to is the exempla of the triad of Deborah, Judith and Esther, and the Amazon, Penthesilea. Dupuy seems to value the odd remark in DMV that the Maid "exposes her body to supreme peril, in evidence of her mission" as a chief characteristic of her person. Even though he cites the examples of Esther, Judith, and Deborah from sacred history, he does not specifically identify them as saviors of the people of God, nor does he make a connection with Joan on this account. Instead he groups them with the Amazon Penthesilea under the rubric of "the bellicose exploits of women" (*mulierum actus bellicosi*) and unflinchingly relates aggressive and violent details about them: because of Deborah's

---

[9] The Spanish manuscripts read: "potius censenda sunt divina *aut angelica* quam humana" (emphasis mine), Dondaine "Dupuy" [pt. 2] (1968), p. 34.

presence "the whole enemy army was annihilated at the point of the sword"; Judith not only decapitated Holophernes, but ordered the men to arm themselves, and "with shouting and ululating pursued the Assyrians."[10] For Esther, Dupuy has no bellicose acts to relate, but, interestingly, he includes her story among his "mulierum actus bellicosi," showing the tendency, given the strength of the grouping of the three Old Testament heroines, to retain her, even when emphasis was on the more active and "virile" heroines, Deborah and Judith.

Invoking the surpassing topos, Dupuy argues Joan's superiority to the previous examples, emphasizing her extraordinary, yet virile, courage:

> That our maiden equals or surpasses [*equiparetur . . . seu supergrediatur*] all these women is made obvious by extraordinary acts of bravery [*actibus strenuissimis*], courage [*virtuosissimis*] and daring [*bellicosissimis*].[11]

But although Dupuy stresses the physical prowess of his heroines and includes the Amazon Penthesilea among his exempla, he does so ultimately as a Christian proof, similarly to the way in which Christine handles the theme in the *Ditié*. Like Christine who declares Joan superior to Esther, Judith, and Deborah, which to Christine proved Joan's greater miracle, Dupuy also states that by comparison with other women, Joan's combat seems "still more miraculous" (*amplius mirabiliores*). Thus Dupuy's deployment of the surpassing topos, by which Joan is claimed to outdo other human exemplars, is to prove a miracle, not to vaunt her prowess. The use of the word "miraculous" instead of "incredible," is no doubt significant – the word "incredible," as Gerson implied in *De distinctione*, being more appropriately used of actions which stretch our belief than of true miracles.[12] Dupuy has thus enlisted the example of three Hebrew women and one pagan to underscore a Christian message, the supernatural mission of Joan. How different this is from the author of DMV, who inexplicably cites the exempla of Deborah, Saint Catherine, Judith, and Judas Maccabaeus, not to prove phenomena above the natural order, as one would expect, but to show that "included in all these cases, there is constantly an aspect of natural order" (*aliquid naturale*).[13]

Why Dupuy should mention an Amazon at all, is unclear, unless reliance on DMV is responsible. If this were the case, however, we would need to explain why he rejected Camilla in favor of Penthesilea. First, we might entertain the possibility, which has rarely seemed meritorious in discussing these texts, that an outside party, logically Charles VII, urged both authors to adduce examples of their own choosing, perhaps from pagan, Jewish, and

[10] Delisle, "Nouveau témoignage," p. 663.
[11] Delisle, "Nouveau témoignage," p. 664.
[12] Gerson, *De distinctione*, Boland, *Concept*, p. 79; Glorieux, *Oeuvres* 3: 38.
[13] Wayman, "The Chancellor," p. 300.

Christian history. Dupuy states that he will recall stories from sacred history, but in fact he draws only upon the Old Testament. But without more evidence, the idea of an official royal directive guiding the composition of our treatises is not compelling. If we remind ourselves of Dupuy's residence in Rome at the time he wrote about Joan, we might hypothesize a heightened awareness of his so-called Trojan forebears and the notion of "translatio studii." In fact, a certain analogy exists between Penthesilea's intercession on behalf of king Priam and Joan's coming to the aid of Charles. Ultimately, however, the outward similarity between Joan and the Amazons may simply have dictated the choice.

There is evidence to suggest that in describing the victory at Orléans Dupuy changed from one source to another. Returning to the conventional Christian proofs brought to bear on Joan's case, Dupuy suddenly paints the Maid as an ignorant and simple shepherdess. DMV had noted Joan "following her sheep," but Dupuy goes further, insisting that she "never knew anything but the care of her flocks" (*numquam aliud noverat quam peccorum custodiam*).[14] This is the familiar argument that dispels the accusation that Joan was instructed as part of a plot. Dupuy also makes the customary claim that Orléans was "reduced to such extremity that the inhabitants could no longer hope for aid except from God (*preter Deum nullus auxiliari poterat*)."[15] Arguing further that Joan was victorious with few soldiers rather than many, in a three-day battle that might be expected to take a month, and against a formidable enemy, Dupuy comes to the expected conclusion. Drawing on 1 Maccabees 3:18, he asks: "To whom should we attribute this if not to he 'who can have many shut up by means of a few: and there is no difference . . . to deliver with a great multitude, or with a small company."[16] Unconventionally, however, he cites Psalm 88:11 to announce that the proud have been humbled and the force of God's arm has controlled their adversaries,[17] instead of calling on the much more prevalent 1 Corinthians 1:27 announcing the weak overcoming the strong. The effect of this change is to eliminate any mention of Joan, except, by implication, as the instrument of the humbling.

It is Joan, however, who occupies Dupuy for the remainder of his discussion. Aside from the investiture incident, which is appended more or less as an afterthought, introduced by the words "What else?" (*quid plura*), the final segment of the chapter about Joan focuses directly on the interests of *discretio spirituum* as Dupuy builds toward his theological pronouncement. Showing more resemblance to DMV or a Burgundian text than a normal French treatise in the debate, Dupuy mixes references

---

[14] Delisle, "Nouveau témoignage," p. 664.
[15] Delisle, "Nouveau témoignage," p. 664.
[16] Delisle, "Nouveau témoignage," p. 664.
[17] *Biblia Sacra: iuxta vulgatem versionem*, ed. Bonifatio Fischer . . . [et al.], 2 vols., Stuttgart, c.1969, repr. 1983, 1: 882.

to Joan's physical prowess into the list he presents of her feminine virtues, the proof of her good life. Since he has not thought to directly emphasize Joan's weakness as proof of God's presence, he is comfortable speaking of her strength (*fortitudo*) and physical prowess (*aptitudo corporalis*). Paralleling DMV, he argues that she seeks no temporal advantage, and is not given to superstitions and spells. But he adds several positive traits of which we find no trace in DMV: simple infrequent speech, prudence regarding her mission (*in facto sue legationis prudentissima*), an irreproachable and sober life (*vita honestissima, sobria*).[18] Of this slightly odd collection of virtues, only the last two are frequently cited in French sources, although later he speaks of her frequent confession and communion, two very conventional proofs.

When Dupuy turns to three characteristics by which one can avoid mistaking miracles accomplished by good spirits from those produced by evil spirits, he seems to wrestle under the weight of the inquisitorial spirit, with its fears of heresy and witchcraft. The negative aspect of the debate is fully in view, even if he ends by discounting it. Thus Dupuy does not evaluate whether or not Joan has been sent by God, but "whether she is exempt from superstition and spells."[19] For his first point, Dupuy enters the problematic realm of whether Joan's actions are beyond human nature or necessarily natural. He argues that although they appear to surpass human nature, they operate through divine power. The second point addresses the very legitimate requirement that miracles prove to be of true utility. Gerson also noted this as an essential ingredient to a divine mission. But as if Dupuy had been reading an inquisitors' manual, he specifies that futile or harmful miracles can entail flying through the air or the possibility of numbing men's limbs. The third sign of a genuine miracle, according to Dupuy, involves the end result (*finis*). As he indicates, and Gerson and other experts concur, a true miracle works toward the improvement of the faith and the amelioration of morals (*ad hedificationem fidei et bonorum morum*).[20] Here Dupuy faces the fact that Joan's behavior is out of character for her sex (*quanquam sui actus vires transcendunt feminei sexus*),[21] but argues that because she fights for peace in the kingdom she demonstrates utility and just cause.

He then extends his argument to make the crucial connection showing how that which benefits France also benefits the Catholic faith, although he does not envision the crusade hinted at in Joan's *Lettre aux Anglais*, which we have seen invoked so often. From peace in France, he argues, will follow the lifting up of the faith (*fidei sublevatio*), which would not have suffered so, without the distraction and disaster of war.[22] Indirectly, he is signaling France's importance as a key player in the maintenance of the

[18] Delisle, "Nouveau témoignage," p. 664.
[19] Delisle, "Nouveau témoignage," p. 664.
[20] Delisle, "Nouveau témoignage," p. 665.
[21] Delisle, "Nouveau témoignage," p. 665.
[22] Delisle, "Nouveau témoignage," p. 665.

Christian church. He has nothing to say, however, about the frequent argument that Christian nations who fight one another particularly encumber the faith.

Satisfied that he has justified the theological opinion he is now prepared to make, Dupuy draws his conclusion. From the forgoing "it must necessarily be concluded [that Joan is] from God [*oportet necessario concludere a Deo*] and does not proceed from spells [*non sortilege procedere*], as the jealous claim." This proclamation, with the refuted proposition ("does not proceed from spells") fully in evidence, is most unusual. The convention of French writers, even when they entertain counter-arguments to Joan's case, is to conclude with a simple statement of belief in her divine mission. Perhaps to an inquisitor, the angel of darkness always lingers in the background of an angel of light. Apparently free of the uncertainty or self-doubt regarding Joan's case, which often plagued theologians engaged in discernment, Dupuy still never forgets that a debate entails both thesis and antithesis.

10

Reply of a Parisian Cleric

A document of superlative importance exists for the dialectical debate over Joan of Arc's mission. It is a tract written in late September 1429 or early 1430, from the Burgundian point of view, as a reply to the treatise DMV (hereafter the Reply). Accusing the French in the very area of their pride, it faults them on their theological investigation of the Maid (*discretio spirituum*), saying they praise Joan "vigorously and without consideration" (*valde et indiscreta*).[1] The document charges the Maid with suspicion of heresy and calls for her case to be turned over to the Inquisition, and as the editor of the text, Noël Valois, alone seems to have recognized: "[the Parisian cleric] already sketches and more or less summarizes the whole act of accusation of 27 March 1431."[2] This fact should be given particular significance, for while it is recognized that the University of Paris sought to have Joan tried on ecclesiastical grounds before the English took specific steps against her politically, scholars have supported this point with a 25 May 1430 letter from the University of Paris to Philip the Good, in which Joan is found "vehemently suspect of several crimes [touching upon] heresy,"[3] which the Parisian cleric's tract clearly antedates.

The cleric's tract, signaled uneventfully by Michel Denis in 1800[4] and only "rediscovered" in 1906 by Noël Valois, has been published twice without significant increase to its visibility.[5] Importantly, the document is the sole

---

[1] Valois, "Réponse d'un clerc parisien," p. 176.
[2] Valois, "Réponse d'un clerc parisien," p. 166.
[3] M. G. A. Vale, "Jeanne d'Arc et ses adversaires: Jeanne, victime d'une guerre civile?" in *Jeanne d'Arc, une époque, un rayonnement (Colloque d'histoire médiévale, Orléans, Octobre 1979)* (Paris, 1982), p. 210, citing Henri Denifle and Emile Chatelain, "Le procès de Jeanne d'Arc et l'Université de Paris," *Mémoires de la Société de l'Histoire de Paris et de l'Ile-de-France* 24 (1897): 1.
[4] Michel Denis, *Codices manuscripti theologici bibliothecae Palatinae Vindobonensis latini aliarumque Occidentis linguarum*, vol. 2 (Vindobonae, 1800, in-fol.), col. 2292.
[5] The first publication by Noël Valois in 1907 was followed by a reprint by Théophile Cochard in *Bulletin de la Société archéologique et historique de l'Orléanais* 14, no. 187 (1907): 524–30. The text is ignored by Pernoud and Clin (1986), Warner (1981) and Gies (1981), and was not seen by Margolis (see entry 955 in her *Joan of Arc*). Barstow, *Joan of Arc*, pp. 48–49, construes the text as a preacher's sermon to his congregation,

159

representative of the Anglo-Burgundian side of the religious debate before the time of the condemnation trial, although DMV is possibly answering another such document no longer extant.[6] The peculiarity of the disproportion between the large number of French tracts, as compared to this single Burgundian treatise, owes to the fact that most French theological discussions were apparently directed at a French audience. Even when it was deemed useful to publicize the *Poitiers Conclusions*, for instance, the target audience was either loyal Frenchmen or sympathetic foreigners. DMV, on the other hand, although finding its way mainly to sympathizers (Jean Dupuy, Martin Le Franc, and Pancratio Justiniani), traveled in a different circuit from the chancellery documents, and thereby made its way into the hands of the opposing side.[7] Since most of the Anglo-Burgundian arguments against Joan are disclosed only in French tracts which anticipate and dispel objections to her case, the evidence of the Parisian cleric's reply offers a complement to the indirect evidence in writings by her own party, and provides an invaluable example of the raw anger DMV drew from the Burgundian side.

In the single extant manuscript of the Parisian's reply (Vienna lat. 4701) the text in question occurs after a partial transcription of DMV.[8] The relationship of the cleric's reply to DMV is established by the heading "Against which the following in reply" (*Contra quem replicantur sequentia*), which links the two tracts dialectically. The words "1435. In Concilio Basiliensi," which directly precede the text of DMV in the manuscript, clarify that the transcription occurred at the council of Basel. The manu-

---

without acknowledging its relationship to DMV. For the fullest discussion, see Peyronnet, "Gerson," pp. 358–59.

[6] As Pernoud remarks in *Joan of Arc*, pp. 103–104: "In May a memorandum drawn up by a clerk of the university, but which has not been preserved, was accusing Joan of heresy; and it may have been in defence of her and in reply to this *libelle* that Jean Gerson . . . composed the work [DMV]." The assumption has to be made that Pernoud is talking about a document other than the Parisian cleric's reply, written in the fall.

[7] While the pairing of DMV and the cleric's refutation might at first appear to reinforce Wayman's unusual assertion that DMV is a forged version of Gerson's document "eagerly [seized] upon for the purpose of refuting it and delating Gerson and Jeanne d'Arc to Rome" ("The Chancellor," p. 280), we know that Jean Dupuy living in Rome intended to quote it in sympathy with the Maid's cause. Never does Dupuy imply that he has intercepted a text detrimental to Joan's reputation, nor does he indicate that the text was distributed with hostile intent by the University of Paris. In many ways, however, he offers a more solid theological defense of Joan than DMV itself which remains puzzling. Furthermore, if DMV were "circulated widely by the Burgundian faction" ("The Chancellor," p. 280), as Wayman asserts, one wonders why there is no manuscript evidence. While DMV may well have been widely available at the council of Basel, we know that Martin Le Franc, at least, avidly mined it for his defense of Joan.

[8] Perhaps as little as half of DMV is included. DMV goes from fol. 322r to fol. 323v, while the two texts together take up fols. 322r to 325r of the manuscript, Valois, "Réponse d'un clerc parisien," p. 162.

script, in fact, consists of a collection of documents presumably gathered at the council.[9] What is not known is whether the two documents were already paired when the scribe recopied them, or whether he himself, recognizing their relationship, first brought them together in a single manuscript. The Basel cleric clearly did not write the Reply himself. The urgency with which the Parisian cleric calls for something to be done about Joan, coupled with editor Valois's arguments – the author's use of the present tense, his complaint that Joan is venerated as a saint in her lifetime, and his failure to exploit arguments provided by her defeat at Compiegne – verify that the Reply was written during Joan's lifetime.

What the cleric at Basel understood by this pair of documents is unclear. Since by 1435 both documents were approximately six years old, one wonders how they arrived at Basel. DMV might have been brought to Basel by a member of the University of Paris, perhaps a Rouen judge, in which case the Reply would have accompanied it; but DMV could also have been brought singly by a sympathizer like Jean Dupuy, who knew DMV and also attended the council. Perhaps the Basel copyist transcribed the refutation of DMV given him by a University friend, or even the author himself, since we know by the words "matris meae Universitatis" that the reply was written by someone from the University. But if, on the one hand, those still wishing to defame Joan's memory circulated DMV at Basel paired with the Parisian cleric's refutation, on the other hand, there may have been a second copy of DMV circulating as well, unaccompanied by the Reply. This is what we are led to believe by the evidence of Martin Le Franc, another council participant, who plausibly obtained DMV (an identifiable source for the *Champion des dames*) at Basel, but never touches on any of the Parisian cleric's arguments, leaving his Adversary's very different anti-Joan argumentation rather thin.

Intriguingly, these documents were still of interest well after the fact. Was it because the clergy was still curious about a life that they recognized as sensational? Was her case – in these years between her condemnation and nullification trials – still felt to be an unresolved issue, or maybe *again* becoming a subject of dispute? Could the texts, as they are juxtaposed in Vienna lat. 4701 – which together represented historically what DQP's author had created artificially (two sets of contradictory arguments offered side by side for purposes of analysis) – have served at Basel as a dialectical tool of juridical or ecclesiastical interest, for evaluating the Hussite and Vaudois heresies? The author of DQP had perspicaciously anticipated the

---

[9] See *Tabulae codicum manu scriptorum praeter graecos et orientales in Bibliotheca Palatina Vindobonensi asservatorum*, ed. Academia Caesarea Vindobonensis (Graz, repr. 1965), vol. 3, pp. 356–57 for a description of the manuscript but which omits mention of the Reply. By far the greatest number of treatises in this manuscript are those of Thomas Ebendorfer of Haselbach. Others include Gerson's *De schismate* and tracts by Nicholas of Cusa and pope Eugenius IV.

usefulness of the debate surrounding Joan's case in treating those future cases which were "altogether similar," but at Basel it was DMV and the Parisian cleric's Reply which are the only texts known to have continued the dialogue.

Not only is it virtually assured that the Reply was composed within a scant few months of DMV, but its identification as a reply specifically to DMV, independently of the rubric, is equally well assured, since the cleric establishes this relationship through pointed allusions to DMV. Some points refute arguments not specifically made in DMV,[10] which implies that the Parisian cleric also used other sources, but the matching of the two texts was not done erroneously, since the Reply is primarily a rebuttal of DMV. Much less certain is the assertion by Noël Valois, agreeing with Michel Denis,[11] that Gerson is the author of this "apology of the Maid."[12] The heading in the manuscript identifies DMV as "the treatise of Jean Gerson, chancellor of Paris," and the subject of the tract is given as "the faith that can be placed in the Maid,"[13] but the text itself never bears this identification out. There is probably little doubt that DMV was understood to be Gerson's treatise by everyone at Basel, but when Noël Valois claims that the Parisian cleric, "without naming Gerson, nevertheless refers to him in the most obvious way,"[14] he proves only that the cleric is responding to DMV, not that Gerson wrote it. Valois thinks that the Parisian cleric recognizes that he is refuting a man of high reputation, but Gerson is never named in the tract,[15] nor is the author of DMV ever referred to as chancellor.[16] In fact, the author of DMV is only referred to in the Reply as "the aforesaid master who compiled the treatise in question."[17] The cleric does not even demonstrate that he knows who wrote the treatise.

Moreover, a certain mocking tone by the Parisian cleric and perhaps an intention of irony, could imply that he felt someone of lower stature than Gerson to be his opponent. Either to highlight the ineptitude in DMV, or perhaps, confronted with the DMV author's unleashed anger, the cleric

[10] For instance, he uses the same text that Gelu cites in defense of Joan in the *Dissertatio* (Matthew 7:20: "Wherefore by their fruits you shall know them") to argue against her.
[11] Denis, *Codices* 2: col. 2292.
[12] Valois's article bears the subtitle: "Reply of a Parisian cleric to the apology of the Maid by Gerson," p. 161. See also p. 162, n. 1.
[13] Valois, "Réponse d'un clerc parisien," p. 162, n. 1: "tractatus domini Johannis de Jarson, cancellarii Parysiensis." The subject of the treatise follows in the usual form: "de Puella et credulitate sibi adhibenda."
[14] Valois, "Réponse d'un clerc parisien," p. 163.
[15] A similar failure to name Gerson as the author of DMV occurs on the part of Jean Dupuy, author of the *Collectarium*.
[16] Although a Parisian cleric in 1429 might reasonably resist calling Gerson "cancellorius," since from 1418 the controlling Burgundian faction at the University no longer recognized Gerson as chancellor, the French and their sympathizers still referred to him as chancellor. See, for instance, Dorez and Lefèvre-Pontalis, *Morosini* 3: 235.
[17] Valois, "Réponse d'un clerc parisien," p. 176: "prefatus magister, qui compilavit pro prefata Puella tractatum prefatum."

returns like for like. In a direct denial of DMV's assertion that Joan's case supports the circumstances for pious belief, the cleric repeats the DMV author's own words, but inserts the word "non" which effectively contradicts his opponent's point.[18] The anonymous Parisian takes aim at the DMV author's very claim that believing in Joan is not, strictly speaking, a necessity of faith, but a pious belief, and that belief in her should thereby be refused even less than a popular cult without canonization.[19] He remarks that only those "approved and canonized by the church" (*ab Ecclesia ... approbatus et canonizatus*) may be "venerated as a saint" (*pro sancto venerari*).[20] But the cleric also astutely points out that a popular cult had *already* arisen around Joan "in many countries" where her portraits or statues were venerated.[21] Where DMV cites the *Disticha Catonis*, the cleric comes back with a verse of his own.[22] And in a citation dripping with sarcasm, the cleric calls for action by the Inquisition by using the words of Ovid: "Resist beginnings [of love]; too late is the medicine prepared."[23]

Much harder to understand is the charge by the editor Valois that elsewhere in the text the Parisian cleric twists citations, buttresses his points with "very inappropriate" examples – the impudence, Valois claims, of one "who deludes himself that no one will verify [his citations]."[24] Whether the Parisian cleric intentionally seeks to underscore the DMV author's inept examples by imitating them or is merely as ineffectual as that author, remains open to further examination.

Not every theological tract on Joan, coming into the hands of a Parisian cleric, would have elicited the same irate response as DMV. Nor were other French writers on Joan writing in such a controversial context as DMV. Neither DQP's pro and con format nor the *Poitiers Conclusions'* provisional decision left them as vulnerable to reprisal as did DMV's insistent conclusions. But DMV's hyperbolic account of the French men-at-arms, obeying the Maid's command "with one same heart" while the enemy hides "failing as a woman giving birth," could be expected to have especially exasperated the Parisian cleric. Without distinguishing between the "bad" English and the merely "blind" or "ill-advised" Burgundians, as Christine does in the *Ditié*, DMV divides people sharply into two camps, "the friends of justice"

18 Valois, "Réponse d'un clerc parisien," p. 178: "Item, quod de 'pietate fidei katholice et devotionis sincere' ... *non potest sustineri*." Cf. Wayman, "The Chancellor," DMV, p. 298: "Concudendum est tandem ex praemissis quod pie et salubriter *potest* de pietate fidei et devotionis *sustineri*." (Emphasis mine.)
19 This was the claim of DMV. See Wayman, "The Chancellor," p. 299.
20 Valois, "Réponse d'un clerc parisien," p. 178.
21 Valois, "Réponse d'un clerc parisien," p. 178. Pierre Lanéry d'Arc basically confirms this point in a fascinating pamphlet, *Le culte de Jeanne d'Arc au XVe siècle* (Orléans, 1887).
22 Valois, "Réponse d'un clerc parisien," p. 163 and p. 176.
23 Valois, "Réponse d'un clerc parisien," p. 179; Ovid, *Remedia amoris* 1: 91.
24 Valois, "Réponse d'un clerc parisien," p. 165.

and its "enemies." Those opposed to Charles's goals are "pertinacious enemies." The Parisian cleric's palpable anger at DMV, which is reminiscent of DMV's own outrage at the charges *it* refutes, was probably heightened by Joan's recent assault on Paris (8 September 1429), a major concern in this treatise. The Parisian cleric is particularly condemnatory because the attack took place on a holy day, and perhaps also because the English were disappointed in their desire to capture Joan that day.

The cleric's seven major objections to the Maid's claim to be God's representative are, in short: first, the lack of sufficient evidence of her divine mission; second, the wearing of men's clothes and her usurpation of a masculine role; third, doubt as to whether God intervenes on behalf of nations, in particular, that he would aid one Christian nation against another; fourth, Joan's non-observance of holy days; fifth, her lying predictions (failure to realize her miracles); sixth, idolatry; and seventh, the use of spells.[25]

At the head of the list is the Parisian cleric's opinion that the French have rushed to a careless judgment in favor of the Maid (*adherendo tam leviter*), as if the danger of too hasty belief, outlined in the *Poitiers Conclusions* (*ne doit croire en lui tantôt et légièrement*), had come to pass. As a canon lawyer, he does not employ the term *discretio spirituum* but twice signals the two main requirements of a prophet, which he considers unfulfilled: the support of a miracle, and direct testimony from Scripture in evidence of a divine mission. The problem raised at Poitiers – that Joan expected people to believe in her based on her mere personal affirmation – is apparently what the Parisian cleric means when he refers to her "invisible" mission (*invisibilis missio*).[26] Unlike the Poitiers investigation, which weighed the options 'sent by God' or 'not sent by God,' the cleric reads the alternatives as 'sent by God' or 'suspect of heresy.'

The cleric's second point is his strenuous objection to Joan's male dress. He disagrees with DMV's argument that Deuteronomy's prohibition has lost its force, and fortifies his position by the authority of canon law. Gratian's *Decretals*, according to him, carry the weight necessary to prohibit Joan's dress in the current era. With a confirmable citation to Gratian,[27] he writes:

> If she were really sent by God, she would not take clothing prohibited by God and proscribed to women in canon law, under pain of anathema in the chapter *Si qua mulier*, distinction 30.[28]

---

[25] A slightly different list is given by Valois, "Réponse d'un clerc parisien," p. 166.

[26] Valois, "Réponse d'un clerc parisien," p. 175.

[27] Gratian, Decretum *Corpus iuris canonici*, Emil Friedberg, ed., vol. 1 (Leipzig, 1879; repr. Graz, 1959). D. 30 c. 6: "Si qua mulier suo proposito utile iudicans, ut virili veste utatur, propter hoc viri habitum imitetur, anathema sit." This "capitulum" is preceded by three others dealing with women and questions of marriage, separation, and virginity.

[28] Valois, "Réponse d'un clerc parisien," p. 176: "Juncto quod, si a Deo mitteretur, non

The cleric, who is a decretalist rather than a theologian, argues that even when the debate is lifted out of the realm of pure theology, Joan's male clothing is nonetheless prohibited through a second line of authority, the exercise of canon law. Responding to DMV's second supporting argument for Joan's dress (which justifies weighing all circumstances and allows considering what "time, necessity, purpose, manner and other similar conditions demand"),[29] the cleric accuses DMV's author of deviousness:

> In the case where those who let themselves be deceived by the said Maid would try to excuse and justify her dress in consideration of the mission for which she is sent, such cunning [*calliditates*] will lead nowhere.[30]

Those are only the excuses spoken of by the psalmist, he adds, which "accuse more than they excuse."[31] Outraged at the libertinism he sees encouraged when a woman wears men's clothes, the cleric – alone among commentators on Joan's dress, perhaps echoing a statement from Aquinas directed against "lasciviousness" (*luxuriam*) – envisages a worse possibility: "Furthermore, if a woman could without impunity dress at will in male attire, women would have ready opportunities for fornication."[32] There is disagreement among contemporary documents as to whether male clothes aided or discouraged the maintenance of virtue,[33] but the re-creation in the *Chronique de la Pucelle* of Joan's attitude, told as if in her own words, may well summarize the Maid's thinking:

> I well believe that you think it [wearing men's clothes] strange, and not without justification; but it is necessary, since I must arm myself and serve the gentle Dauphin in arms, that I take suitable and necessary clothes for

assumeret habitum a Deo prohibitum, et de jure canonico mulieribus sub pena anathematis interdictum in capitulo *Si qua Mulier*, 30a distinctione."

29 Wayman, "The Chancellor," DMV, p. 302: "quod observare debet circumstantias omnes ut quando oportet, cur oportet, qualiter oportet," and also "vel necessitatis vel evidentis utilitatis vel approbatae consuetudinis vel ex auctoritate seu dispensatione superiorum."

30 Valois, "Réponse d'un clerc parisien," p. 176: "si vellent seu [n]itterentur tales decepti per predictam Puellam excusare se quod susceperit habitum predictum juste attento negocio ejus pro quo mittebatur, non juvant tales calliditates."

31 Valois, "Réponse d'un clerc parisien," p. 176.

32 Valois, "Réponse d'un clerc parisien," p. 176: "Item, si mulier posset impune pro libito voluntatis habitum virilem accipere, daretur libera occasio mulieribus fornicandi ac exercendi actus viriles sibi de jure prohibitos secundum doctrinam." Aquinas, *Summa* 29: 223 [1a2ae. 102, 6], states that women could not wear men's clothing and vice versa because of crossdressing pagan cults, but "the second reason was to deter from lasciviousness."

33 Christine implies that women in armor were considered anything but seductive. She states in Richards, *City of Ladies*, p. 46, that when Hercules and Theseus saw the Amazons without their armor "their joy doubled; they had never captured prey which pleased them so much."

that [task]; and also when I am among men, being in men's clothes, it seems to me that in that state I will better conserve my virginity in thought and deed."[34]

For a woman to dress as a man also introduces a broader problem, mentioned by more than one ecclesiastical writer, that of assuming roles forbidden on the basis of sex, rank, or class. The problem is not just the male dress itself, writes the cleric, but that it provides occasion for "exercising virile acts," which are juridically prohibited to women. "In a general way," he continues, "all masculine office is prohibited to women, for instance, preaching, teaching, bearing arms, absolving from sin, excommunicating, etc."[35] On these points he follows canon law.[36] It is known that, basing himself on Aristotle, Aquinas viewed women as deficient mentally and therefore inferior.[37] Although a bias against women is reflected in canon law, the real question, as Gelu showed in the *Dissertatio*, was that people were considered to belong to a given rank in the world that they were intended to maintain. Proving to us that it is not just women who face such role restriction, Gelu acknowledged differences in religious roles as a reference point, noting that not all men were allowed to preach, to minister the sacraments, or make sacrifices. But whereas the cleric condemns Joan's transvestism, Gelu argued an exception, saying that God, who does well whatever he does, was free to break his own rules. However, as if zeroing in on the one prohibition which, if applied to Joan, would quickly remove her from the whole military scene, the cleric includes an injunction forbidding bearing arms (*arma deferre*) to the general list of prohibitions, an issue which rarely figures prominently among the concerns of royalist treatises, but is hardly negligible as an issue to contemporaries, despite its often being overpowered then as now by the problem of male dress.[38]

The third topic addressed by the cleric involves a question that we know

---

[34] Vallet de Viriville, *Chronique de la Pucelle*, pp. 276–77.

[35] Valois, "Réponse d'un clerc parisien," p. 176: "Item, generaliter, virile officium mulieribus est interdictum, scilicet predicare, docere, arma deferre, absolvere, excommunicare, etc."

[36] Violations of these restrictions were always considered prohibited practices. Innocent III strictly forbade certain abbesses from continuing to preach. See René Metz, "Le statut de la femme en droit canonique médiéval," IV, pp. 59–113 in Metz, *La femme et l'enfant dans le droit canonique médiéval* (London, repr. 1985), p. 102. When, in the time of Gratian, some cited the Old Testament Book of Judges for the freedom women exercised there, he lashed back: "Under the reign of the Old Law, many liberties had been granted women, which are refused them in our own day," Metz, "Le Statut," IV, p. 103.

[37] Metz, "Le Statut," p. 77: "Naturaliter femina subjecta viro, quia naturaliter in homine magis abundat discretio rationis," Aquinas, *Summa* I. 92, 1. Roman law confirms this by the terms used to refer to women: "infimitas sexus," "imbecillitas sexus" and "levitas animi," Metz, "Le Statut," p. 78.

[38] See for instance, Thomassin, *Registre* in Quicherat, *Procès* 4: 304.

bothered even royalist theologians. Would God intervene directly on behalf of a people? The underlying issue is whether God's aid would target another Christian people. A complicating factor was whether the French were "restoring" a kingdom as they claimed,[39] and thereby regaining something once possessed, or, as the Parisian cleric would have it, "acquiring" one (*acquisitione regni*), with the aggressiveness that this term suggests toward the putative holder of the throne, Henry VI of England. Gerson's *De distinctione verarum visionum a falsis* (1401) endorses the deep-seated Valois assumption that divine intervention can take place on behalf of kingdoms, counting among worthwhile revelations those which benefit, improve, or honor "morals, the State [*rem publicam*] and divine worship,"[40] although Gerson qualifies this statement elsewhere by insisting that any miracle lacking religious significance is suspect or must be rejected.[41] The Parisian cleric charges that canon law has been violated for political ends, and he accuses Joan of escalating war "among Christian people," obviously touching on a delicate issue. Here he argues the general principle that the end does *not* justify the means – which was implicit in French argument every time they spoke of ultimate goals (*finis*) – by citing Augustine (*non oportet facere malum ut inde eveniat bonum*).[42] The cleric also makes the argument, a bit self-serving in the light of Burgundian collaboration with the English, that the French should simply have sat by, even if they "regarded as a scandal the transference of the kingdom to the English."[43]

Inasmuch as DMV never fully enunciates the Valois arguments used to justify war – that war is alone defensible when the final objective is peace, that England's aggression and usurpation creates the context for a just war, that a victory that stops war between Christian nations agreeably frees all parties to advance the faith – and offers only a garbled version, in passing, of what DQP spoke of as God's use of "the weak sex and of the age of innocence to offer . . . kingdoms the happiness of salvation,"[44] the treatise DMV does little, in advance, to parry the blows of an attack like that of the Parisian cleric. Ultimately DMV's enthusiastic description of Joan's military operations gives the Parisian cleric ample room to insist that Joan's behavior is contrary to the *rex pacificus* and contrary to the virtues of modesty and a pacific nature.[45]

[39] Wayman, "The Chancellor," DMV, p. 298: "restitutio regis ad regnum suum."
[40] Gerson, *De distinctione*, Boland, *Concept*, p. 84; Glorieux, *Oeuvres* 3: 41.
[41] Gerson, *De distinctione*, Boland, *Concept*, p. 97; Glorieux, *Oeuvres* 3: 51.
[42] Valois, "Réponse d'un clerc parisien," p. 177.
[43] Valois, "Réponse d'un clerc parisien," pp. 176–77: "Item, si bene inspexisset regulam juris *Qui scandalizaverit, De regulis juris*, pretextu acquisitionis regni, veritatem fidei non permitteret quovismodo violari occasione prefate Puelle, etiam si reputaverit scandalum quod regnum ad A[ng]licos transferatur."
[44] Wayman, "The Chancellor," p. 299: "Sacris consonat litteris per fragilem sexum et innocentem aetatem exhibitas a deo fuisse populis et regnis laetam salutem."
[45] Had DMV given as extensive a defense of violence and killing as did Gelu's *Dissertatio* or Christine's *Ditié*, which was based on the justification in the *Lettre aux Anglais* of

The fourth point, the only accusation from the pen of the cleric whose defense is never found in pro-Joan treatises, is her failure to observe holy days. This accusation is directed at Joan's attack on Paris during the observance of the Nativity of the Virgin on 8 September 1429. The cleric, who has so recently experienced this attack on his city, brims with outrage at this violation, occurring at so late a date in the theological debate that he alone of the treatise writers can mention it. It is here that he actually describes Joan performing the devil's work. In direct antithesis to the Valois rhetoric, where God's miracles are performed "through the Maid," in this text the devil's work is done "through the aforementioned woman" (*per medium prefate mulieris*). And demonstrating plainly to us where his allegiance lies, the cleric expresses glee that the tables were turned in the assault on Paris. Whatever massacres did occur by the grace of God, he notes, "did not turn out as the enemy planned" (*non tante [qu]od affectabat prefata hostis*).[46] The words that Christine aimed in the *Ditié* at the English and Burgundians, when she wrote: "A short time ago, when you looked so fierce, you had no inkling that this would be so" (lines 309–310), could now be redirected against the French, making a sad commentary on the failure of the *Ditié* to influence political outcomes.

When the Parisian cleric accuses Joan of lying in her predictions – his fifth point – much more is involved than mere prevarication. By charging Joan with not delivering the miracles she promised, the cleric again concludes not simply that she is in error but that she is led by the devil. Making his pronouncement against her divine mission, he states: "And thus, she was not conducted by the blessed spirit of truth, from which all truth proceeds, but by the devil, father of lies, whose deeds she strives to accomplish."[47] He goes this far because the assertion of a divine mission has been established in DMV based on Joan's signs and confirming miracles. But DMV needed to rationalize the "Maid's waiting," stating that "a first miracle does not always produce all the effect men expect of it." Thus the Parisian cleric calls DMV's author to account for lacking proof to support Joan's mission. Bringing up exactly the criticism voiced by Guillaume Aimeri at Poitiers,[48] he insists that an interior mission, in which someone "affirms purely and simply [*nude . . . asserere*] to be sent by God [*missus a deo*]," is not enough.[49] In fact, he states, it is the pretension of all heretics.

the use of force for enemies who refuse to surrender, the Parisian cleric would have had less cause for complaint, but DMV seems not to know of Joan's letter.
[46] Valois, "Réponse d'un clerc parisien," p. 177.
[47] Valois, "Réponse d'un clerc parisien," p. 177: "Et sic illa benedicto Spiritu veritatis, a quo omnis veritas procedit, non ducebatur, sed a Dyabolo, patre mendacii, cujus desideria nititur perficere."
[48] Duparc, *Procès* 4: 151.
[49] Valois, "Réponse d'un clerc parisien," p. 175.

To the cleric, Joan is "without a miracle" (*sine miraculo*).[50] He feels she has had ample time to prove herself, and in his words, "since through none of these ways has she proven that she was sent by God,"[51] he concludes his treatise with the dire charge that she is suspect of heresy. DMV curiously failed to play its best card by arguing that Orléans was the miracle that substantiated Joan's claims, despite the rubric on certain manuscripts identifying the treatise as "about a miraculous victory" (*de mirabili victoria*).[52] DMV leaves the impression, instead, by an allusion to St. Catherine of Alexandria "converting the philosophers," that, as far as the author knows, Joan's main miracle might only have been her ability to hold her own against the persistence of her judges at Poitiers, which, given the inadequacy of this proof, allows the anonymous cleric room to claim that she failed the test of one sent by God.

In introducing the sixth objection, the charge of idolatry, which the cleric calls the most serious of all (*gravissimum*), because it involves usurping honor due only to the creator,[53] he describes the veritable cult that had already grown up around Joan within one year. His statement that "in many countries people have already erected and venerated portraits and statues of this Maid, just as if she were already beatified" is a stunning revelation of her influence from the "enemy" side.[54] He also protests that Joan has received lighted candles offered by children on bended knee, a sign he sees as idolatry. In a tone recognizable to those familiar with inquisitional or witchcraft-trial rhetoric, throughout his treatise the Parisian cleric continually expands the scope of his accusations. Where Christine warned that it was wrong to support Joan in one's heart but remain silent, this decretalist warns that to remain silent about Joan's *error* could result in "grave problems, divisions, scandals, and very great dangers to the faith [*pericula maxima contra fidem*]."[55]

The cleric's seventh point addresses the Maid's seeming use of spells (*sortilegiis*). He has heard it reported (*ut fertur*), in relation to the children offering candles, that Joan placed three drops of candle wax on each child's head, which he calls "spells complicated by heresy" (*sortilegium involutum heresi*).[56]

The editor of the Reply, without appreciating how completely interest in the Maid before 1430 was dominated by the one point that all considered

---

[50] Valois, "Réponse d'un clerc parisien," p. 175.
[51] Valois, "Réponse d'un clerc parisien," p. 175: "Item, cum dicta Puella nullo predictorum modorum probaverit se missam a Deo fuisse."
[52] See Monnoyeur, *Traité*, p. 19, n. 1.
[53] Valois, "Réponse d'un clerc parisien," p. 178: "et videtur in hoc usurpasse laudem et honorificentiam que debetur Creator."
[54] Valois, "Réponse d'un clerc parisien," p. 178.
[55] Valois, "Réponse d'un clerc parisien," p. 178.
[56] Valois, "Réponse d'un clerc parisien," p. 179.

central (her claim to be sent by God), is still able to identify this point, rather than the Rouen judges' interest in her saints and their messages, as the Parisian cleric's principal focus: "He limits himself to remembering that Joan called herself [*se dit*] sent by God, without entering into the detail of the 'voices' or apparitions."[57] The Parisian cleric, since he is not a theologian but a canon lawyer, bases his case against Joan on the *Decretals* of Gregory IX.[58] A look at this source gives us a deeper understanding of why royalist treatises and early writing on Joan scarcely mention "visions," "apparitions," or "voices," stressing instead her claim to be "sent by God." For the role of someone sent by God, as decretalists also confirm, is that of prophet, a role no one acquires haphazardly. The *Decretals* cite the apostle in Romans 10:15 asking: "And how shall they preach unless they be sent?" (*mittantur*); those sent by God (*invisibiliter mittuntur a Deo*) are compared to those sent by man (*visibiliter mittantur ab homine*); and John the Baptist is "not sent by man, but by God" (*non . . . missus ab homine, sed a Deo*). Significantly, instead of aligning her with mystics of questionable credentials, both Joan and her supporters aimed high, linking her, through their very choice of words, with the likes of John the Baptist, as someone directly sent by God.[59]

This French presumption must have further fueled the Parisian cleric's vehement reaction to Joan. Gerson had once written:

> It would be perverse to ask us to accept as coming from the Mouth of God, and therefore to be believed with the certainty of Faith, all the visions that go on multiplying to extraordinary limits.[60]

But in the case of Joan, the author of DMV wants her words accepted this way; we have only to recall his audacious conclusion that further dialogue should cease because it is "dangerous, presumptuous and foolhardy to blame and to criticize things which have been instituted by God [*a deo . . . ordinata sunt*]."[61] Moreover, the anonymous Parisian cleric does not even acknowledge the lesser form of faith – "pious belief in the Maid" – as acceptable, given that he reversed DMV's statement: "It is pious, salutary, of true and

---

[57] Valois, "Réponse d'un clerc parisien," p. 166.
[58] Several specific references to the *Decretals* of Gregory IX can be found in the footnotes to the Latin text of the treatise published by Valois.
[59] The words "sent by God" almost become a leitmotif of the cleric's treatise. See Valois, "Réponse d'un clerc parisien," for examples: "a Deo . . . mittatur," "missus a deo," "missam a Deo," "a Deo mittatur" and "a Deo missa."
[60] The reference is to *De probatione* cited by James L. Connolly, *John Gerson, Reformer and Mystic* (Louvain, 1928), pp. 238–39: "Perversum esset, ne dicamus vanum, visiones super visiones in immensum multiplicantes debere recipere tanquam ab ore Dei prolatas ac deinde certissima fide credendas." Connolly's text differs slightly from Du Pin and Glorieux, *Oeuvres* 9: 181.
[61] Wayman, "The Chancellor," p. 302.

devout belief to support the Maid's case" (*potest . . . sustineri*),[62] by slipping the negative "non" into DMV's statement, so that the assertion reads "cannot be supported" (*non potest sustineri*).[63]

What better way for the cleric to personally put an end to Joan's career than to use his skill as a canon lawyer to find objections to her that would nourish the charge of heresy. The treatise culminates in a tense plea for the immediate involvement of the Inquisition in Joan's case. The cleric explains that expeditiousness is of the essence, as he paints an increasingly dire picture of the consequences of Joan's activities, until he has involved the fate of all Christendom in her error. And like any Burgundian writing against Joan, he not only criticizes her, but charges her with drawing others into her deception, one of her crimes being the desire to be believed. But he also accuses the French of credulity, and he warns that her superstitions, which represent a peril to the soul (*periculum animarum*) tend toward the subversion of the Christian faith (*subversionem fidei christiane*).[64] "Consequently, it is the responsibility of the Inquisitor of the faith, through his office," writes the cleric, "to inform himself on [this] crime of heresy." And further, the author states:

> the result from the preceding [material] is that all this manifestly contains error and heresy, causing, directly or indirectly, openly or secretly, damage to orthodox faith. That is why it is in the interest of every faithful Christian, but especially my mother, the University, the bishop, and the Inquisitor of the faith to combat such superstitions . . . without gentleness and with promptness.[65]

From early in the treatise, when the author indicates that Joan had in no way proved her divine mission,[66] his conclusion was in preparation: "there are no grounds for believing her on her word, but there are grounds for proceeding against her as suspect of heresy."[67] His tract contains an implicit condemnation of the decision of the Poitiers commission. Taking Joan's case beyond the date of that decision, he sees her "fruits," by which her mission would be confirmed, as no more than a series of acts tending to the

---

[62] Wayman, "The Chancellor," p. 298.
[63] Valois, "Réponse d'un clerc parisien," p. 178; Cf. Wayman, "The Chancellor," DMV, p. 298.
[64] This is the opposite message to that which we see in Jean Dupuy who finds in Joan the "raising of the faith" (*sublevatio fidei*).
[65] Valois, "Réponse d'un clerc parisien," p. 179.
[66] Valois, "Réponse d'un clerc parisien," p. 175: "Non sufficit cuiquam nude tantum asserere quod ipse sit missus a Deo."
[67] Valois, "Réponse d'un clerc parisien," p. 175: "Item, cum dicta Puella nullo predictorum modorum probaverit se missam a Deo fuisse, nullo modo sibi credendum est quod a Deo mittatur, sed contra ipsam, tanquam suspectam de heresi, procedendum."

destruction of the Christian faith.[68] All these allegations are summarized in the cleric's conviction, expressed in his concluding entreaty, that Joan needs investigation, immediately, by the Inquisition, as an individual suspect of heresy. Based on the Parisian cleric's treatise, it appears that, in his opinion, by this date the problems raised by Joan's case could not have been dissolved, had she suddenly agreed to leave the army and return home. For the protection of the orthodox faith, this Burgundian cleric feels that her case must be tried. The mechanism has already been set in motion by which she will become an instrument, through her error, for the instruction of the faithful.

[68] Valois, "Réponse d'un clerc parisien," p. 177.

11

Martin Le Franc's
Le champion des dames

The last text deserving our consideration in the theological debate is a poem called *Le champion des dames*, which was completed in 1442 by Martin Le Franc, and was conceived as a reply to the attack on women in Jean de Meun's *Roman de la Rose*. The poem is structured as a debate mounted by two protagonists, the Champion, who argues in favor of women in the literary *querelle des dames*, and the Adversary, who takes the side of the misogynistic opposition. The thirty-two stanzas devoted to Joan of Arc in Book Four of the *Champion* (stanzas 2102–133) are set within the framework of the theological debate: the Champion argues in favor of Joan's divine mission, and the Adversary against it. Although the passage on Joan constitutes an essentially self-contained discussion, separated from the rest of the poem by its focus on Joan's theological legitimacy, the Johannic section of the poem is in fact a debate within a debate.

Martin writes about Joan from outside the boundaries of the kingdom of France, probably from Basel while the great ecumenical council was in session. Unlike Christine de Pizan, however, who wrote during the English occupation yet with distinctly royalist sources, Martin pieces together his discussion from hearsay and from only one clearly identifiable written source, the treatise DMV. The orientation of his information is Burgundian. In fact, comparison of Martin's account with the writings of the Burgundian Monstrelet demonstrates at times an overlap of information perhaps indicating a second source. He may well have obtained at Basel his one pro-Joan source, DMV, which, as we have seen, is better attested outside France than within, and was available at Basel. At Basel, Martin must have had more contact with the Burgundian delegation than the French, since he had been educated at the University of Paris during the English occupation, and he was in the employ of Amadeus VIII, the uncle of Philip, duke of Burgundy. As we learn in the *Champion*, however, he remained French at heart. Because it is important to understand Martin's mixed loyalties in order to sort out the strands of his discussion of Joan, we begin with a brief biography.

Martin Le Franc was born either in 1395 or about 1410 in Aumale,

Normandy,[1] which belonged to the house of Harcourt, notable as a preserve of supporters for the French crown.[2] Fleeing his Norman homeland when it was seized by the English, he nonetheless remained in Burgundian territory and studied at the University of Paris, then composed of sympathizers of the English. He never received a doctorate in theology, apparently leaving Paris as a master of arts, but we know that he studied under Thomas de Courcelles, the professor of theology notorious for his role in Joan's trial at Rouen, and who was later a major figure at the council of Basel.

Over many years Le Franc functioned as an arbiter in both secular and religious disputes, traveling extensively through northern France and many parts of Europe. Many of his negotiations were conducted in service to the antipope Felix V (Amadeus VIII of Savoy), who was elected at Basel in 1439, whom he served as papal secretary with the title 'apostolic protonotary.' Martin undoubtedly participated in Amadeus's persistent efforts to promote and prolong truces between his nephew Philip the Good, duke of Burgundy, and Charles VII. At the same time that Martin served Amadeus as secretary, Aeneas Silvius Piccolomini, the future Pope Pius II, held a similar position. Aeneas's *Dialogues on the Authority of a General Council* of 1440, a work contemporaneous with the *Champion des dames*, consists of Latin dialogues on conciliar theory between Stephano da Caccia and Nicolas of Cusa, which alternate with minor dialogues in which Martin (*Martinus Gallicum*) plays the role of interlocutor to Aeneas.[3] Both clerics were presumably at the pope's side in Basel, participating in the general council and writing for themselves as time permitted.

In 1435 Martin attended the signing of the treaty of Arras, which marked the reconciliation of Philip the Good and Charles VII. Also in attendance were Joan's chief prosecutor Pierre Cauchon, who maintained Henry VI's right to the crown of France down to the final moment, and assessor Thomas de Courcelles, who had suddenly become such a fine spokesman for national unity that those hearing his words at Arras declared that "it seemed as if an angel of God were speaking."[4] There were certainly many others at that gathering in northern France as well who were capable of exchanging information about the recent death of Joan, but not a single reference to her can be connected to Arras in 1435.

By 1443 Martin had became provost of Lausanne, a lucrative post undoubtedly conferred on him by Amadeus during a stay of several

[1] Arthur Piaget, *Martin Le Franc, prévôt de Lausanne* (Lausanne, 1888), p. 12, places Martin's birth in 1395, but Paris, "Un poème inédit," p. 393, sets it around 1410.

[2] Paris, "Un poème inédit," p. 393.

[3] The *Dialogues* are contained in Adám Ferencz Kollár, *Analecta monumentorum omnis aevi vindobonensia: Opera et studio Adami Francisci Kollarii*, typis et sumptibus, Ioannis T. Trattner, 2 vols. (Vindobonae, 1761–62) 2: 691–790. See also Cecilia M. Ady, *Pius II (Aeneas Silvius Piccolomini): The Humanist Pope* (London, 1913), p. 68.

[4] Barrett, *Trial*, Champion, "Dramatis personae," p. 426.

months in the city by the antipope that same year.[5] Soon after the abdication of Amadeus as pope in 1449, an action which permitted the reunification of the church, Amadeus died. However, Martin succeeded in maintaining his post as papal secretary under the new pope, Nicolas V (1447–55). Martin died in 1461, a year after a complaint was filed against him in Lausanne for his frequent absences from his duties in that city. It is believed that he died in Rome[6] – where his former fellow papal secretary Aeneas had by then become Pope Pius II – far from his birthplace in the country he referred to as "very gentle France" (*la tres doulce France*).[7]

When Quicherat, until recently the sole modern editor to reproduce the Joan of Arc passage from Martin's *Champion des dames*,[8] introduces the excerpt, he alerts the reader to be prepared for a "curious discussion." In his view, the passage "merits full consideration" for two reasons, both crucially important: the passage was written sixteen years before the nullification trial and the work was dedicated to the Burgundian duke Philip. What Quicherat is suggesting, however briefly, is that to reopen the debate on Joan, after the emphatic statement handed down by her condemnation and burning in 1431, to which the Burgundians were a party, was a curious course of action. Martin's work breaks a virtual moratorium on writing about Joan between the two trials. Furthermore, to dedicate the work to Joan's mortal enemy, the duke by whom she was sold to the English, complicates the situation further. Others besides Quicherat have also commented on these contradictions, noting that Martin's passage seems "more or less dangerous"[9] but that he fully admires Joan and "does not hesitate to say it."[10] However, the matter was left there, and Martin simply retained the right to perplex us.

Quicherat worried still less about another odd circumstance arising from the Joan of Arc passage as he presented it. In Martin's multi-faceted work, which despite its attention to political and historical factors, was conceived as a feminist apology against Jean de Meun, the Adversary, the voice against women, has the last word on Joan. In an anticlimactic ending to Joan's case, the Adversary exclaims to the Champion, woman's defender: "You have preached too much, think of another woman to praise. You could not have adduced a worse example to accomplish what you wish."[11] Taking into account that Martin, nominally a Burgundian, since he was born in Normandy, dedicated his poem to the Burgundian duke, Quicherat may

---

[5] Paris, "Un poème inédit," p. 397.
[6] Paris, "Un poème inédit," p. 400.
[7] Piaget, *Martin Le Franc*, p. 16.
[8] A complete edition of the *Champion des dames* is now available by Robert Deschaux, *Le champion des dames*, Classiques français du Moyen Age, 127–31, 5 vols. (Paris, 1999).
[9] Gustave Cohen, *Sainte Jeanne d'Arc dans la poésie du XVe siècle* (Paris, 1948), p. 86.
[10] Piaget, *Martin Le Franc*, p. 201.
[11] See Appendix V for an English translation of Martin's passage on Joan of Arc. References to Quicherat are to the French text.

have thought that mentioning the Maid at all, so shortly after her condemnation, and to the man responsible for her capture, was enough of a show of courage on Martin's part; her side would not have to win the debate as well. Quicherat, thinking no doubt of Joan's Rouen judges, must also have believed that Joan had no following in Normandy, for elsewhere he wrote of a Norman chronicler who spoke favorably of Joan, stating "this was very noteworthy on the part of a Norman."[12] He might, too, have dismissed the problem as a sign of literary prudence. Martin deemed the duke to be the best patron with whom to place his work, someone enthusiastic about the *querelle*, whom Martin would not have wished to aggravate, in seeking his patronage, by praising a heretic.

Nothing could be further from the truth. Through error or oversight, Quicherat omitted from his edition the final thirty-two lines of Martin's discussion of Joan. In this concluding passage, it is revealed that the Champion and his pro-Joan arguments win the debate, that Martin defends the Maid's right to fame and honor, and thereby her inclusion in his gallery of famous women, and that he closes the section enlisting her *exemplum* as a tool of propaganda for emulation by the chivalric elite so that peace may return to France. In Martin's discussion we are witness to an odd phenomenon: a poet whose knowledge of Joan arises in a Burgundian context, returns to his French roots to praise her and reinvigorate the French cause through her example. It is this complex setting in which the discussion of Joan in the *Champion des dames* takes place.

There is another adjustment that needs to be made to Quicherat's excerpt from Martin. In 1893 six supplementary stanzas to the passage on the Maid were discovered in Brussels manuscript 9466 of the *Champion des dames*.[13] Quicherat had used B.N. fr. 12476, which, similarly to all others, lacks the extra stanzas.[14] The position of the additional stanzas is signaled by a marker between the two stanzas where they belong, and they are transcribed on the final folio of the manuscript. The most important revelation in the supplement is the identification of "Jan Jarson" as the author of the "little treatise" (DMV) on which Martin depends. But it was obvious, with or without the name of Gerson, that DMV was Martin's source. There is no way to guess why the stanzas were left out; nor does there seem to be any compelling reason not to reinsert them, if we bear in mind the fact that these stanzas alone contain the attribution of DMV to Gerson. The last three supplementary stanzas are the first three stanzas in Martin's defense of Joan's male clothing, based on the "three truths" of DMV. Thus the

[12] Quicherat, *Procès* 4: 339.
[13] Arthur Piaget, "Huitains inédits de Martin Le Franc sur Jeanne d'Arc," *Le Moyen Age* 6 (1893): 105–107.
[14] For information on the manuscripts, see Martin Le Franc, *Le champion des dames* (lines 1–8144) in *Société d'Histoire de la Suisse romande*, Arthur Piaget, ed., *Mémoires et documents*, 3rd ser., vol. 8 (Lausanne, 1968), p. vii.

addition seems to make the passage complete. It also eliminates the awkward and unlikely circumstance that Martin began two stanzas in a row with the word "also."

Martin's passage begins with a theme already familiar to the theological debate: the dual recognition that France's most powerful had failed to protect the kingdom from devastation, and that if a savior could not be found the national cause was lost. Similarly to Christine, who expressed the belief in the *Epistle to the Queen of France*, that only the powerful, because of their superior gifts, could make a difference and negotiate peace, Martin seems to have first trusted in potentates for solutions, only to be deceived. His opening lines also immediately undercut the main premise on which his collection of illustrious women, and certainly the entire classical branch of the genre, is founded: that the famous are not the meek but the powerful. "What can duchesses do," exclaims the Champion, "against their harmful enemies, or queens or princesses?" Martin has prepared the way for the weak to confound the strong. Joan, against all expectation, will be the anticipated savior, as inferiority becomes superiority.

Martin thus opens the debate acknowledging its foundations in the narrative of France brought to despair, but he focuses on human solutions, making no reference as yet to providence as the sole hope of France. A fuller exposition of France's desolation has in fact been told in the *Champion*, at an earlier moment in the poem, where love, however, rather than a human redeemer, is envisioned as the factor capable of saving France. Cast as a literary lament and prosopopoeia, in which the author gives speech to an inanimate entity, Martin permits "France" to express her grief over the tragic desolation which has brought her down. In roughly three hundred lines, Martin discloses how hatred has "caused the beautiful lily to be trampled" (*fait flatrir la belle fleur de lys*).[15] Thus some fifty pages before the Joan of Arc passage, Martin demonstrates that France herself is no longer a "powerful queen" (*puissant royne*). He describes her now as "wandering without a path or route, dressed as a poor maid [*poyre meschine*], all covered with ruin."[16] Pronouncing in her own name the ills she suffers, France especially laments the spilling of the blood of her own people which spreads "like a flood," whereby even "heaven cannot water the land enough to keep it from running red."[17] A list follows of social and economic evils: uncultivated land, murder, rape, hunger, and fear. Those who knew France when she was peaceful and complete (*paisibles et entiers*) look upon the cruelty with pity; France is one-third gone (*fondue*) and the enemy and marauders devour what remains of her. At the end of the lament there is a warning: France will sink still lower without returning to flower unless love checks all felonious hearts; whereas if

---

[15] Piaget, *Martin Le Franc*, p. 206.
[16] Piaget, *Martin Le Franc*, p. 206.
[17] Piaget, *Martin Le Franc*, p. 207.

such evil can be conquered, France will rule and flourish as before, and the present world will become a paradise on earth.[18]

Returning to the lines on Joan we see that the stage is now set for Joan to enter the picture. "What will those who understand [*les congnoissans*] such things think?" asks the Champion, as if posing the very question that had confounded the experts. For now he introduces Joan: "a maid" (*pucelle*) who "a short time ago" (*naguères*) "broke [the backs] of the powerful and put the swiftest men to death."[19] Wealth has become an unexpectedly irrelevant concomitant to power, since in contrast to duchesses, queens, and princesses, the Maid possesses "few earthly goods" (*sans / Habondance de biens mondains*), an anomalous first description of the Maid when compared to other texts, although it adequately conveys, popularly construed, the concept of 1 Corinthians 1:27 (*infirma confundat fortia*), since it configures poverty as lowliness. It also anticipates the widespread Anglo-Burgundian charge that Joan's unacknowledged objective was personal gain, a point touched upon twice in DMV, where that author both denied that she tried to "secure her own interests" (*ad quaestum proprium*)[20] and emphasized, implying Joan's innocence of such a charge, that divine grace is not conferred for "social profits" (*ad mundanos questus*).[21]

After this brief introduction, the Champion circles back to position his topic with more precision. That Martin is paying homage to Joan by entering her in the canon of illustrious women immediately brings to mind the poet Christine whose *Ditié* serves as an intermediate measure to such an induction. Unfortunately, we cannot answer the intriguing question of whether Martin knew the *Ditié*. His enthusiastic recommendation of Christine and her talent elsewhere in the *Champion* suggests that he would happily have added Joan to his collection of illustrious women for Christine's sake alone.[22] Yet despite his claim to have read her "beautiful poems both long and short" (*beaux dictiers longs et courts*),[23] there is no sign that he knows anything of her works other than her love poetry. He does not even specifically acknowledge the *Cité des dames*, in whose pathway he composes his own collection of biographies.

At first the incongruity between Martin's opening focus on chivalric deeds and Christine's sharply contrasting interest in sacred history makes one think that Christine, were she still alive, would have mourned Martin's substitution of a misshapen narrative of worldly prowess for the supernatural in Joan's mission. When Martin announces: "I wish to tell [*dire veul*] of the Maid who delivered Orléans, where Salisbury lost an eye, and then was struck by vile

[18] Piaget, *Martin Le Franc*, p. 208.
[19] Quicherat, *Procès* 5: 44.
[20] Wayman, "The Chancellor," p. 298.
[21] Wayman, "The Chancellor," p. 301.
[22] Paris, "Un poème inédit," pp. 415–16.
[23] Paris, "Un poème inédit," p. 415.

death,"[24] the dissimilarity to the way Christine casts the story, with the words: "I wish to relate [*vueil raconter*] how God . . . accomplished all this through his grace," despite the parallelism in the utterances, stands out. But more than a decade had passed by the time Martin wrote. With the Maid's burning as a heretic at Rouen, it is impossible for Martin to hold out assurances or bolster optimism with declarations that God has guaranteed future French victories. The story has ended a few chapters short of the anticipated finish, yet other observers, including the king of France, seem content to consider the Maid's case in silence.

Hampered by his inability to bear witness to any new sequence of successes, Martin must describe the (unsuccessful) assault on Paris, which was so anxiously awaited by Christine, in carefully selected terms, stating that "the king came forth . . . and with a great French army went before Paris [*ala devant Paris*]." There was, of course, no victory to report. Martin seems willing to settle for crediting Joan with her psychological contribution, her boost to French courage and morale, when he states the grounds for including her name in his collection: "It was she who recovered French honor to such a degree that she will rightfully enjoy perpetual renown."[25] Then in the last six lines of his speech, the Champion suddenly asserts that writing about Joan requires acknowledging the "divine spirit" (*divin esprit*) behind her miracles.[26] With this statement Martin accepts that the Maid's story must be told in the context we have described in these pages, as a debate over her divine mission. Thus he makes an earlier-than-usual pronouncement, at the end of the Champion's first speech, of his belief in Joan's supernatural mandate, which he supports as he proceeds through his discussion.

By granting the Champion this early pronouncement, and then transferring speech to the Adversary, Martin permits a situation to develop which Christine refused to tolerate in the *Ditié*. In Martin's lines, there will be no hazy evocation of detractors – which was the only outward evidence of a debate that Christine would permit – but a rightful opponent prepared to contest. Yet already in the Champion's first speech Martin declares certain points to be beyond consideration, but which from our vantage point are clearly debatable. He does this not from intransigence but through an assumption that the facts are universally admitted. Consequently, we will not learn his version of "where she came from, why or how."[27] And on a point to which French writers would take vigorous exception, Martin's protagonists concur that Joan was "taught to wield a lance and bear armor." Here Martin faces the difficulty of writing a pro-Joan commentary with Burgundian sources. To the French, the fact of an untaught Maid accentuates

[24] Quicherat, *Procès* 5: 44.
[25] Quicherat, *Procès* 5: 45.
[26] Quicherat, *Procès* 5: 45.
[27] Quicherat, *Procès* 5: 45.

the miracle of her achievements, but Burgundians prefer to explain away these claims by insisting on her training. It appears that the notion of Joan's military preparation was so prevalent in Burgundian territory, that Martin was unaware of hampering his Champion with this contradiction.

The Adversary replies to the declaration of Joan's divine mission with the conventional counter-argument of the danger of false prophets. In an effort to make theology accessible, through the use of historical example, Martin includes the story of Thomas Couette as a popularization of 2 Corinthians 11:14: "For satan himself transformeth himself into an angel of light." His theme is the gullibility of the masses and his lesson essentially the same warning as the *Poitiers Conclusions*, that one must not "believe . . . immediately or lightly" (*tantôt et légièrement*). The Adversary seeks to demonstrate that the cult which developed around Couette was a symptom of the times. According to him, foolish people (*la gent fole*), who leave themselves open to trickery, do not detect a fraud: "And a great fraud conceived and conducted by a clever mind, in the current day is not recognized by all people."[28] With a lesson for those who believe in Joan, the Adversary points out to the Champion the discrepancy between appearances and reality: "Did you not judge and affirm that he lived a very saintly life? Was it not commonly cried: Here is a saint arrived on earth" (*un saint sur terre venu*)? In addition to mocking the excesses of the public veneration which grew up around Couette, the Adversary also notes pointedly Couette's overstepping the boundaries of allowable roles, a charge also easily applicable to Joan's appropriation of a masculine role: "He was neither priest nor subdeacon, and still he sang mass."[29]

In an outcome to Couette's story, worthy of Gelu's image of the volcano of evil which erupts to the surface when made to stand the test of time, the Adversary relates that after Couette had long been taken for a saint, his deception was finally disclosed (*sa malice véue*) and he was subsequently burned at Rome. Martin allows the lesson in this exemplum to penetrate slowly until the discussion arrives at Joan's death at Rouen, but the error of trusting in an outward show of virtue is already patent. Here also is a serious challenge to the ubiquitous idea among French writers that the ability to offer a list of a person's virtues serves as a fully valid proof.

The Adversary is allotted exactly twice the number of lines as the Champion. Thus he has time to move his discussion from the counterfeit behavior of Couette to the idea that Joan was involved in a plot. This is a vintage Burgundian argument, but no surviving source on the Anglo-Burgundian side testifies to the plot theory prior to Martin's *Champion des dames*.[30] He offers two versions of the plot theory, one which he presents

---

[28] Quicherat, *Procès* 5: 46.
[29] Quicherat, *Procès* 5: 46.
[30] Quicherat believed that Jean Wavrin du Forestel was the first to represent Joan as part

as conventional but untrue, the other a supposedly genuine, unimpeachable version, known to him through a private source. Neither account is precisely duplicated in any other text. Analogously to the argument that Joan underwent military training, when the Adversary claims her involvement in a plot, he does so to explain away the miraculous through rational explanation. The Adversary rejects, however, that "someone who loved Orléans" galvanized Joan and "taught her what to say."[31] The account he prefers is part of a broad two-tiered deception. He now offers the first episode.

In the plot theory which the Adversary claims to know "for a certain thing" (*pour chose certaine*), training plays its popular role. But Martin's unique description is an intensified version of Monstrelet's avowal that Joan worked as a chambermaid at an inn where she grew strong tending to the horses.[32] The Adversary contends that in her youth Joan served as a page to a certain captain, who dressed her in armor and taught her to wield a lance "when the bloom of youth ... chose to reveal her sex" (*jonesse ... voulut son sexe monstrer*).[33] This is apparently a transposition of Baudricourt's early role in Joan mission, which included furnishing her with men's clothing. From this simple miscommunication the true plot develops. Joan would "come to Orléans" [sic] to dupe the king. Although trained as a knight, she would present herself "as a simple shepherdess" (*comme simplette bergière*), offering signs to the king and his parliament "by which it would be understood that she was divinely sent" (*qu'elle venist divinement*).[34] Contradicting the cherished French notion that providence rather than fortune lay behind Joan's accomplishments, the Adversary derides French gullibility relating to Joan, as he had earlier scoffed at it for Couette. As if he were simultaneously scorning the voice of the patriotic poets, the general French enthusiasm for theological proof, and the era of great peace predicted in *Virgo puellares*, the Adversary dismantles the sacred French tale. With time, he indicates, the French came to believe in this "contrived farce" (*farse controuvée*), while "fortune increased her accomplishments" (*la fortune acrut / Ses faiz*). "There, the voices are raised," the Adversary mocks, "Now the war will be over, if God and Saint Avoie aid us!" "Surely the thing is amply proven," he states with a final show of disdain, "God sends the Maid to France!" (*Dieu la Pucelle en France envoie*).[35] Through the scorn of his last line the Adversary proves his refusal to accept the Maid's supernatural mission.

Undeterred by the Adversary's sneering attitude toward theological proofs,

of a political plot, but Wavrin, according to Quicherat, wrote between 1455–60 well after Martin had completed the *Champion des dames*. See Quicherat, *Procès* 4: 406.

[31] Quicherat, *Procès* 5: 46.
[32] Enguerrand de Monstrelet in Quicherat, *Procès* 4: 361–62.
[33] Quicherat, *Procès* 5: 46.
[34] Quicherat, *Procès* 5: 47.
[35] Quicherat, *Procès* 5: 47.

the Champion offers all the validation he can. To stock the Champion's arsenal of arguments, however, Martin appears to have no theological text to fall back on except DMV, whose weaknesses we have previously discussed. Stranded by DMV's failure to explain the "unquestionable signs" by which that author recognized Joan's divine mission, Martin can only make the pathetically weak statement that without divine power she could not have produced her signs, a point that is self evident. He then alleges the useful argument of speed: "Moreover, she did in a moment what had not been accomplished in twenty years,"[36] but follows it imprudently with the claim that "those to whom God gives strength always conquer and move forward," a point which, given the abrupt end put to Joan's mission by her capture, does not make for his case.

Turning next to the perilous argument of DMV's angels, the Champion avows his own (pious?) belief (*je croy en bonne foi*) that angels accompanied Joan "for as we see in Jerome, they love and embrace chastity."[37] Then going beyond DMV, the Champion claims to "hold as true" (*tien pour vray*) that angels helped her defeat the English, adding by way of explanation, in the first of the six supplementary stanzas attested in Brussels manuscript 9466, that God permits the destruction of those who disrupt peace. Although one must doubt that Martin knows anything directly about the *Lettre aux Anglais*, if we except the allusion to the angels, his explanation is by and large the argument of that document. But by speaking of Joan's helping angels, he has followed DMV into the arena of Joan's condemnation. For instead of insisting upon her direct inspiration from God, he has sworn belief in the intermediaries whom her Rouen judges would cast as diabolical spirits and with whom they would induce Joan to admit forbidden relationships.

Martin offers a more direct expression of the topos of the weak confounding the strong in the second supplementary stanza. Instead of being merely poor, as she was in the passage's opening stanza, Joan is portrayed here – like the Joan in Christine's *Ditié* – as "a humble little creature" who "confounds the pride of the English" (*Pour abessier . . . / L'orgueul des Anglois*).[38] This is the last proof offered by the Champion before he embarks on a six-stanza defense of Joan's male clothes, a defense and illustration of the "three truths" in the supplementary portion of DMV. First, however, he claims that "a thousand reasons" could establish a saintly depiction of the Maid, but protests that her detractors would only submit them to "false interpretation" (*male interpretacion*).[39] Yet, in fact, Martin is already beginning to curtail the Adversary's opportunities for rebuttal.

Joan's resumption of masculine clothing after abjuring this fault was the technicality on which she was declared a relapsed heretic and burned at the

---

[36] Quicherat, *Procès* 5: 47.
[37] Quicherat, *Procès* 5: 48.
[38] Piaget, "Huitains inédits," p. 106.
[39] Piaget, "Huitains inédits," pp. 106–107.

stake. That Martin may have understood the importance of the male-dress issue in the Maid's condemnation is suggested in the *Champion des dames* by the fact that the full six-stanza defense of Joan's male attire is simply juxtaposed with the Adversary's announcement of her burning at Rouen. If so, it is here that we particularly wish for more than the arguments of DMV. Was there nothing else he could learn on the subject at the council of Basel or does he refuse to put what he learned into the mouth of his Adversary?

The slow beginnings of the assembly at Basel in 1431, the scattered departures of disaffected participants at various stages of the council (especially during the *Conciliabulum* between 1437 and 1449), and the flight of members in 1433 due to an infestation of plague,[40] combined with our inability to exactly pinpoint the period of Martin's attendance, make it impossible for us to know whether Martin passed up better opportunities for knowledge than the now ten-year-old treatise DMV. A slight air of self-importance surrounds the revelation in the first supplementary stanza that his authority is the celebrated chancellor: "Don't you know what Gerson said? I'm talking about master Jean Gerson,"[41] a piece of information that he may have discovered only upon arriving at Basel. He seems pleased with DMV as a resource and never indicates that there might have been whispering in the halls at Basel capable of adding the last chapter – the Rouen chapter – to the male-clothing debate.

Although Martin calls DMV, which he terms "a little treatise composed about her" (*d'elle ung petit traictié fit*), "more subtle than we think" (*plus soubtil que nous ne penson*), he unveils nothing about the "three truths" which was not already distinctly stated in DMV. In fact, the three points defending Joan's male clothing in DMV constitute the plainest truths and the most straightforward writing found in that tract. The objections of the Parisian cleric notwithstanding, the three points, as we have seen, are grounded in Aquinas, and do not seem to merit the Parisian cleric's designation of "such artfulness" (*tales calliditates*).

It is probable that for the popular audience Martin envisaged for the *Champion des dames*, he felt he needed to make the theology of DMV's "three truths" more accessible. Thus he oddly personalizes Deuteronomic law, citing the lifting of the Old Testament's dietary laws as proof that restrictions on clothing are similarly unimportant in the new era of Christ. He introduces a rhetorical couple, "Robin and Joanne," to serve as everyman, so that he can demonstrate Joan's case to be no different from theirs. It is as if the anonymous pair have been incongruously lifted from a *pastourelle*, to be told that they, like Joan, are not bound by a law under which they do not live. In his third stanza on the Deuteronomic prohibition, Martin relaxes

---

[40] Barrett, *Trial*, Champion, "Dramatis personae," p. 426.
[41] Piaget, "Huitains inédits," p. 107.

the tone still more. Referring to the forbidden meats of the dietary laws, he notes: "Nowadays if someone offered you some [hare or pork], you would take second helpings [*maint morseau*]!"[42] He has outdone himself in the effort to make theology approachable.

The second principle of DMV's "three truths" insisted that the moral aspect (*aliquod morale*) of any law remained binding. For Joan this principle had bearing on the decency of her dress. To the anonymous author of DQP the question was whether the Maid could manage to conduct her mission in a more feminine way, since Esther and Judith had reached their objectives in woman's dress. But Martin draws exclusively on DMV to justify the Maid's male dress, and that document recommends weighing "all circumstances" (*circumstantias omnes*), with the clear suggestion that "time, necessity, purpose, manner and other similar conditions" can remove the charge of indecency.[43]

Martin does not hide details about Joan's dress that make her circumstances worse rather than better. He admits that she dressed in doublet (*pourpoint*) and a hammered breastplate (*heuque frapée*), signs of a well-fitted knight. To him, however, it is a question of dignity that she be allowed to dress in this manner, a sign of the respect due her station, as well as an enhancement to her knightly presence. This is not a moment for the Champion to stress her humility: "She was more dreaded . . . and was taken for a proud prince [*fier prince*], not a simple shepherdess [*simplette bergière*]."[44] But Martin knows a still more compromising fact: the Maid rejected long coats in favor of a short ones (*robes courtes*).[45] In "weighing the circumstances" the Champion maintains that a short coat makes her more agile (*aperte*) and her clothing lighter (*legière*). Anticipating the third point (dress appropriate to a given activity), he argues that "long coats . . . are not good for warfare." Using the proverb "a monk's habit does not a monk make" (*l'abit ne fait pas le moine*), to persuade the Adversary that an exterior need not match an interior, he also acknowledges "that her circumstances were not those of most women" (*aussy aultre estoit / Son fait, que cil des femmes toutes*).

The final point (DMV's third truth) the Champion by now takes to be self-evident: "Arms require appropriate dress; there is none so foolish that he does not know this." Contrasting the life of the warrior to that of the inhabitant of a city, he insists on the different requirements of attire. Making a single oblique reference to the general charge that Joan "unsexed" herself [*se effeminare*] by wearing men's clothes,[46] he resorts to a parallelism from falconry. Joan, who traded the hanging panels of a long coat for a short tunic

[42] Piaget, "Huitains inédits," p. 107.
[43] Wayman, "The Chancellor," p. 302.
[44] Quicherat, *Procès* 5: 48.
[45] Quicherat, *Procès* 5: 48.
[46] Wayman, "The Chancellor," DQP, p. 304.

in order to engage in battle, is compared to the falcon whose jesses are cast off as he is sent out for prey.

Following this analogy, the Champion's important final argument about Joan's short coat loses its ascendancy. Martin either knows or senses that toward the end of her military career any Englishman or Burgundian able to capture the Maid would be striking gold. In fact, when the time came after Joan's capture to purchase her from Jean de Luxembourg and the bastard of Vendôme, Pierre Cauchon, who was especially eager to wrest control of Joan from her captors, offered six thousand *livres* ransom, a pension to the bastard of Vendôme, and the chance that the ransom could be raised to ten thousand *livres*, if six were not enough.[47] Thus Joan's ability to protect herself may have increasingly depended on her skill at blending in with other knights, rather than cutting a conspicuous figure at the front of the army as before. So the Champion offers his last point: "Also whoever hides from his enemies has no need of a long coat."[48] This last argument is not cast theologically or legally as a right to self-protection. It is merely a closing thought, like so many of Martin's arguments, an isolated observation on her male dress.

With the end of Martin's defense of Joan's clothing, he can follow DMV no further. After a quick allusion to the coronation, he leaves Joan's *gesta* and enters the arena of her reputation after her death. The Adversary is quick to draw parallels with Couette. Just as Couette's error was confirmed by his burning, so justice "sent her to burn at Rouen in Normandy."[49] He also adds his assessment of Joan to the theological debate: "For never did God send her" (*Car oncques Dieu ne l'envoïa*).[50] But the Champion rejects that a supposition of guilt can be drawn from the fact of Joan's death. The unspoken theology behind the Champion's reply is that judgments through discernment performed by humans may be in error. Beginning to outline his own version of the company she keeps after death, the Champion aligns her not only with saints but with Jesus himself: "How many saints do we celebrate who died shamefully! First think of Jesus and then of his blessed martyrs."[51] Having generally failed to depict the Maid with the typical feminine virtues, he now adduces the adjective "innocent" (*la Pucelle innocente*), but it has double value, for he is primarily using it juridically to claim a reversal of the Rouen trial's pronouncement, from a verdict of guilt to one of innocence.

In addition to wishing to celebrate her part in the coronation, Martin wants Joan to be remembered for her "courage" (*vertu*) (attested twice), her bravery (*vaillance*), her strength (*force*), and her victory (*victoire*). This is

[47] Henry Charles Lea, *A History of the Inquisition of the Middle Ages* (New York, 1922) 3: 358.
[48] Quicherat, *Procès* 5: 48.
[49] Quicherat, *Procès* 5: 49.
[50] Quicherat, *Procès* 5: 49.
[51] Quicherat, *Procès* 5: 49.

indeed a flavorless and secular set of adjectives, although sincerely proposed. The Adversary, now disadvantaged by Martin, is allowed to speak his final lines, but not have the last word on Joan, as Quicherat believed; he concludes his role with an equally lackluster speech: "You have preached too much [*trop preschié*]; think of another woman to praise. One could not adduce a worse example to accomplish what you wish."[52] There is not a trace left in either protagonist of the theological debate.

Giving full thought to Joan's detractors, Martin envisions that they will play the role of his Adversary well into the future. Thus the Champion states: "Let them say what they will of her – they are free to speak or to remain silent – but her praises will not lack, for the lies they know how to make."[53] And so, in the first stanza following the termination of Quicherat's excerpt, the Champion anticipates his critics and justifies his own decision to include Joan: "And if I have praised three or four complete foreigners, why would I remain silent about she who chose to fight for France? Surely I will not do that."[54] There is more in these lines than meets the eye. We must look briefly at the contest between poet and patron.

It was no doubt Quicherat's sense, when he excerpted the passage on Joan from the *Champion des dames*, that Martin wished to please his patron Philip the Good, duke of Burgundy, by granting the Adversary the final opinion on Joan. Therefore, he must have read no further than the Adversary's tedious last claim that to include Joan in a book praising women did the Champion's cause more harm than good. But although Martin was writing after the treaty of Arras in 1435, which reunited France and Burgundy, not all animosities had by then been eradicated, by any means, and Joan's case remained a delicate subject. According to one scholar, Philip was engaged in a bid not to become first among princes, but to rise in rank equal to kings.[55] What he apparently desired was to extend his holdings to cover all the ancient crown of Lotharingia. At the council of Basel, through his spokesman Jean Germain, Philip had sought ascendancy in a protocol dispute by invoking his illustrious forebears. Aligning Philip with the likes of Francus, the Trojan prince, Charles Martel, Pepin, and Charlemagne, and affirming Philip's adherence to the orthodox faith and his dedication to the service of Christianity, Germain was creating a Burgundian mythology through which Philip could assert his preeminence.[56]

Deprecating Joan, who had been such an assiduous promoter of the Valois

---

[52] Quicherat, *Procès* 5: 50.

[53] Quicherat, *Procès* 5: 48–49.

[54] Martin Le Franc, *Le champion des dames* (continuation of Joan of Arc passage), print edition for Galiot Du Pré (Paris, 1530).

[55] Joseph Toussaint, *Les relations diplomatiques de Philippe le Bon avec le concile de Bâle (1431–1449)* (Louvain, 1942), p. 207.

[56] Yvon Lacaze, "Philippe le Bon et le problème hussite: Un projet de croisade bourguignon en 1428–1429," *Revue historique* 241 (1969): 69–98.

sacred mythology, thus became a means of honoring the duke of Burgundy. Germain, for instance, who throughout his career was a loyal servant to the duke, wrote a scurrilous attack on the Maid.[57] The practice is also attested as late as 1459, in a speech at Mantua by Jean Jouffroy, a representative of Philip the Good. Speaking three years after the nullification trial at Rouen, Jouffroy did not temper his remarks just because of the reversal of official opinion on the Maid (although he pretended to shorten them in mock deference to Charles VII). Jouffroy was even willing to embroider the truth of Philip's role in the capture of Joan: "Now Philip, whom ghosts could not frighten . . . first stopped the progress of the Maid at Charité-sur-Loire . . . he first pushed her back from the attack on Paris, and he alone captured her."[58] Jouffroy continued:

> Once Philip was master over her, he would not deign to look at her. . . . He scarcely thought it worthy for him to have conquered [the Maid] who had spread so much terror or at least delusion throughout Champagne, Reims, Sens and Senlis.[59]

It must have been very clear to Martin, long before Jouffroy's speech, how one portrayed the Maid to the duke. Yet in deciding which of his two protagonists should win the debate on Joan, Martin faced a dilemma. In the context of his work as illustrious female biography, it was impossible for him to glorify Philip, the person responsible for the demise of the woman he had elected to praise. Since the Adversary censures Joan, the Adversary must be seen as the representative of Philip's views. This leads to the extraordinary inference that if the Champion represents Martin and the Adversary, Philip, the debate actually pits the poet against his benefactor. A further complication develops from a statement in the introduction of Martin's work. Protecting himself from the criticism that the Adversary would be speaking unpopular lines against women, Martin stated that "one must consider the nature of the person who is speaking."[60] For the Joan of Arc passage this has curious implications. If the Adversary, who is also called "Small-Understanding" (*Court Entendement*) speaks foolishness, his criticism of Joan, which concurred with Philip's opinion, could not be discredited without embarrassment to Philip.

From Martin's own pen we hear the reaction of the duke to Martin's decision to speak his mind in the *Champion des dames*.[61] The *Complainte du livre du Champion des Dames à maistre Martin Le Franc son acteur* is Martin's

---

57 Jean Germain, "De laudibus Philippi" (chap. 14) in Ayroles, *Jeanne d'Arc* 3: 640–41; French translation in same vol. 3: 535–38.
58 Jean Jouffroy, "De Philippo Burgundae duce oratio," in Ayroles, *Jeanne d'Arc* 3: 641; French translation in same vol. 3: 537.
59 Ayroles, *Jeanne d'Arc* 3: 641; in French 3: 538.
60 Piaget, *Le champion*, p. 4.
61 See the text of Martin's *Complainte* in Paris, "Un poème inédit," pp. 423–37.

description of the poem's failure to find favor with the duke. In this poem the rejection of his manuscript at the Burgundian court is told by the book itself in a dialogue with its author. It was whispered in the ear of the duke that Martin's book should be burned, "for it carries poisons in its belly," claimed the anonymous adviser, "and thus Martin should be ordered to rewrite [*rescripre*] it for several reasons."[62] Among the accusations directed at Martin was the following charge: "You praised several as you pleased [*a ta guise*], some openly [*devant*], others surreptitiously [*derriere*]."[63] The young Martin had recklessly believed that he could honor his Norman roots and speak his mind about Joan, but Philip was not pleased with poetry that countered his politics.

Certainly the matter of whether or not to include the Maid in his work was the most serious decision Martin faced in dealing with Joan's case. But he also had to make a judgment about where to place her among his heroines. Martin may have relied heavily on DMV and stated his conviction that no one could write about her unless he acknowledged Joan's "divine spirit." But ultimately it was more as a secular warrior than as a divine envoy that Martin understood her example. He included her among his female fighters (*cheveleresses*),[64] yet not in direct proximity to the Amazons, as if the significance of the Christian context in which her mission arose was in fact adequately understood by him. Martin never indicates that he knew how powerful the Old Testament analogies between the French and the people of God were to the early debate over Joan's mission. Intuitively, however, he decides to treat her directly after Deborah, Jael, and Judith. But his connections are nonetheless hazy. Although he labels Deborah a prophetess, his own portrayal of Joan completely omits this aspect of her career; there is but a single reference to her "making signs" with God's help, if that can in fact be considered a reference to her prophecies. The rubrics for Jael and Judith refer to them as killer of Sisera and killer of Holophernes, respectively. Joan has been included as part of Martin's effort to "praise women warriors" (*louer les batailleresses*).

As if consciously highlighting the new element Joan brought to the conduct of women in war and peace, Martin concludes his stanzas on the Maid with an exhortation to "you barons, you princes, and you lords of France."[65] The structure likely owes nothing to the *Lettre aux Anglais*, which Martin never demonstrates he knew, but to the duchesses, queens, and princesses of his opening lines on Joan. Elsewhere in his poem, Martin gave high praise to the mediating abilities of Philip's wife, Isabelle of Portugal, during the signing of the treaty at Arras.[66] But, like Christine and archbishop

---

[62] Paris, "Un poème inédit," p. 428.
[63] Paris, "Un poème inédit," p. 430.
[64] Martin, *Le champion* (1530), p. cclxxxv.
[65] Martin, *Le champion* (1530), p. cclxxxv.
[66] Piaget, *Martin Le Franc*, p. 90.

Gelu, Martin finds in Joan an alternative to the passive tradition of women as peaceweavers. In its place emerges the strategy advocated by Joan, the *voie de fait*, which stands in direct contrast to the female mediator tradition and must be considered a new chapter in the history of French heroines. Here is another sign of the new readiness to accept Joan's vision that military intervention can serve as a woman's contribution to peace.

When Martin employs the Maid as a stimulus to male courage in his final stanza of the passage, it is an earnest but somehow hollow appeal. He asks that the barons, princes, and lords of France "have the courage and endurance of this one woman to overcome and destroy your enemies quickly."[67] What pathos there is in his words comes from the requirement that he reinvest his hope in French nobles and knights ("on whom we still place the hope of our deliverance"), whom Martin believed had failed France, but were once again France's single chance. But he writes within the framework of a long tradition of the praise and blame of women, where certain conventions prevail. In this literature, upon the introduction of men to the narrative, the noble deeds of women become the embarrassment of men. Boccaccio, for instance, praised Veturia for success that was made possible only by the vacuum left by men, "since men . . . seemed unable to defend the Republic,"[68] and he described Penthesilea as "much more manly in arms than those who were made men by Nature."[69] If Martin is attempting to shame the chivalric class with sarcasm, he has left no signs to make this clear.

A few stanzas later he claims to wish "that women had ruled [because] I know that the English would not have led France into such grief" (stanza 2139). Not only is any wholesale statement of this type destined to disappoint our emotions, but in the setting of a palinode, where our author atones for the misogyny of Jean de Meun's *Roman de la Rose* by praising women, this indiscriminate praise of women is as much in error as the indiscriminate blame of the misogynists. In his discussion of Joan, Martin avoids most of the pitfalls of this artificial genre by adhering to the theological debate. But there is a problem. The mixing of the preordained rhetoric of the praise genre with the vocabulary of sincere patriotic emotion allows each discourse to blunt the effect of the other.

Martin's shortcomings as a writer in the theological debate are more serious. As a displaced Norman, he lived more or less as an itinerant ecclesiastic after leaving his Norman birthplace. Because, in effect, Martin spent his life in exile, this meant that Charles VII was never the focal point of his thinking about Joan. To be sure, his poem is about the lives of women.

[67] Martin, *Le champion* (1530), p. cclxxxv.
[68] Giovanni Boccaccio, *Concerning Famous Women*, Guido A. Guarino, trans. (New Brunswick, N.J., 1963), p. 119.
[69] Boccaccio, *Famous Women*, p. 66.

But nothing relating to the perpetuation of the Valois dynasty informs his discussion of Joan, or even seems to move him. His attachment is more genuinely to the land. Thus there is no allusion in his verse to the disinheritance effectuated by the treaty of Troyes, nor is there any sense of the importance of Charles's right to the title of "true heir." Furthermore, Martin does not recognize that through the preservation of Charles great deeds were promised for the benefit of all Christendom. Lost also is the lesson of how these elements conferred just cause on Joan's military mission and excused her from the charges of renewing warfare and the accusation of cruelty through war. The receipt of the three propaganda documents would have made these and other crucial aspects of the debate available to him. In particular, the *Poitiers Conclusions* would have illustrated to him the connection between Joan's prophecies and the nature of the proofs, which he tries to record yet perhaps only marginally comprehends. In any event, wherever he came upon the manuscript of DMV which he utilizes for his discussion, the propaganda documents were nowhere to be found.

The passage by Martin on Joan of Arc in effect signals the decline of a spirit, a mood, and a system of beliefs which pervaded France for approximately the year-and-a-half of the Maid's mission, persisting weakened, but still in recognizable form, until 1442 when the *Champion des dames* was completed. At the time Martin wrote, he still recognized that the debate which defined Joan's career was the ecclesiastical debate over her heavenly mandate. He lists his proofs, however scattered and incomplete, and both the Champion and the Adversary make pronouncements on Joan's case, the Champion insisting on the "divine spirit" which inspired her and the Adversary claiming that "never did God send her." From Martin's vantage point, however, at a distance of ten years from the events and with only DMV to guide him, it is inevitable that his discussion of Joan, while theological, veers away from the ideals of *discretio spirituum*.

If we forgive Martin for the limited intellectual resources available to him, over which he had no control, we can nonetheless harbor significant regret at lost opportunities for more information. The point was introduced briefly with regard to Thomas de Courcelles, but it merits amplification. It was said that at Joan's trial, in words which Cauchon forbade to be included in the official record, three assessors, and a fourth on the following day, explained to Joan, in an effort to gain her submission to the church, that at the council of Basel, which was then in session, there were as many of her friends as enemies.[70] This is likely a gross overstatement, but it points to the fact that at Basel the debate over Joan's case surely experienced an afterlife. We know from the anonymous cleric's transcription at Basel of DMV, paired with the Parisian cleric's reply, that there was textual representation at the great council of both points of view. However, the list of assessors at Joan's trial

[70] Lea, *Inquisition* 3: 366.

who sooner or later participated in the assembly at Basel suggests that Joan's enemies must have far outnumbered her friends.

At least twenty-four of Joan's judges at Rouen participated in the council of Basel.[71] Among them were men bearing particular distinction as enemies of Joan. Pierre Cauchon, the instigator of the trial, who had pleaded the case for tyrannicide against Gerson at the council of Constance in 1415, was put in charge of Joan's trial as a "special mission," after being expelled from his bishopric of Beauvais in August 1429 by French forces. He attended the council in 1435 as a deputy of England.[72] Gilles de Duremort, abbot of Fécamp, who was entrusted with the English embassy to Basel in 1431, held the distinction of formulating the charge of Joan's relapse into heresy at the trial session of 29 May.[73] The Norman Nicolas Loiseleur, a deputy who proceeded directly from Rouen to Basel, had played the contemptible role of false confessor.[74] Jean Beaupère, a Burgundian ambassador at Constance with Cauchon in 1415, left Rouen on 28 May 1431 to attend Basel, where he arrived in early November 1431.[75] Testifying in 1452 for the nullification trial, he insisted on his original position against Joan's divine inspiration.[76] Nicolas Midi, friend of Loiseleur, Beaupère, and the English regent Bedford, was responsible for drafting the final twelve articles of accusation, a misleading summary of the previous seventy articles.[77] Thomas de Courcelles, Martin's professor of theology, goes down in history as one of those who favored torture in order to extract a confession from Joan. When charged with the creation of an official translation into Latin of the French minutes of the trial, he systematically expunged his name from the record to imply falsely that his role in the trial had been minor.[78] These were the most vigorous opponents of Joan at Basel, but others with names such as Pierre Maurice, Jean Massieu, Nicolas Lami, Denis de Sabrevois, Guillaume Evrard, Philibert de Montjeu, and Zanon de Castiglione surely gave their own hostile accounts of the Maid in off-the-record conversations in between the official sessions of the council.

Among Joan's supporters at the council, we can name one particularly pivotal figure, Jourdain Morin. This prelate not only bore the distinction of having attended the council of Constance, as a member of the French delegation headed by Gerson, but he was, as we have seen, one of the Poitiers assessors. As an evaluator of Joan in those early days of theological

---

[71] See Barrett, *Trial*, Champion, "Dramatis personae." Champion notes participation at Basel in the assessors' biographies.
[72] Barrett, *Trial*, Champion, "Dramatis personae," p. 406.
[73] Barrett, *Trial*, Champion, "Dramatis personae," p. 412.
[74] Barrett, *Trial*, Champion, "Dramatis personae," p. 416.
[75] Barrett, *Trial*, Champion, "Dramatis personae," p. 423.
[76] Barrett, *Trial*, Champion, "Dramatis personae," p. 424.
[77] Barrett, *Trial*, Champion, "Dramatis personae," p. 425.
[78] Barrett, *Trial*, Champion, "Dramatis personae," p. 427.

examination, one imagines that he would have been in a position to disseminate the important *Poitiers Conclusions* at the council, had he deemed it appropriate. Also at Basel was the key figure Pierre l'Hermite, who had corresponded with the likes of archbishop Jacques Gelu to obtain outside opinions on Joan virtually from the point of her arrival.

It is, then, with a sense of regret and unfulfillment that we read Martin's passage on Joan. Daring and not without interest, it is ultimately unsatisfying. He is the final spokesman for Joan, writing without direct knowledge of the testimonies of the condemnation and nullification trials – the first a document he clearly never read, and the second not yet composed in 1442. Given the multiple ways in which discourse on Joan will change with the advent of the two trials, we now arrive at the end of the theological debate.

Conclusions

Based on the narrative of the preceding chapters, it is now appropriate to ask what changes occur in our understanding of Joan of Arc when she is approached, not biographically, but, as her contemporaries apparently viewed her, as an object of theological debate. The phenomenon referred to here as "the early debate," began with Joan's personal assertion that she was "sent from God" and her demand to be believed. There is, then, a sense of undeniable authenticity in the witnesses we have examined, who, without necessarily shunning the biographical facts, decide to consider only the case for Joan's divine mission. Such an analysis of Joan, as we have seen, when performed by theologians, involves a formal procedure known as *discretio spirituum*, a tool used in canonization trials or applied in the evaluation of any self-proclaimed prophet. Knowing, through the evidence of the *Poitiers Conclusions*, that Joan's assessors thoroughly understood the formal requirements of the procedure, we no longer need to hesitate in identifying the Maid's approbation as religious. It was not military, not secular, and, above all, not haphazard.

In the later Middle Ages, refinement of this procedure had grown out of the perception, by many, of a growing tide of false prophets. The calendar of entire phases of the councils of Constance (1415 – 1418) and the Basel (1431 – 1449) was devoted to the question. At Constance, when the dust settled, the Czech reformer John Huss and his disciple Jerome of Prague had been burned alive as heretics. Through Gerson's treatise *De probatione* and other means, the council of Constance also addressed, by reopening the case of St. Bridget, the question of female prophets. The difficulty – despite a growing number of texts defining procedure – of making secure pronouncements can be gauged by the reappearance on the docket at Basel of the Hussites, whose zeal had not lessened with the loss of their leader, and of St. Bridget. Although Bridget's cause found a second defender (after Alphonso of Jaén) at Basel in John of Torquemada,[1] it is clear that the independent inspiration of Bridget continued to provoke theologians, drawing them, as if by a magnet, to her case. Since the purpose of conducting a discernment investigation at Poitiers was to test Joan as a prophet, a focus often lost sight of during both the condemnation and nullification trials, we might do well to frame Joan's case in the broader context of the councils, situating it in a period marked by the councils of Constance and Basel.

Through the series of works under discussion, we have seen how gradual

---

[1] Vandenbroucke, "Discernement," *Dictionnaire* 1: col. 1946.

was the process of belief in the Maid. As if in answer to those who feel that Charles's party seized upon Joan immediately for political benefit, we have been reminded not only by Gelu, who warned the dauphin not to make himself ridiculous in the eyes of foreign nations (considering the reputation of the French for the ease with which they let themselves be duped), but by the author of DMV and the chroniclers who described Joan's arrival at the court, that at the outset no one knew whether endorsing Joan or sending her away was a beneficial political action. From the early handling of Joan's case in Gelu's correspondence to the king and in DQP, we notice the utter openness of both theologians to the dark side of Joan's case. In fact from French sources we can learn most of the serious charges against her, whether it be from Seguin Seguin who stated at Poitiers that no one could recommend belief in Joan on her mere say-so, or the declaration in DQP that the Maid wore male clothes in violation of Deuteronomy 22:5.

By the time the *Poitiers Conclusions* were written, we see Charles's theologians beginning to protect their investment in Joan, at least by eliminating any mention of the negative arguments that led up to the consensus expressed in the document. They also ostensibly exceed their own authority by allowing her to proceed to Orléans without first producing a miracle. It seems inaccurate, however, to draw from these considerations the view that the doctors did not genuinely agonize over their decision, or that anything but the Orléans miracle would have kept Joan's career secure.

Already in DQP we found the religious narrative that would assimilate Joan taking shape. There the image of the Old Testament shepherd or shepherdess endorsed the humble as victors in God's wars and explained the source of their strength through the topos *infirma confundat fortia*. Furthermore, invoking Deborah, Esther, and Judith provided a precedent for women who obtained salvation for the people of God. Regarding the reference to France's necessity in the *Poitiers Conclusions*, it has been argued here that the term is not exclusively political, but that it has a religious dimension which makes divine intervention possible. In Gelu's *Dissertatio*, he elaborates on this theme, insisting that the desolation of France is meant for its correction, not its annihilation.

The *Lettre aux Anglais* and the prophecies about the Maid constitute a more self-conscious effort to solve difficulties in the French narrative. In the face of the disinheritance of Charles, it is apparent that the *Lettre* tries to make light of English claims in France by challenging the titles of the principal players. It addresses the issue of violence through the act of issuing the summons itself, and justifies defeating other Christians as a necessary prelude to the future exaltation of the faith by the French. As for the prophecies, the *puella* in the supposedly ancient Merlin prophecy helps to reduce the sense of novelty of a girl on the battlefield, and the EVA / AVE prophecy counteracts the sin of Isabeau de Bavière by the purity of a redeeming virgin.

There is compelling evidence that in order to include the treatise DMV in the debate examined here, we must shift the focus away from a royal setting to some other geographical location. The indicators which suggest Paris as the hub from which DMV reached its satellite locations include the early manuscript connection of DMV to the abbey of St. Victor; the ease with which the *Morosini* chronicle correspondent Justiniani, who credits Paris sources with a substantial part of his information, obtained DMV in Bruges; the accessibility of the tract to the Parisian cleric who refuted it, and Guillaume Bouillé's ability to uncover DMV in a search conducted in Paris, among other places, for documents pertinent to Joan. DMV, however, is noticeably absent from Christine's sources, which are the most complete of any author taken into account in these pages, despite her proximity to Paris. Since Justiniani mentions DMV only in a letter of 20 November 1429, based on information received "yesterday" from Paris, it is possible that Christine's *Ditié*, the last of the documents in the early phase of the debate, was simply written before DMV was composed.

Even if we impute DMV's divergences from the remarkably consistent core of other debate documents to a later date of composition, this alone cannot account for the skewed treatment of familiar themes. Limiting ourselves to two examples, we can point to the author's purely secular representation of France's just cause, or his serious lapse in never specifically mentioning that theologians (not just the "king's council and the men at arms") had been led to believe in the Maid or had conducted the investigations of her. Although it is certain, from the testimony of the Italian Justiniani, from the rubricator of the *Reply of the Parisian cleric* manuscript, from the appended verses to the Joan passage in the *Champion des dames*, and from the evidence of Guillaume Bouillé, that DMV circulated as Gerson's work, it must be emphasized that neither the *Collectarium*, the *Reply*, nor the body of the text of the *Champion*, names Gerson as the author of DMV. While DQP may not be a treatise by Gerson on the Maid, the weight of the evidence points away from ascribing DMV to Gerson, unless, viewed as a compilation, certain fragments, as yet unidentifiable, can be attributed to him. On balance, DMV appears to be a successful piece of pro-French propaganda, which even theologians who had better sources, such as the author of the *Collectarium*, were willing to trust, but it is unclear how we can account for this or other riddles that originate with DMV.

It would be a vast undertaking to compare the theological investigation in the early debate with that of the theological investigations embarked upon at Rouen, those of the condemnation and nullification trials. Nevertheless, certain observations immediately stand out, much more for the trial of 1431 than that of 1456. The eyewitness accounts of the second trial, transcribed roughly a quarter of a century after the events, while sometimes valuable, are often formulaic in nature or excessively hagiographic. Only recently have the extra-judicial treatises, the more logical counterpart to the texts of the early debate, begun to spark interest.

The condemnation trial is a different story. Just as the technical deficiencies of the Rouen trial of 1431 can be identified by a legalistic approach, so can the practice of *discretio spirituum* at Rouen be judged by comparison with the treatises of the early debate. Conversely, we can see where the French argument was solid or weak, and whether Joan's Anglo-Burgundian assessors recognized the weaknesses and knew to exploit them. On the matter of Joan's male dress, the French appear to have been on quite solid ground. Thus the judges at Rouen shifted to new details such as her receiving communion in men's clothes, her alleged love of rich clothing, her declaration that she donned male dress specifically at God's request, or her resumption of male attire in prison in order to make their case. Regarding Joan's aversion to negotiating peace with the English, her judges held a trump card which they hardly exploited. Her only answer, when accused of dissuading Charles from negotiating any peace treaty with his enemies (article 18), was to refer to overtures of peace made to the duke of Burgundy, and to insist that peace with the English would only result from their return to England. In article 57 of the original seventy accusations, the English identified a potent charge against Joan, which Gelu's *Dissertatio*, the *Ditié* of Christine, and particularly DMV, with its acknowledgment that "a first miracle does not always produce all the effect men expect of it," tried to address. It is the allegation that "she made many promises and uttered many prophecies . . . which in no way came true."[2] Neither article 18 nor article 57, however, survives in the definitive twelve articles against Joan.

Sometimes it was enough for Joan's judges to trap her by exploiting her ignorance of *discretio spirituum*. Thus they accused her of presuming to "know the future" and of "discovering things secret or hidden," claiming that this was an "attribute of God."[3] They did not acknowledge that this was also the means by which humans demonstrated the gift of God. We saw earlier how these same assessors induced Joan to say that she would "certainly know" if it were St. Michael or a counterfeit in his likeness who appeared before her. She had no counsel to inform her that the significance of 2 Corinthians 11:14 ("For satan himself transformeth himself into an angel of light") is to underscore the element of doubt inherent in such discernments.

Nowhere, perhaps, is Joan's need for theological advice at Rouen more pronounced than on the question of her role as divine envoy and the nature of her heavenly counsel. Throughout our discussion of the early debate, we have not once come upon a reference to St. Michael, St. Catherine, or St.

---

[2] Barrett, *Trial*, p. 220; Quicherat, *Procès* 1: 298.
[3] Barrett, *Trial*, p. 184; Quicherat, *Procès* 1: 251.

Margaret as the "voices" delivering the expression of divine will to Joan. The single exception to this is DMV, ever running counter to the French mainstream, which alludes momentarily to "Saint Catherine converting the philosophers," a remark suggesting a post-Poitiers connection between St. Catherine and Joan, and in which no effort is made to identify her as one of Joan's saints. It is dangerous to contradict Joan herself, who contended at Rouen that whatever her judges wished to know about her relationship with Saints Catherine and Margaret was in the Book of Poitiers, but everywhere we look in the early debate we find virtual unanimity that Joan declared inspiration, without intermediaries, directly from God, the highest category of inspiration. Maybe we can reconcile this discrepancy through a chance statement in the Rouen trial record (article 10 of the seventy articles), in which it is stated that Joan informed Robert de Baudricourt "according to the command of St. Michael and of St. Catherine and St. Margaret" of "revelations made to her by God."[4] Thus celestial orders emanated from God, but Saints Michael, Catherine, and Margaret provided only minor quotidian counsel.

If this is the case, Joan's French coaches, counselors, and mentors very carefully kept the saints hidden from view, and rightly so. For at Rouen, the assessors exulted in what they had found when Joan began to speak of the corporeality of her saints, whom she claimed to see with her bodily eyes, and of their smell, their touch, and the language they spoke. This was a slippery slope, unidentified by Joan as such, which led her into an entirely different realm of culpability. Indeed, one-fourth of the definitive articles of accusation (articles 1, 2, and 11) converge on this question.

Quite apart from the dire consequences that speaking of her saints eventually resulted in for Joan at Rouen, if we return to the period of the early debate, it is evident that confining herself to the pure and unadorned declaration, heard so many times in the French texts, that she was "sent by God," held its own considerable power. There is evidence everywhere that this statement left people from theologians to common parishioners in a quandary, and that the urge to "pronounce," whether in favor of belief or against, was inherent in the way that contemporaries experienced Joan of Arc. How ardently invested in this question even foreigners could be is demonstrated in one assessment, conscientious to the point of being comical, from the Italian Cosma Raimondi de Cremone, who wrapped up his judgment in the following terms:

> What I see as possible, even though it be very extraordinary and unheard of, by the fact that it is possible, even if I do not believe it completely, I do not think, for all of that, that it is to be entirely rejected.[5]

[4] Barrett, *Trial*, p. 157; Quicherat, *Procès* 1: 216.
[5] Mercati, "Una lettera," p. 308.

Even well into the sixteenth century, we can still find an occasional isolated pronouncement on Joan's divine mission, the last vestiges of the discernment debate. Thus we find the outraged French chronicler Etienne Pasquier condemning those who judged the Maid to be "feigning that she was sent from God," asserting about the calumniators:

> Not only do I not pardon them, but, on the contrary, they seem to me to be worthy of an exemplary punishment for being worse than the English. . . . For my part, I judge her story a true miracle of God.[6]

More emphatic still is Guillaume Postel, author of a collection of illustrious female biographies, who proclaims:

> Whoever does not believe in Joan of Arc deserves to be exterminated as a destroyer of the fatherland [*la Patrie*] . . . her deeds are a thing as necessary to maintain as Scripture.[7]

There seems to be a serious possibility that Joan brought substantial harm to her own case in front of the Rouen judges by talking in human terms about her saints and herself – embracing, bowing, speaking French, and climbing the steps to the castle – in short, all the actions performed by mere mortals. The supporters from her own side knew her only as a maiden "sent by God," and there is good reason to believe that had she held firmly to this attitude at Rouen, she would have fared better against her judges. Under the constant pressure of the trial, and because Joan did not know what the prelates wanted from her when they posed their questions, it appears that, by any fair estimate, Joan sometimes changed her tune when she provided them with answers. However, in one instance, related in article 25, we catch a glimpse of the Joan of the early debate, that enigmatic entity, not from Domrémy, but "from God," who had created such an upheaval. Taken from the Rouen trial, the statement nevertheless captures the mood of the maid who arrived at Chinon, impatient with procedure, clear in her goals, and owing first allegiance to someone other than they. "On Saturday, February 24th," reads the Latin record, "she said she came from God and had no business here, in this trial, and asked to be sent back to God from Whom she came."[8]

---

[6] Etienne Pasquier, *Les recherches de la France, revues et augmentées de quatre livres* in *Oeuvres choisies d'Etienne Pasquier*, Léon Feugère, ed., 2 vols. (Paris, 1849) 1: 176.
[7] Cited by Lanéry d'Arc, *Livre d'Or*, p. 64.
[8] Barrett, *Trial*, pp. 177–78; Quicherat, *Procès* 1: 243: "Sabbati, XXIIII. februarii, confessa fuit, quod venerat ex parte Dei, et quod in judicio in quo erat coram nobis, non habebat quid agere aut negotiari; et quod remitteretur ad Deum a quo venerat."

Appendix I

De quadam puella[1]

(CONCERNING A CERTAIN YOUNG GIRL)

A medley-like work concerning a certain young girl, who formerly rode in France, published by Master Jean Gerson.

To the glory of the blessed Trinity and ever glorious Virgin Mother of God and also to that of all the celestial Curia.

I was carried away by the Lord when I was following my flock and he said to me: "Go prophesy to my people Israel," Amos VII – "People of Israel," the people of the Kingdom of France can, without impropriety, be so called. We know it has always blossomed, thanks to the faith in God and to the observance of Christian religion.

So, there came to see the Dauphin of this Kingdom a very young person, the daughter of a shepherd who, it is reported, had herself looked after the flocks. She affirmed that she had been sent by God so that, through her own intermediary, the said kingdom should be brought to obey her. In order that her claim should not be considered adventurous, she, moreover, makes use of supernatural signs, such as revealing secret thoughts and foreseeing what is about to occur. It is also reported that she had her head shaved like a man and that, when she wants to leave for war, she dresses in men's clothes, takes men's weapons, then gets on horseback; and on horseback and carrying her standard, at once she becomes marvelously active; as if she were an experienced troop chief, she draws up her army, and (finally it is reported) that her relatives too are filled with ardor. On the opposite side, her adversaries, filled with fear, are as if they had lost their strength. But having climbed down from her horse and recovered her usual feminine manners, she becomes extremely naive, inexperienced in secular matters, like a defenseless lamb.

It is reported that she lives in chastity, sobriety and continence; since she is devoted to God, she prohibits murder, plundering and forbids any other violence [inflicted] upon all those [women] who want to give proof of the obedience she has demanded.

On account of such facts and others which are similar, states, fortified places and castles submit to the Dauphin, pledging themselves to remain faithful.

[1] Quicherat, *Procès* 3: 411–21. The English translation is that of Francq, "Gerson," pp. 74–80.

199

With these given facts, a few questions come to one's lips, prompting learned minds to formulate them. For instance, should one go to the extent of believing that she is a true young girl of human nature, or could she be the transmutation of an effigy of the same ghostly appearance?

Second question: Should it really be believed that her actions could be, on the human plane, accomplished by herself, or else, through her, by some superior cause?

Third question: If it is through a superior cause, could it be really through the intermediary of a good one, that is to say of a good spirit, or through the intermediary of a bad cause, [and] as it is thought, of an evil spirit?

Fourth question: Should one really have faith in her words, approve her actions as if their origin were divine, or should one consider them as fabricated and misrepresented?

Because in fact, on such minor questions or similar ones, people have different opinions as to the extent to which the two parties are capable of drawing evidence from the Holy Scriptures for the defense of their views, the present opus, well balanced, offers certain suggestions in favor of one viewpoint only, not in affirming but, so as to put them in order, in dictating.

Then, it offers certain suggestions which are in favor of the other debated opinion, inviting the finest minds to reason more deeply. However, in writing from sheer memory, such elements which must permit the formulation with assurance of a judgment on such a subject, what is needed is the preliminary and clear knowledge of the mores of this young girl, of her words, her feats and acts, those which characterize her as a private person, and those which characterize her when she is with other people, in public, as well as the rest of the circumstances of her life; further, whether, incidentally, the revelations she makes and even her predictions could always be found to be true. But for what follows, principles must be admitted at once after the report which trustworthy persons have left for the formation of the present deliberate stands:

First "propositio"

It must be simply affirmed that such a person is really a young girl, of a truly human nature.

This proposition is patent, because there is no rule adhered to by the philosophers which does not proclaim that action proves existence, but there is better still: Our Savior too gives evidence that it is proper to draw from accomplishments the idea that a person exists. Therefore, since the present young person constantly conforms with other men in human acts: to speak, be hungry, eat, drink, sit up, sleep and other actions of this kind, who would dare say that the young girl in question is not a veritable individual of human nature as much as others, her companions, amidst quite similar signs revealing human nature? (*Igitur,* etc. . . .)

Second "propositio"

The normal period of the Prophecy is that before the coming of Christ and continues in the course of the beginning of the dawning Church, with the accomplishment of miracles.

This proposition is formulated by the theologians in accordance with the fact that the epoch of the Old Testament was, in its entirety, symbolic in announcing the coming of Christ and the future condition of His Mystic Body.

In an analogous way, in the Primitive Church, there were many Prophets and, because predictions which go beyond any understanding of human faculty were then made, it was indispensable to add signs to them by means of miraculous achievements in order to confirm these sayings. Otherwise, the salvation of mankind could not have been sufficiently provided for. As a consequence, Gregorius notices that a plant recently transplanted needs more water afterwards so that it recovers when it has taken root. (*Igitur*, etc. . . .)

Third "propositio"

It is not considered a disgrace in the passage of time that from time to time certain persons are granted the Spirit of prophecy and directed towards the execution of miracles. Such a proposition is by Augustine in the *City of God*, and can be drawn again from Gregorius' teaching. And the affirmation of this point is still evident by the fact that with His lips the Savior promised us to be in Person with us up to the end of time, leading mankind by the hand of his Providence in accordance with what is opportune for our salvation.

Thus in the same way, in effect, as He did not attach His Might to sacraments, so He did not attach it either at any time to places or individuals. Even, in his boundless commiseration, He rather stands always at man's side, providing us with efficient remedies and succor.

"The hand of the Lord has not been shortened in effect," says Isaiah, "so that it could not redeem."[2] (*Igitur*, etc. . . .)

Consequently, when through the revelation of what is concealed, and by the performance of miracles, human nature needs to be awakened and made aware, sometimes in one people, sometimes in another, [that] one must believe with piety that such advantages are not denied to us. (*Igitur*, etc. . . .)

Fourth "propositio"

It is in harmony with the Holy Scriptures that God made use of the weak sex and of the age of innocence to offer peoples and kingdoms the happiness of salvation.

Such a proposition is evident because, according to the Apostle's testimony, God chose what was weak in the world to confound all that which was strong. From there, proceeding with examples, one can read about Deborah, Hester, and Judith, how they obtained salvation for the people of

---

[2] Isaiah 59:1: "Behold, the hand of the Lord is not shortened that it cannot save, neither is his ear heavy that it cannot hear."

God. Daniel too, in his boyhood, was called to liberate Susan. Similarly, David, in his youth, felled Goliath.

And this does not take place without purpose because, in such a way, the gift of Faith in God becomes more apparent, in order that man claim not his own strength, when he should rather render to God actions of grace. For it is thus, through a humble Virgin, that Redemption of the whole of mankind was born. (*Igitur*, etc. . . .)

Fifth "propositio"

In speaking of the aforementioned young girl, it is not part of the Holy Scriptures that God sent men leading a bad life under such an appearance or nature as is evidenced by fame.

The evidence of such a proposition surprises because, as the Apostle says, there is no accord between Christ and Belial, and He has not felt He should enter demons' society or engage Himself with them, as with their servants or tenants. Although the Apostle says that certain bad men have sometimes prophesied, in passing, as for instance Balaam prophesied that Jacob would make a star rise, and as Saul and Caiaphas likewise prophesied. But it is quite different with the present young girl who possesses, at her discretion, the power of supernatural gifts to manifest what is concealed and to predict the future, to prohibit what is unfavorable to the service she provides and, in addition to that, to forbid, as has already been said, murders with their sequel of sins.

On the contrary, she encourages people to acts of virtue and to other achievements of honesty in which God is glorified. In the same way as Joseph, being possessed by the Spirit of God, was sent first into Egypt, before his father and brothers, and Moses with the view of liberating the people of Israel, and Gideon and the women who were named hereabove – likewise the present very young person, whom it is not inopportune to count among the good people especially sent by God, the more so since she is not in quest of presents and since she works with fervor to establish this good: Peace.

That is not, in effect, the work of the Spirit of evil, which is an agent of discord rather than of peace.

Sixth "propositio"

So to speak, this proposition, as an addition, follows from the foregoing ones.

Such a girl, a true individual among mankind, was sent on purpose by God for works which are accomplished not by human but by divine means, and one must grant her credit for it. The evidence accompanies the present proposition which corresponds to questions previously dealt with.

Whether she is, in effect, a real human being, is evident according to the first proposition. Besides, because God, even nowadays, has not ceased to make use, in our favor [and] on purpose, of supernatural signs, it is not abnormal for God to take an innocent girl. It is, especially, a consequence of the fourth proposition.

And because the gift that you know of dwells in herself permanently for a godly end, and thanks to Virtue and Honor as the fifth proposition claims, it seems, by way of consequence, that the present proposition will have to agree.

Then, one should not be surprised that, as a rider, she is more enlightened by a second light than in her usual feminine condition because even David, when he wanted to consult the Lord, would wear the ephod, and used to take his psalterio. Moses too, as long as he carried his rod, accomplished miracles. Because, as Gregorius says, "The Holy Spirit settles inwardly according to conditions found externally."

Thus, from what has been revealed formerly, there is a possibility for anyone who is a partisan of the present issue to take the opportunity to defend her cause by progressing even farther towards more important developments.

But because there are other people who feel more inclined to take side with the opposite party, it remains to bring forward certain testimonies drawn from the Holy Scripture on which they may lean for their point of view in examining the propositions hereunder written.

First "propositio"

Many pseudo prophets about to come will claim that they are sent by God, that their origin is divine.

Here is a proposition which is from the Lord when He says that "in the very last days which belong to the law of the Gospel, many will come who will say they come in my name, and many through their intervention will be deceived." From there too, the Apostle declares that the Angel of Satan takes the appearance of an Angel of Light. And, very surely, one must not be surprised. That one, who reigns by wickedness on all the sons of Pride, endeavors without respite to reach the perfection of the Divinity.

And to this end, he takes care of the false prophets who, in the Lord's name, have been sent to deceive. (*Igitur*, etc. . . . .)

Second "propositio"

Usually, pseudo prophets reveal secret thoughts as well as the issue of events which are part of the immediate future.

Here is a proposition which, usually, is granted by the doctors. The reason given for this is that the higher its value, the more it aims at greater enterprises. On the other hand, we know that the intelligence of Demons is much greater than human intelligence and thus what is hidden from us, even future events unknown to us, are known to the Evil spirit.

Third "propositio"

Judging from external appearances and signs, the distinction is not easy to make between a true and a false prophet.

Here is an evident proposition because it is not necessary that a prophet lead a virtuous life or that he be in a state of grace.

It is also in the power of demoniac prophets to reveal what is hidden from us, like the future, and in this way, as on many other points, they act like the true prophets. Whenever from time to time they happen to make false announcements, they are able to remedy this by giving a second interpretation, or by giving themselves, as an excuse, the fact that the real prophets have from time to time prophesied a few events which did not occur. To be precise, one can read something of this nature about the prophets Isaiah and Jonah. It is because of this fact that even the Apostle says that one should not trust any Spirit. But one should test them since those spirits come from God,[3] [the Apostle] suggesting that it is difficult to make a distinction between the good and the wicked prophets. (*Igitur*, etc. . . .)

Fourth "propositio"

At the present time which is the epoch of Grace, the fact that God proceeds in making a particular grant tending to the good cause of temporal happiness, does not have the appearance of reality.

The present proposition can be drawn from considerations which Augustine recalls frequently. For the goods of the present existence are granted in an equal proportion to the good and to the wicked, to the just and to the unjust, principally at the present epoch of Grace – so that the good do not tie their love to passing possessions which the wicked very much care for; [and] even, so that they direct their attention to those possessions that [the Lord] keeps for His friends in the future life, whereas, in the present life, He provides in abundance temporal goods to His enemies.

Therefore, the creation of a mission, which tends to provide happiness in the present time and which tends likewise to foreshadow what contempt the Scriptures teach, seems to have little chance to come about. Yet, in the Old Testament, as long as the celebrated people were the servants of God, they had in exchange such temporal goods. And one can read that from time to time a mention of such a kind is made. (*Igitur*, etc. . . .)

Fifth "propositio"

The present young girl commits two actions whose interdiction is found in the Holy Scriptures.

Here is an evident proposition because the law of Deuteronomy XXII forbids a woman to wear men's clothes. Besides, the Apostle forbids a woman to shave her head as a man does.

However, infringements of the two interdictions at the same time are underscored in what is told about the young girl. And, in the conclusion that is drawn at once, in the case of very young people, the fact that the young girl is on horseback, dressed in men's clothes, suggests indecency, and, while God cherishes the measure, people judge that she fails her divine mission when stripping the woman she is to appear as a man. Neither do they find that such behavior agrees with a confidential mission, because such

---

[3] As Francq points out, the quotation from St. John suggests that the translation should be worded: "But one should try to find out whether these spirits come from God."

a confidential mission occurs through the spirit which, internally, sanctifies the soul. Attention: later comes the famous saying of Wisdom VII: "The Wisdom of God passes into holy souls; it has made the friends of God and the Prophets." And, supposing the mission of our young person is prophetic, this is really why the person in question should be of an uncommon saintliness and should have a divine soul. Whereas, given the sex and personality, it is judged that the transformation into a secular man-at-war is indecent. On the other hand, nothing of the kind is found about Hester or Judith; they may have adorned themselves with particular care, but nevertheless feminine, to please those people more for whose attention they had played their part. (*Igitur*, etc. . . .)

Sixth "propositio"

Whether the said young girl has been sent on purpose by God, and whether God is acting through her as an intermediary, implying that she should be trusted, cannot be shown with satisfactory evidence.

Well, here is a proposition which is evident: it comes, so to speak, as a gift, in addition to what has been said at first, because, should many false prophets show up, they will be similar to the real ones.

And pay attention whether, for the progress of temporal happiness, no purposeful mission is made under the reign of Grace.

Take good care! Since her arrival occurs contrary to divine orders, how could it be affirmed or held that a girl of such a kind was chosen especially by God to pursue those achievements which fame brings about?

After these remarks, one can see how the partisans of this present direction could give some color to their pleas by attacking the channel open in an opposite direction. And moreover, to discover what lies beneath, they might, starting from preceding propositions, find in this an opportunity.

Also, the present reflections (after having drawn from them, here and there, to put them together, and having placed them according to a method that gathers the whole) are presented to those people who will look at them so that (in this case as in another altogether similar) they will be capable of making an answer by themselves to those who would ask questions similar to these.

For ever to the glory of God, who reigns for centuries, [and] who is blessed. Amen.

[Here] ends the compilation of arguments [*opusculus collativium*] about the young girl who formerly rode armed in France.

Appendix II

The Poitiers Conclusions[1]

This is the opinion of the doctors requested by the king regarding the case of the Maid sent by God.

The king, given his necessity and that of his kingdom, and considering the continuous prayers of his poor people to God and to all others who love peace and justice, ought not to turn away [*deboutter*] nor reject the Maid who says she is sent by God [*envoyée de par Dieu*] for his succor, even though her promises consist only of human works; nor should he believe in her immediately [*tantôt*] or lightly [*légièrement*]. But following Holy Writ, he must test her [*la doit esprovier*] in two ways: that is, by human means, inquiring about her life, behavior [*meurs*], and her intentions, as the apostle Saint Paul states: *probate spiritus, si ex Deo sunt*; and by devout prayer, requiring the sign either of divine works or hope from heaven [*d'aucune euvre ou spérance divine*] through which to judge whether she has come by the will of God. Thus God commanded Ahaz to ask for a sign, when God promised him victory, telling him: *pete signum a Domino*; and the same with Gideon, who requested a sign, and several others, etc.

The king, since the coming of the said Maid, has observed and [investigated her?] in the two ways, that is, by human prudence and asking for a sign from God. As to the first manner, which is by human prudence, he has caused the said Maid to be tested [*esprouver*] as to her life, birth, moral comportment [*meurs*], and her purpose [*entention*], keeping her with him for the space of six weeks, presenting her to all manner of people, be they clerics, churchmen, pious people, men-at-arms, women, widows, or others. She has conversed with everyone publicly and privately. But in her is found no evil, only goodness, humility, virginity, piety [*dévotion*], honesty, and simplicity; and of her birth and life marvelous things are related as true [*plusieurs choses merveilleuses sont dites comme vrayes*].

As to the second manner of testing [*probacion*], the king has requested a sign from her to which she replies that before the city of Orléans she will show it, and nowhere else: for so it is commanded her by God [*de par Dieu*].

The king, given the investigation conducted [*probacion faicte*] of the said Maid, as far as he is able [*en tant que luy est possible*], and that no evil is found in her, and considering her reply, which is to give a divine sign at Orléans; seeing her constancy and perseverance in her purpose, and her

[1] I have followed the text in Ayroles, *La vraie Jeanne d'Arc* 1: 685–86. It can also be found in Quicherat, *Procès* 3: 391–92.

insistent requests to go to Orléans to show there the sign of divine aid, must not prevent her from going to Orléans with her men-at-arms, but must have her led there in good faith [*honnestement*], placing hoping in God. For doubting her or dismissing [*delaissier*] her without appearance of evil, would be to repel [*repugner*] the Holy Spirit, and render one unworthy of the aid of God, as Gamaliel stated in a council of Jews regarding the apostles.

Appendix III

Lettre aux Anglais

JHESUS MARIA

King of England, and you duke of Bedford, who call yourself regent of the kingdom of France; you, William Pole, count of Suffolk; John Lord Talbot, and you, Thomas Lord Scales, who call yourselves lieutenants of the said duke of Bedford, make satisfaction to the King of Heaven; surrender to the Maid who is sent here by God, the King of Heaven, the keys of all the good towns which you have taken and violated in France. She is come here by God's will to reclaim the blood royal. She is very ready to make peace, if you are willing to grant her satisfaction by abandoning France and paying for what you have held. And you, archers, men-at-war, gentlemen and others, who are before the town of Orléans, go away into your own country, in God's name. And if you do not do so, expect tidings [*attendez les nouvelles*] from the Maid, who will come to see you shortly, to your very great harm. King of England, if you do not do so, I am chieftain of war [*chef de guerre*], and in whatever place I meet your people in France, I shall make them leave, whether they will it or not [*vueillent ou non veuillent*]. And if they will not obey, I will have them all put to death. I am sent here by God, the King of Heaven, body for body, to drive you out of all France. And if they wish to obey, I will show them mercy. And be not of another opinion, for you will not hold the kingdom of France from God, the King of Heaven, son of Saint Mary; for the king Charles, the true heir [*vray héritier*], will hold it, as is revealed to him by the Maid, [and] he will enter Paris with a good company. If you do not believe these tidings from God and the Maid, in whatever place we find you, we shall strike therein and make so great a *hahay* [tumult] that none so great has been in France for a thousand years, if you do not yield to right. Know well that the King of Heaven will send greater strength to the Maid and her good men-at-arms than you in all your assaults can overwhelm; and, by the blows [*aux horions*] it will be seen who has greater favor [*meilleur droit*] with the God of Heaven. You, duke of Bedford, the Maid prays and requests that you not bring destruction on yourself. If you will grant her right, you may still join her company, where the French will do the fairest deed ever done for Christianity. Answer if you wish to make peace in the town of Orléans; and if you do not, you will be reminded shortly to your very great harm. Written this Tuesday of Holy Week. [22 March 1429]

Appendix IV

De mirabili victoria[1]

In conformity with these premises, and the circumstances being considered with their good result, in particular the object of so just an enterprise as the restoration of the king in his kingdom and the very just expulsion and defeat of his so obstinate enemies: it is pious, salutary, of true and devout belief to approve the Maid's case.

Furthermore, let us add that in her practices, this Maid does not appear to resort to spells forbidden by the Church, nor to disapproved superstitions, nor to frauds of cunning people. Neither is she trying to secure her own interest, since she exposes her body to supreme peril, in evidence of her mission.

Finally, in regard to the numerous rumors spread by the malevolence and hatred of so many talkative, light-minded or malicious people, it will suffice to answer with this line by Cato:

We do not have to judge what everyone says.

But we have to judge what is believed and professed, while remaining, within the limits of discretion, reserved and detached from tumultuous discussions, for, as the Apostle said: *A servant of the Lord should not contest;*[2] *We have no such custom,* that is to contest. Therefore these opinions should be tolerated, or one should seek the decision of Superiors, as has been done for former canonisations of saints of which, strictly speaking, many are not so by necessity of faith but of pious belief, and which however cannot be blamed, despised or rejected lightly by anyone. In effect, everything being equal, one must repudiate them still less than a cult propagated without canonization.

In favor of our cause be the following circumstances added:

1 The king's council and the men at arms have been led to believe in the word of the Maid and to obey her in such a way that, under her command and with one same heart, they exposed themselves to the dangers of war, ignoring all fear of dishonor. What a shame, indeed, if fighting under the leadership of a young woman, they had been vanquished by such audacious enemies! What a derision on behalf of all those who would have heard about such an event!

2 The people are thrilled with delight, a pious and deep persuasion has

---

[1] The original Latin text can be found in Quicherat, *Procès* 3: 298–306. The English translation is that of Francq, "Gerson," pp. 61–64.

[2] 2 Timothy. 2:24.

filled them; they are transported in the praise of God to the enemies' confusion.

3 These enemies, it is assured, even their chiefs, hide, overtaken by a thousand fears. They feel languorous and failing as a woman giving birth. This is the accomplishment of the invocation contained in the hymn to Mary, sister of Moses, when in the midst of the dance, rhythmed by the sound of the tambourins, she exclaimed: "Cantemus Domino gloriose enim magnificatus est,"[3] adding "Irruat super eos formido et pavor."[4] This hymn should be reread and sung again with a devotion suitable to the present event.

4 Finally, let us examine this last consideration. The Maid and the men at arms, her followers, do not neglect the means of human prudence: they act according to what they feel; one cannot see that they are tempting God more than is reasonable. It is evident that the Maid is not obstinate in her own sentiments and that she does not go beyond the orders and inspirations she is convinced she received from God. Still, many circumstances of her life, since her early childhood, could be presented. They were submitted to research and thorough investigations which have been carried on by numerous investigators. No mention of them will be made here.

Similar facts could be reported: those of Deborah, Saint Katherine converting the philosophers no less miraculously; and many others also, such as the examples of Judith, of Judas Maccabaeus. Included in all these cases, there is constantly an aspect of natural order.

A first miracle does not always produce all the effect men expect of it. So, even though the Maid's waiting and ours were frustrated, and may God forbid, one should not conclude that what has been accomplished is the evil spirit's doing and is not God's achievement.

Our ingratitude, our blasphemes, other reasons could attract the divine anger, and, through a secret but just judgment of God, make it so that we would be frustrated in our hopes. May God turn away from us his anger and make everything turn out well!

The Maid's four official warnings of civil and religious order should be added.

The first concerns the king and princes of the blood; the second, the militia of the king and the kingdom; the third concerns the ecclesiastics and the people; the fourth, the Maid herself. These documents tend to the same end: to bring one to live in righteousness, in pity toward God, in justice toward other people, in sobriety which is in virtue and temperance toward oneself.

The fourth notice, in particular, demands that God's grace, manifested in the Maid, be neither for her nor for other people a subject of vain curiosity,

---

[3] Let us sing to God, for He has made His glory shine magnificently.
[4] May terror and distress fall on them.

of social profits, hatred of parties, seditious quarrels, vengeance for the past, inept bragging. God's grace must, on the contrary, be received in a spirit of compassion, of supplications and actions of grace. May everyone bring generously to such an enterprise the contribution of his possessions, so that peace come back to his home and so that, through God's favor, all of us "being delivered from the power of our enemies, we may serve Him every day of our lives with sanctity and justice worthy of His regard . . ."[5] *A Domino factum est istud.*

Following are three principles to justify the wearing of man's clothes by the Maid elected as she was while following her sheep.

First principle: The prohibition of the ancient law against the wearing of man's clothes by woman and against the wearing of woman's clothes by man, insofar as it is a Law which is still in force, does not carry any obligation under the new Law, for it is a constant truth and it is by necessity of salvation that judicial precepts of the ancient Law are abrogated and, as such, do not make it an obligation in the new one, unless the Superiors have again instituted and confirmed them.

Second principle: The Law in question included a moral aspect which must remain in any legislation. It can be defined thus: it is prohibited to man as to woman to wear indecent clothes which do not comply with conditions required to keep one's virtue, which command us to weigh all circumstances and to consider what time, necessity, purpose, manner and other similar conditions demand, which are taken into account in the judgment of the wise. It would be out of purpose to stop here at these peculiarities.

Third principle: This Law, neither insofar as it is judicial, nor insofar as it is moral, condemns the wearing of manly and warriorlike clothes by the Maid who is a warrior and acts in manly manner, while unquestionable signs prove that she has been chosen by the King of Heaven as His standard-bearer in the eyes of everyone to crush the enemies of justice and to revive its defenders; to overthrow by the hand of a woman, a young girl, a virgin the powerful weapons of iniquity; this Maid, finally surrounded by helpful angels with whom her virginity forms a link of friendship and relationship, as Saint Jerome says and as it is frequently seen in the history of saints – Cecile's for instance – where they appear with crowns of lilies and roses.

In that, too, the Maid is justified in having had her hair cut, despite the prohibition that the Apostle seems to have made against women doing so.

Conclusion: May the tongues of iniquity be stopped and silenced. For, when divine power operates, it establishes means in harmony with its aim and it becomes dangerous, presumptuous and foolhardy to blame and to criticize things which have been instituted by God.

Many other reasons still could be added: borrowing examples from sacred

---

[5] Luke 1:71, 75.

and secular history, recalling Camilla and the Amazons, noting that these facts find their justification in necessity, is an evident usefulness, in accepted customs, in command or dispensation of Superiors. But what we have said suffices though briefly to establish the truth.

Ah! henceforth, may the party which has justice on its side take care not to stop in its course and render useless, by disbelief, ingratitude and other prevarications, the divine help whose commencement manifested itself in such an evident and marvelous manner. It is, as we read it in the Scriptures, the misfortune that once befell Moses and the sons of Israel who had received so many divine promises. Indeed, God, without changing His schemes, varies the application of His decrees according to the change in the merits of men.

Appendix V

Martin Le Franc's *Le champion des dames*
(JOAN OF ARC PASSAGE)

The Champion:

What can duchesses do against their harmful enemies, or queens or princesses? What will those who understand such things think, when a short time ago a maid with few worldly possessions broke the backs of the most powerful and put the swiftest men to death?

I wish to tell of the Maid who delivered Orléans, where Salisbury lost an eye, and then was struck by evil death. It was she who recovered French honor to such a degree that she will rightfully enjoy perpetual renown.

You know how she was taught to wield a lance and bear armor, how the English were beaten by her great undertaking; how the king came forth under [the influence of] her confidence, whether from Bourges or Blois, and with a great French army went before Paris in France.

Where she came from, why or how, you know very well, so I'll not speak of that. But whoever wishes to record her miracles in books or commentaries, it seems this cannot be done without acknowledging the divine spirit in Joan, which inflamed and inspired her to accomplish such things.

The Adversary replies to the Champion, and describes briefly the faults and errors of Joan the Maid.

Small-Understanding [The Adversary]:

When you heard of brother Thomas,[1] replied Small-Understanding, did you not judge and affirm that he lived a very saintly life? Was it not commonly cried: Here is a saint arrived on earth? Nevertheless, you know for certain to what end he came.

He was neither priest nor subdeacon, and still he sang mass to subdeacons and deacons. No one who was not there could consider himself fortunate. People almost kissed the ground he had walked on; he did whatever he wanted with the people, there was no other alternative.

---

[1] Thomas Couette, native of Mans, was burned in Rome. See the chronicle of Monstrelet for the years 1428–32.

213

Then came his burning in the Roman Capitol, his malice seen. Therefore, I say that the foolish mob is very easily deceived, and a great fraud conceived and conducted by a clever mind, in the current day is not recognized by all people.

To say nothing of the various ways [describing] how the Maid took up arms. Could someone not have taught that saint, someone who loved Orléans, who emboldened and inflamed her and taught her what to say? But the way it was told to me, by God, it happened very differently.

I was told as a certain thing, that she served a captain in her youth, as a page, where she observed the art of bearing armor. And when the bloom of youth overcame her and chose to reveal her sex,[2] she was advised to dress in armor and bear a lance.

Then necessity taught her the manner by which she would come to Orléans [sic], and, as a simple shepherdess [*simplette bergière*], would ask questions and reply, and how she would give the king and his parliament signs by which it would be understood that she was divinely sent [*venist divinement*].

Necessity also instructed those who told her to employ certain tactics [?]. A number of Englishmen believed that she used the art of necromancy, that therefore their confidence soon faltered and that she took advantage of their fantastic courage in diverse ways [?].

After that [we saw] how people believed in this contrived farce, as soon as fortune increased her accomplishments. There, the voices are raised, now the war will be over, if God and Saint Avoie aid us! Surely the thing is amply proven: God sends the Maid to France!

The defense of Joan the Maid

The Champion:

She could not have made the signs, said the Champion bluntly, if by his dignified power God had not been allowing her to advance. Moreover, she did in a moment what had not been accomplished in twenty years. Those to whom God gives strength always conquer and move forward.

Also I piously believe [*je croy en bonne foy*] that angels accompanied her, for as we see in Jerome, they love and embrace chastity. And I hold as true that they helped her win the outer bulwarks, and at Patay plucked the eyes out of the vanquished English.

---

[2] I wish to thank Nadia Margolis for suggesting this phrase and several others adopted in this translation.

Le champion des dames

[The next six stanzas are the supplementary stanzas found only on fol. 180 of Brussels manuscript 9466. A marker on fol. 125 indicates their proper position and signals their transcription at the end of the manuscript.]

For we should all assume that God, who is the author of peace, permits all those who do not want it to be devastated and destroyed, [and] we ought to say that he never allows those to last long who, either by word or deed, do not want peace to endure.

Also, I surmise, it was fitting that lofty pride was unseated by a humble little creature. In that way, one supposes that to bring down and confound the pride of the English, God wanted to send the Maid.

A thousand reasons are apparent through which my opinion and others like it appear[3] of heavenly design [*saincte imaginacion*], but the envious do not know how to speak forthrightly and they put an evil interpretation on something where there is no finding fault with it.

It seemed scandalous to people that she dressed in men's clothes, for we read in Deuteronomy that Moses prohibited it. Don't you know what Gerson said? I'm talking about master Jean Gerson who composed a little treatise about her, more subtle than we think.

The ancient law of Moses, inasmuch as it is judicial, does not apply to Robin and Joanne living under the sacramental law, unless, by decree or decretal, such things as were customary then, for a special reason, are confirmed anew.

Do you not see that it was prohibited that anyone eat animals if they did not have cloven hoof and chew their cud? No one dared eat hare or sow or hog. But nowadays if someone offered you some, you would take second helpings.

Also do not marvel, however unusual it is, that the Maid dressed in doublet and short coat, for she was the more dreaded, skillful, and unencumbered, and she was taken for a proud prince, not a simple shepherdess [*simplette bergière*].

She wore a felt hat, hammered breastplate [?][4] and short surcoat; I admit it. But her circumstances were not those of most women. Long coats (you realize) are not good for warfare. Again, very frequently you hear that a monk's habit does not a monk make.

---

[3] Here the sense requires 'pareir' (to appear) rather than 'perdre' (to lose).

[4] The French gives "heuque frapée," but whereas 'heuque' is a synonym for 'hoqueton' which is a cloth surcoat, often quilted, the word 'frapée' or 'hammered' suggests something more substantial and made with metal. It appears that the miniature in B.N. manuscript fr. 12476 of Joan wearing a breastplate and standing next to Judith who holds the head of Holophernes depicts this description.

215

Arms require appropriate dress; there is none so foolish that he does not know this. There is dress suited for town, and other dress for bearing a lance or battle-ax. When a falcon is released for prey his long jesses are removed. Also, whoever hides from his enemies has no need of a long coat.

Let them say what they will of her – they are free to speak or to remain silent – but her praises will not lack, for the lies they know how to make. What else should I add? Through her bravery and courage, in spite of all opposition, the king of France was crowned.

The Adversary:

I hold that talk to be frivolous, for never did God send her, said the adversary with the deceitful face, very annoyed with Joan. Ha! he said, she was too much led astray by presumptuousness, whatever they say! Justice sent her to burn at Rouen in Normandy.

That is mistaken, know-it-all, replied Free-Will [*Franc-Vouloir*] rapidly. How many saints do we celebrate who died shamefully! First think of Jesus and then his blessed martyrs. It is clear that you will conclude that you have no knowledge about this subject.

Your arguments scarcely amount to anything against the Maid [who is] innocent, [or wherever?] one senses something worse regarding God's secret judgments on her. It is right that each of us agree to grant her honor and glory for her excellent valor, for her strength and victory.

The Actor:

Then the Adversary, angry at being lectured about Joan, told him: You have preached too much; think of another woman to praise.[5] You could not have adduced a worse example to accomplish what you wish. It is enough to drive one crazy or make him pull his hair out.

The Champion:[6]

You have a very cowardly heart [*courage leger*] and are much too opinionated, said Free-Will, who makes it dangerous to conspire against [*colauder*] those of his own hearth. And if I have praised three or four complete foreigners, why would I remain silent about she who chose to fight for France? Surely I will not do that.

Likewise, since she did these deeds, and in no time at all, everyone owes her everlasting thanks [*immortelles graces*]. Do I not have cause to repeat an

[5] The word "blasonner" means both 'to praise' and 'to blame,' which offers the Adversary the chance to imply that the Champion's praise is worthless.
[6] The following four stanzas, copied from the Paris printed edition of 1530, are not reproduced in Quicherat, *Procès* 5: 44–50.

abundance of good things heard about her, as much as I am able? If you say that I am not right, you are biased.

For whatever one may say, she was led into battle in grand array and fought valiantly and conducted herself honorably. Therefore I have remembered her among the women cavaliers [*cheveleresses*], for I have undertaken [here] to praise women warriors [*batailleresses*].

Now let it please God that you barons, you princes [and] you lords of France, on whom we still place the hope of our deliverance, have the courage and endurance of this one woman [*cette femme seulement*] to overcome and destroy your enemies quickly.

Bibliography

SOURCES

Alphonso of Jaén. *Alphonso of Jaén: His Life and Works with Critical Editions of the Epistola Solitarii, the Informaciones and the Epistola Serui Christi*, ed. Arne Jönsson. Studia Graeca et Latina Lundensia, 1. Lund, Sweden, 1989.

Aquinas, Thomas. *Summa theologiae.* [Latin text and English translation]. 61 vols. New York, 1964–81.

Ayroles, J.-B.-J. *La vraie Jeanne d'Arc.* 5 vols. Paris, 1890–1902.

Barrett, W[ilfred] P[hilip], ed. and trans. *The Trial of Jeanne d' Arc: Translated into English from the Original Latin and French Documents.* With Pierre Champion "Dramatis personae," trans. Coley Taylor and Ruth H. Kerr. New York, 1932.

Benoit de Sainte-Maure. *Le roman de Troie,* ed. Léopold Constans. 6 vols. Paris, 1904–12.

Biblia Sacra: iuxta vulgatam versionem. Ed. Bonifatio Fischer . . . [et al.]. 2 vols. Stuttgart, c. 1969, repr. 1983.

Blondel, Robert. *Oeuvres de Robert Blondel, historien normand du XVe siècle,* ed. A. Héron. 2 vols. Rouen, 1891–93.

Boccaccio, Giovanni. *Concerning Famous Women,* trans. Guido A. Guarino. New Brunswick, N.J., 1963.

Boland, Paschal. *The Concept of* Discretio Spirituum *in Jean Gerson's* De Probatione Spirituum *and* De Distinctione Verarum Visionem A Falsis. The Catholic University of America: Studies in Sacred Theology, 2nd ser., 112. Washington, D.C., 1959.

Bower, Walter. *Scotichronicon,* ed. and trans. D. E. R. Watt, et al. 9 vols. Aberdeen, 1987–98.

Bridget of Sweden. *Sancta Birgitta Revelaciones, Lib. IV.,* ed. Hans Aili. Samlingar utgivna av Svenska Fornskriftsällskapet. 2nd ser., Latinska Skrifter; bd 7: 4. Göteborg, 1992.

Champion, Pierre, ed. "Ballade du sacre de Reims (17 juillet 1429)." *Le Moyen Age* 22, 2nd ser., 13 (1909): 370–77.

Champion, Pierre, ed. and trans. *Procès de condamnation de Jeanne d'Arc.* 2 vols. Bibliothèque du XVe siècle, 22, 23. Paris, 1920–21. Geneva, repr. 1976.

Chartier, Alain. "Letter to a Foreign Prince.' In *Procès de condamnation et de rehabilitation de Jeanne d'Arc dite la Pucelle,* vol. 5, ed. Jules Quicherat, 131–36. Paris, 1849.

Chartier, Jean. *Chronique.* In *Procès de condamnation et de rehabilitation de Jeanne d'Arc dite la Pucelle,* vol. 4, ed. Jules Quicherat, 51–93. Paris, 1847.

Christine de Pizan. *The Book of the City of Ladies,* trans. Earl Jeffrey Richards. New York, 1982.

Christine de Pizan. *Ditié de Jehanne d'Arc,* eds. Angus J. Kennedy and Kenneth Varty. Medium Aevum Monographs, n.s. 9. Oxford, 1977.

Christine de Pizan. *The* Epistle of the Prison of Human Life. *With An Epistle to the*

Queen of France *and* Lament on the Evils of the Civil War, ed. and trans. Josette A. Wisman. Garland Library of Medieval Literature, 21. Ser. A. New York, 1984.

Christine de Pizan. "The *Livre de la cité des dames* of Christine de Pisan: A Critical Edition," ed. Maureen Cheney Curnow. Unpublished doctoral dissertation. 3 vols. Ann Arbor, Mich., 1978–79.

Christine de Pizan. *Poems of Cupid, God of Love: Christine de Pizan's* Epistre au dieu d'Amours *and* Dit de la Rose, *Thomas Hoccleve's* The Letter of Cupid, eds. Thelma S. Fenster and Mary Carpenter Erler. Leiden, 1990.

Chronique des Cordeliers. Extracts in "Supplément aux témoignages contemporains sur Jeanne d'Arc," ed. Jules Quicherat. *Revue historique* 19 (1882): 60–83.

Chronique du Mont-Saint-Michel (1343–1468), ed. Siméon Luce. 2 vols. Paris, 1879–83.

Chronique de la Pucelle. In *Chronique de la Pucelle ou Chronique de Cousinot, suivie de la Chronique normande de P. Cochon, relatives aux règnes de Charles VI et de Charles VII,* etc., ed. Auguste de Vallet de Viriville. Paris, 1869.

Chronique de Tournai. In *Corpus chronicorum Flandriae,* ed. J.-J. de Smet. Collection de chroniques belges inédites. Vol. 3. Brussels, 1856.

Clément de Fauquembergue. *Journal de Clément de Fauquembergue, greffier du Parlement de Paris, 1417–1435,* eds. Alexandre Tuetey and Henri Lacaille. 3 vols. Société de l'Histoire de France. Paris, 1903–1915.

Cochon, P. *Chronique normande.* In *Chronique de la Pucelle ou Chronique de Cousinot, suivie de la Chronique normande de P. Cochon, relatives aux règnes de Charles VI et de Charles VII,* etc., ed. Auguste Vallet de Viriville. Paris, 1869.

Cosma Raimondi. "Una lettera di Cosma Raimondi Cremonese sulla Ven. Giovanna d'Arco," G. Mercati. *Studi e documenti di storia e diritto* 15 (1894): 303–309.

Dean of Saint-Thibaud of Metz. Extract from *Tableau des rois de France.* In *Procès de condamnation et de réhabilitation de Jeanne d'Arc dite la Pucelle,* vol. 4, ed. Jules Quicherat, 321–28. Paris, 1847.

Deschamps, Eustache. *Oeuvres complètes d'Eustache Deschamps,* eds. Auguste Queux de Saint-Hilaire and Gaston Raynaud. 11 vols. Société des Anciens Textes Français. Paris, 1878–1903.

Doncoeur, Paul and Yvonne Lanhers, eds. *Documents et recherches relatifs à Jeanne la Pucelle.* 5 vols. Melun, 1952–61. Vol. 3. *La réhabilitation de Jeanne la Pucelle. L'enquête ordonnée par Charles VII en 1450 et le codicille de Guillaume Bouillé.* Paris, 1956.

Duparc, Pierre, ed. and trans. *Procès en nullité de la condamnation de Jeanne d'Arc.* 5 vols. Société de l'Histoire de France. Paris, 1977–89.

Dupuy, Jean *Breviarium historiale* [Also known as *Collectarium*], ed. Léopold Delisle. In "Nouveau témoignage relatif à la mission de Jeanne d'Arc." *Bibliothèque de l'Ecole des Chartes* 46 (1885): 649–68.

Gelu, Jacques. [Correspondence] In *Histoire générale des Alpes-Maritimes ou Cottiennes,* ed. Marcellin Fornier. 3 vols. Paris, 1890–92.

Gelu, Jacques. *Dissertatio.* [Also known as *De adventu Johanne*] In *Mémoires et consultations en faveur de Jeanne d'Arc par les juges du procès de réhabilitation, d'après les manuscrits authentiques, publiés pour la première fois,* ed. Pierre Lanéry d'Arc. Paris, 1889.

Germain, Jean. "De laudibus Philippi." In *La vraie Jeanne d'Arc,* ed. Jean-Baptiste-Joseph Ayroles. Vol. 3. *La libératrice,* pp. 640–41.

Gerson, Jean. *De distinctione verarum revelationem a falsis.* In *Oeuvres complètes [de] Jean Gerson,* vol. 3, ed. P. Glorieux, no. 90, 36–56. Paris, 1962.

[Gerson, Jean?] *De mirabili victoria,* ed. Dorothy G. Wayman. In "The Chancellor and Jeanne d'Arc." *Franciscan Studies* 17 (1957): 273–305.

[Gerson, Jean?] *De mirabili victoria,* trans. H. G. Francq. In "Jean Gerson's Theological Treatise and Other Memoirs in Defence of Joan of Arc." *Revue de l'Université d'Ottawa* 41 (1971): 58–80.

[Gerson, Jean?] *De mirabili victoria,* ed. and trans. J.-B. Monnoyeur. In *Traité de Jean Gerson sur la Pucelle.* Paris, 1930.

Gerson, Jean. *De probatione spirituum.* In *Oeuvres complètes [de] Jean Gerson,* vol. 9, ed. P. Glorieux, no. 448, 177–85. Paris, 1973.

[Gerson, Jean ?] *De puella Aurelianensi.* [*De mirabili victoria*] In *Oeuvres complètes [de] Jean Gerson,* vol. 9, ed. P. Glorieux, no. 476, 661–65. Paris, 1973.

[Gerson, Jean?] *De quadam puella,* trans. H. G. Francq. In "Jean Gerson's Theological Treatise and Other Memoirs in Defence of Joan of Arc." *Revue de l'Université d'Ottawa* 41 (1971): 58–80.

[Gerson, Jean?] *De quadam puella,* ed. Dorothy G. Wayman. In "The Chancellor and Jeanne d'Arc," *Franciscan Studies* 17 (1957): 273–305.

Glorieux, P. *Oeuvres complètes [de] Jean Gerson.* 10 vols. Paris, 1960–73.

Gratian. Decretum. *Corpus iuris canonici,* ed. Emil Friedberg. Vol. 1. Leipzig, 1879; repr. Graz, 1959.

Griscom, Acton. *The Historia Regum Britanniae of Geoffrey of Monmouth.* New York, 1929.

Hall, Edward. *The Union of the Two Illustrious Families of Lancastre and Yorke* [Hall's Chronicle], ed. Henry Ellis. London, 1548, repr. 1809.

Jerome, Saint. *The Principal Works of St. Jerome,* trans. W. H. Fremantle. A Select Library of Nicene and Post-Nicene Fathers of the Christian Church. 2nd ser., vol. 6. Repr. Grand Rapids, Mich., 1983.

Joan of Arc. *Lettre aux Anglais.* In *Procès de condamnation et de réhabilitation de Jeanne d'Arc dite la Pucelle,* vol. 1, ed. Jules Quicherat, 240–41. Paris, 1841. [English translation in appendix.]

Jouffroy, Jean. "De Philippo Burgundae duce oratio." In *La vraie Jeanne d'Arc,* ed. Jean-Baptiste-Joseph Ayroles. Vol. 3. *La libératrice,* pp. 641–42.

Kaerrymel, A. de. [*Virgo puellares* with French translation.] In *Les manuscrits françois de la bibliothèque du roi,* ed. Paulin Paris, 377–84. Vol. 7. Paris, 1848.

Kollár, Adám Ferencz. *Analecta monumentorum omnis aevi vindobonensia: Opera et studio Adami Francisci Kollarii,* typis et sumptibus, Ioannis T. Trattner. 2 vols. Vindobonae, 1761–62.

Langenstein, Heinrich von. *Heinrichs von Langenstein: Unterscheidung der Geister, Lateinisch und Deutsch,* ed. Thomas Hohmann. Munich, 1977.

[La Rochelle, Clerk of City Hall of]. "Relation du greffier de La Rochelle sur Jeanne d'Arc, extrait du Livre noir de l'hôtel de ville de La Rochelle," ed. Jules Quicherat. *Revue historique* 4 (1877): 327–44.

Martin Le Franc. *Le champion des dames.* [Printed by Pierre Vidoue for Galiot Du Pré.] Paris, 1530.

Martin Le Franc. *Le champion des dames,* ed. Robert Deschaux. 5 vols. Classiques français du Moyen Age, 127–131. Paris, 1999.

Martin Le Franc. *Le champion des dames,* ed. Arthur Piaget. [lines 1–8144] In *Société d'Histoire de la Suisse romande.* Mémoires et documents. 3rd ser. Vol. 8. Lausanne, 1968.

Martin Le Franc. *Le champion des dames.* [Excerpt on Joan of Arc] In *Procès de condamnation et de réhabilitation de Jeanne d'Arc dite la Pucelle,* vol. 5, ed. Jules Quicherat, 44–50. Paris, 1849.

Martin Le Franc. *Complainte du livre du Champion des Dames a maistre Martin Le Franc son acteur,* ed. Gaston Paris. In "Un poème inédit de Martin Le Franc." *Romania* 16 (1887): 383–437.

Martin Le Franc. "Huitains inédits de Martin Le Franc sur Jeanne d'Arc," ed. Arthur Piaget. *Le Moyen Age* 6 (1893): 105–107.

[Mascon, Jean de?] *La délivrance d'Orléans et l'institution de la fête du 8 mai, chronique anonyme du XVe siècle,* ed. M. Boucher de Molandon. Orléans, 1883.

Meyer, Paul, ed. "Ballade contre les Anglais (1429)." *Romania* 21 (1892): 50–52.

Monstrelet, Enguerrand de. *The Chronicles of Enguerrand de Monstrelet,* trans. Thomas Johnes. 2 vols. London, 1840; repr. 1849.

Monstrelet, Enguerran[d] de. In *Procès de condamnation et de réhabilitation de Jeanne d'Arc dite la Pucelle,* vol. 4, ed. Jules Quicherat, 360–404. Paris, 1847.

Morosini, Antonio. *La chronique d'Antonio Morosini: Extraits relatifs à l'histoire de France,* ed. and trans. Léon Dorez. Intro. and notes by Germain Lefèvre-Pontalis. 4 vols. Société de l'Histoire de France. Paris, 1898–1902.

Murray, T. Douglas, ed. *Jeanne d'Arc, Maid of Orleans, Deliverer of France . . . Set Forth in the Original Documents.* New York, 1902.

Pasquier, Etienne. *Les recherches de la France, revues et augmentées de quatre livres.* In *Oeuvres choisies d'Etienne Pasquier,* ed. Léon Feugère. 2 vols. Paris, 1849.

Pernoud, Régine. *The Retrial of Joan of Arc: The Evidence at the Trial for her Rehabilitation, 1450–1456,* trans. J. M. Cohen. New York, 1955.

Pius II. [Aeneas Sylvius Piccolomini] *Memoirs of a Renaissance Pope: Commentaries of Pius II.* An Abridgment, ed. Leona C. Gabel and trans. Florence A. Gragg. Book 6. New York, 1962.

Pius II. *Commentarii rerum memorabilium.* [Latin and Italian] *I commentarii / Enea Silvio Piccolomini, Papa Pio II,* ed. and trans. Luigi Totaro. 2 vols. Classici, 47. Milan, 1984.

Poitiers Conclusions. [Also known as *Résumé*] In *Procès de condamnation et de réhabilitation de Jeanne d'Arc dite la Pucelle,* vol. 3, ed. Jules Quicherat, 391–92. Paris, 1845.

Quicherat, Jules, ed. *Procès de condamnation et de réhabilitation de Jeanne d'Arc dite la Pucelle.* 5 vols. Société de l'Histoire de France. Paris, 1841–49.

Sala, Pierre. *Hardiesses des grands rois et empereurs.* In *Procès de condamnation et de réhabilitation de Jeanne d'Arc dite la Pucelle,* vol. 4, ed. Jules Quicherat, 277–81. Paris, 1847.

Thesaurus novus anecdotorum. Ed. Edmund Martène and Ursin Durand. 5 vols. Paris, 1717.

Thomassin, Mathieu. *Registre delphinal.* In *Procès de condamnation et de réhabilitation de Jeanne d'Arc dite la Pucelle,* vol. 4, ed. Jules Quicherat, 303–12. Paris, 1847.

Valois, Noël, ed. "Un nouveau témoignage sur Jeanne d'Arc: Réponse d'un clerc parisien à l'apologie de la Pucelle par Jean Gerson (1429)." *Annuaire-Bulletin de la Société de l'Histoire de France.* Seconde partie. Documents et notices historiques.

43 (1906): 161–79. Reprinted by Théophile Cochard in *Bulletin de la Société archéologique et historique de l'Orléanais* 14, no. 187 (1907): 524–30.

Virgo puellares. [sixteen-verse Latin poem] In Mathieu Thomassin, *Registre delphinal*. In *Procès de condamnation et de réhabilitation de Jeanne d'Arc dite la Pucelle*, vol. 4, ed. Jules Quicherat, 305. Paris, 1847.

Windecke, Eberhard von. *Denkwürdigkeiten zur Geschichte des Zeitalters Kaiser Sigmunds*. In *Les sources allemandes de l'histoire de Jeanne d'Arc*, ed. and trans., Germain Lefèvre-Pontalis. Société de l'Histoire de France. Paris, 1903.

SECONDARY WORKS

Ady, Cecilia M. *Pius II (Aeneas Silvius Piccolomini): The Humanist Pope*. London, 1913.

Audisio, Gabriel. *Les "Vaudois": Naissance, vie et mort d'une dissidence (XIIme – XVIme siècles)*. Turin, 1989.

Ayroles, Jean-Baptiste-Joseph. "La vénérable Jeanne d'Arc, prophétisée et prophétesse." *Revue des questions historiques* 79, n.s. 35 (1906): 28–56.

Ballet Lynn, Therese. "The *Ditié de Jeanne d'Arc*: Its Political, Feminist, and Aesthetic Significance." *Fifteenth Century Studies* 1 (1978): 149–57.

Barbey, Léon. *Martin Le Franc: Prévot de Lausanne, avocat de l'amour et de la femme au XVe siècle*. Fribourg, 1985.

Barstow, Anne Llewellyn. *Joan of Arc: Heretic, Mystic, Shaman*. Studies in Women and Religion, 17. Lewiston, N.Y., 1986.

Beaucourt, Gaston du Fresne de. *Histoire de Charles VII*. 6 vols. Paris, 1881–91.

Beaune, Colette. "Prophétie et propagande: Le sacre de Charles VII." In *Idéologie et propagande en France*, ed. Myriam Yardeni, 63–73. Paris, 1987.

Beck, Jonathan, ed. *Le concil de Basle (1434): Les origines du théâtre réformiste et partisan en France*. Studies in the History of Christian Thought, 18. Leiden, 1979.

Boissonnade, P. "Une étape capitale de la mission de Jeanne d'Arc: Le séjour de la Pucelle à Poitiers, la quadruple enquête et ses résultats (1er mars – 10 avril 1429)." *Revue des questions historiques*. 3rd ser. 17 (1930): 12–67.

Bonnard, Fourier. *Histoire de l'abbaye royale et de l'ordre des chanoines réguliers de St-Victor de Paris, première période (1113–1500)*. 2 vols. Paris, 1904–08.

Bourgain-Hemeryck, Pascale. *Les oeuvres latines d'Alain Chartier*. Paris, 1977.

Bouzy, Olivier. "Prédiction ou récupération, les prophéties autour de Jeanne d'Arc dans les premiers mois de l'année 1429." *Bulletin de l'Association des Amis du Centre Jeanne d'Arc* 14 (1990): 39–47.

———. "Le Traité de Jacques Gelu, *De adventu Johanne*." *Bulletin de l'Association des Amis du Centre Jeanne d'Arc* 16 (1992): 29–39.

Brownlee, Kevin. "Structures of Authority in Christine de Pizan's *Ditié de Jehanne d'Arc*." In *Discourses of Authority in Medieval and Renaissance Literature*, eds. Kevin Brownlee and Walter Stephens, 131–50. Hanover, N.H., 1989.

Calvot, Danièle and Gilbert Ouy. *L'oeuvre de Gerson à Saint-Victor de Paris: Catalogue des manuscrits*. Paris, 1990.

Cecchetti, Dario. "Un'egloga inedita di Nicolas de Clamanges." In *Miscellanea di studi e ricerche sul Quattrocento francese*, ed. Franco Simone, 27–57. Turin, 1967.

Chaume, Maurice. "Une prophétie relative à Charles VI." *Revue du Moyen Age latin* 3 (1947): 27–42.

Chevalier, J. *Mémoire historique sur les hérésies en Dauphiné avant le XVIe siècle.* Valence, 1890.

Christian, William A., Jr. *Apparitions in Late Medieval and Renaissance Spain.* Princeton, N.J., 1981.

Cohen, Gustave. *Sainte Jeanne d'Arc dans la poésie du XVe siècle.* Paris, 1948.

Colledge, Eric. "*Epistola solitarii ad reges*: Alphonse of Pecha as Organizer of Birgittine and Urbanist Propaganda." *Mediaeval Studies* 18 (1956): 19–49.

Connolly, James L. *John Gerson, Reformer and Mystic.* Louvain, 1928.

Contamine, Philippe. "Jeanne d'Arc et la prophétie." In Philippe Contamine, *De Jeanne d'Arc aux guerres d'Italie: Figures, images et problèmes du XVe siècle,* 53–61. Orléans, 1994.

——— "L'Idée de guerre à la fin du Moyen Age: Aspects juridiques et éthiques." In *Comptes-rendus de l'Académie des Inscriptions et Belles-Lettres* (1979): 70–86.

Cordier, Jacques. *Jeanne d'Arc: Sa personnalité, son rôle.* Paris, 1948.

Cosneau, Eugène. *Les grands traités de la guerre de cents ans.* Paris, 1889.

Coville, Alfred. *Jean Petit: La question du tyrannicide au commencement du XVe siècle.* Paris, 1932.

——— "Pierre de Versailles (1380? – 1446)." *Bibliothèque de l'Ecole des Chartes* 93 (1932): 208–66.

Cowie, Murray A. and Marian L. Cowie, eds. *The Works of Peter Schott (1460–1490)* Vol 2. Chapel Hill, N.C., 1971.

Crane, Susan. "Clothing and Gender Definition: Joan of Arc." *Journal of Medieval and Early Modern Studies* 26, 2 (1996): 297–320.

Dacheux, L. *Un réformateur catholique à la fin du XVe siècle: Jean Geiler de Kaysersberg, prédicateur à la cathédrale de Strasbourg (1478–1510); étude sur sa vie et son temps.* Paris, 1876.

Dassance, Pierre. "Jacques Gélu, archevêque d'Embrun (1370–1432) ou la loyauté vis-à-vis du miracle." *Les Amis de Jeanne d'Arc* 114 (1984): 5–7.

Denifle, Henri and Emile Chatelain. *Chartularium Universitatis Parisiensis.* 4 vols. Paris, 1889–97.

——— "Le procès de Jeanne d'Arc et l'Université de Paris." *Mémoires de la Société de l'Histoire de Paris et de l'Ile de France* 24 (1897): 1–32.

Denis, Michel. *Codices manuscripti theologici bibliothecae Palatinae Vindobonensis latini aliarumque Occidentis linguarum.* Vol. 2. Vindobonae, 1800.

Dingjan, François. *Discretio: Les origines patristiques et monastiques de la doctrine sur la prudence chez saint Thomas d'Aquin.* Assen, 1967.

Dondaine, Antoine. "Le Frère Prêcheur Jean Dupuy, évêque de Cahors, et son témoignage sur Jeanne d'Arc, *Archivum Fratrum Praedicatorum* 12 (1942): 118–84.

——— "Le témoignage de Jean Dupuy O. P. sur Jeanne d'Arc, note additionnelle à AFP XII (1942) 167–184." *Archivum Fratrum Praedicatorum* 38 (1968): 31–41.

Dorange, Auguste, "Vie de Mgr. Gelu, archevêque de Tours au XVe siècle, écrite par lui-même, et publiée d'après un manuscrit de la Bibliothèque municipale." *Bulletin de la Société archéologique de Touraine* 3 (1875): 267–80.

Dulac, Liliane. "Un écrit militant de Christine de Pizan: *Le Ditié de Jeanne d'Arc.*" In

Aspects of Female Existence: Proceedings from The St. Gertrude Symposium, Copenhagen, September, 1978, eds. Birte Carlé et al., 115–34. Gyldendal, 1980.

Fabre, Lucien. *Joan of Arc,* trans. Gerard Hopkins. New York, 1954.

Flavigny, Catherine Moitessier, comtesse de. *Sainte Brigitte de Suède: Sa vie, ses révélations et son oeuvre.* Paris, 1892.

Fraioli, Deborah. "The Literary Image of Joan of Arc: Prior Influences." *Speculum* 56 (1981): 811–30.

—— "Why Joan of Arc never became an Amazon," In *Fresh Verdicts on Joan of Arc,* eds. Bonnie Wheeler and Charles T. Wood, 180–204. New York, 1996.

France, Anatole. "Le siège d'Orléans (1428–1429) [pt. 4]." *La revue de Paris* 15 Feb. (1902): 737–45.

—— *Vie de Jeanne d'Arc.* 2 vols. Paris, 1908.

Francq, H. G. "Jean Gerson's Theological Treatise and Other Memoirs in Defence of Joan of Arc." *Revue de l'Université d'Ottawa* 41 (1971): 58–80.

Gies, Frances. *Joan of Arc: The Legend and the Reality.* New York, 1981.

Glénisson, Jean. "Notes d'histoire militaire: Quelques lettres de défi du XIVe siècle." *Bibliothèque de l'Ecole des Chartes* 107 (1947–48): 235–54.

Goyau, Georges. "Jacques Gelu: Ses interventions pour Jeanne d'Arc." *Revue des questions historiques* 117 (1932): 302–20.

Hotchkiss, Valerie R. *Clothes Make the Man: Female Cross Dressing in Medieval Europe.* New York, 1996.

Huppé, Bernard F., ed. and trans. *The Web of Words: Structural Analyses of the Old English Poems: Vainglory, the Wonder of Creation, the Dream of the Rood, and Judith.* Albany, N.Y., 1970.

Jan, Eduard von. "Das literarische Bild der Jeanne d'Arc (1429–1926)." In *Beihefte zur Zeitschrift für Romanische Philologie,* 76. Halle, 1928.

Jouet, Roger. *Et la Normandie devint française.* Paris, 1983.

Jung, Marc-René. "Situation de Martin Le Franc." In *Pratiques de la culture écrite en France au XVe siècle: Actes du colloque international du CNRS, Paris, 16–18 mai 1992, organisé en l'honneur de Gilbert Ouy par l'unité de recherche "Culture écrite du Moyen Age tardif",* eds. Monique Ornato and Nicole Pons, 13–30. Louvain-la-Neuve, 1995.

Kremple, Frederich Awalde. "Cultural Aspects of the Councils of Constance and Basel." Unpublished doctoral dissertation. Ann Arbor, Mich., 1954.

Lacaze, Yvon. "Philippe le Bon et le problème hussite: Un projet de croisade bourguignon en 1428–1429." *Revue historique* 241 (1969): 69–98.

Lanéry d'Arc, Pierre. *Le Livre d'Or de Jeanne d'Arc: Bibliographie raisonnée et analytique des ouvrages relatifs à Jeanne d'Arc. Catalogue méthodique . . . depuis le XVe siècle jusqu'à nos jours.* Paris, 1894.

—— *Le culte de Jeanne d'Arc au XVe siècle.* Orléans, 1887.

Lea, Henry Charles. *A History of the Inquisition of the Middle Ages.* Vol. 3. New York, 1922.

Lewis, P. S. *Essays in Later Medieval French History.* London, 1985.

Lightbody, Charles Wayland. *The Judgements of Joan: Joan of Arc, A Study in Cultural History.* Cambridge, Mass., 1961.

Liocourt, Ferdinand de, Colonel. *La mission de Jeanne d'Arc.* Vol. 2. Paris, 1981.

Little, Roger G. *The Parlement of Poitiers: War, Government and Politics in France, 1418–1436.* London, 1984.

Bibliography: Secondary Works

Lowell, Francis Cabot. *Joan of Arc.* Boston, 1896.

Lucie-Smith, Edward. *Joan of Arc.* 1976. New York, repr. 1977.

Margolis, Nadia. "Elegant Closures: The Use of the Diminutive in Christine de Pizan and Jean de Meun." In *Reinterpreting Christine de Pizan,* ed. Earl Jeffrey Richards, with Joan Williamson, Nadia Margolis, and Christine Reno. 111–23. Athens, Ga., 1992.

——— *Joan of Arc in History, Literature, and Film: A Select, Annotated Bibliography.* New York, 1990.

Markale, Jean. *Isabeau de Bavière.* Paris, 1982.

Marx, Jean. *L'Inquisition en Dauphiné.* Paris, 1914.

Metz, René. "Le statut de la femme en droit canonique médiéval." In *La femme et l'enfant dans le droit canonique médiéval.* London, repr. 1985.

Motey, Henri Vicomte du. *Jeanne d'Arc à Chinon et Robert de Rouvres.* Paris, 1927.

Neuville, D. "Le Parlement royal à Poitiers (1418–1436) [pt.] I." *Revue historique* 6 (1878): 1–28.

Nichols, Stephen G. "Prophetic Discourse: St. Augustine to Christine de Pizan." In *The Bible in the Middle Ages: Its Influence on Literature and Art,* ed. Bernard S. Levy, 51–76. Medieval and Renaissance Texts and Studies, 89. Binghamton, N.Y., 1992.

Orliac, Jehanne d'. *Joan of Arc and her Companions,* trans. Elisabeth Abbott. Philadelphia, 1934.

Parke, H. W. with ed. B. C. McGing. *Sibyls and Sibylline Prophecy in Classical Antiquity.* Croom Helm Classical Studies. London, 1998.

Pernoud, Régine. [Bibliography section] *Bulletin de l'Association des Amis du Centre Jeanne d'Arc* 16 (1992), p. 65.

Pernoud, Régine. *Joan of Arc, by Herself and Her Witnesses,* trans. Edward Hyams. 1962. New York, repr. 1969.

Pernoud, Régine and Marie-Véronique Clin. *Jeanne d'Arc.* Paris, 1986. Translated and revised by Jeremy duQuesnay Adams as *Joan of Arc: Her Story.* New York, 1998.

Peyronnet, Georges. "Gerson, Charles VII et Jeanne d'Arc: La propagande au service de la guerre." *Revue d'histoire ecclésiastique* 84 (1989): 334–70.

Piaget, Arthur. *Martin Le Franc, prévot de Lausanne.* Lausanne, 1888.

Pinzino, Jane Marie. "Heretic or Holy Woman? Cultural Representations and Gender in the Trial to Rehabilitate Joan of Arc." Unpublished doctoral dissertation. Ann Arbor, Mich., 1996.

Pons, Nicole. "La propagande de guerre française avant l'apparition de Jeanne d'Arc." *Journal des savants* (avril–juin 1982): 191–214.

Rabbe, Félix. *Jeanne d'Arc en Angleterre.* Paris, 1891.

Raguenet de Saint-Albin, Octave. *Les juges de Jeanne d'Arc à Poitiers, membres du parlement ou gens d'église?* Orléans, 1894.

Raknem, Ingvald. *Joan of Arc in History, Legend and Literature.* Oslo, 1971.

Reinach, Salomon. "Observations sur le texte du procès de condamnation de Jeanne d'Arc." *Revue historique* 148 (1925): 200–23.

Roche, Charles de and Gustave Wissler. "Documents relatifs à Jeanne d'Arc et à son époque, extraits d'un manuscrit du XVe siècle de la Bibliothèque de Berne." In *Festschrift Louis Gauchat,* 329–52. Aarau, 1926.

Rousset, Paul. "Saint Catherine de Sienne et le problème de la croisade." *Schweizer-*

ische Zeitschrift für Geschichte / *Revue Suisse d'Histoire* / *Rivista Storica Svizzera* 25 (1975): 499–513.

Sackville-West, Vita. *Saint Joan of Arc.* 1936. New York, repr. 1991.

Sahlin, Claire L. "Gender and Prophetic Authority in Birgitta of Sweden's *Revelations.*" In *Gender and Text in the Later Middle Ages,* ed. Jane Chance, 69–95. Gainesville, Fla., 1996.

Spiegel, Gabrielle M. "The *Reditus Regni ad Stirpem Karoli Magni*: A New Look." *French Historical Studies* 7 (1971): 145–74.

Strayer, Joseph R. "France: The Holy Land, the Chosen People, and the Most Christian King." In *Medieval Statecraft and the Perspectives of History: Essays by Joseph R. Strayer,* 300–314. Princeton, N.J., 1971.

Tabulae codicum manu scriptorum praeter graecos et orientales in Bibliotheca Palatina Vindobonensi asservatorum. ed. Academia Caesarea Vindobonensis. Vols. 3–4. Graz, repr. 1965.

Taylor, Rupert. *Political Prophecy in England.* New York. 1911.

Toussaint, Joseph. *Les relations diplomatiques de Philippe le Bon avec le concile de Bâle (1431–1449).* Louvain, 1942.

Twain, Mark. *Personal Recollections of Joan of Arc by the Sieur, Louis de Conte (Her Page and Secretary).* New York, 1896, repr. 1926.

Vale, M. G. A. *Charles VII.* Berkeley, 1974.

—— "Jeanne d'Arc et ses adversaires: Jeanne, victime d'une guerre civile?" In *Jeanne d'Arc, une époque, un rayonnement (Colloque d'histoire médiévale, Orléans, Octobre, 1979),* 203–16. Paris, 1982.

Vallet de Viriville, Auguste. *Histoire de Charles VII, roi de France et de son époque (1403–1461).* 3 vols. Société de l'Histoire de France. Paris, 1862–65.

Valois, Noël. *Le conseil du roi au XIVe, XVe et XVIe siècles.* Paris, 1888.

Vandenbroucke, François. "Discernement des esprits, III. Au Moyen Age." In *Dictionnaire de spiritualité ascétique et mystique, doctrine et histoire,* ed. Marcel Viller et al. 15 vols. Paris, 1937–67.

Vaughan, Richard. *John the Fearless: The Growth of Burgundian Power.* London, 1966, repr. 1979.

Voaden, Rosalynn. "Women's Words, Men's Language: *Discretio Spirituum* as Discourse in the Writing of Medieval Women Visionaries." In *The Medieval Translator* / *Traduire au Moyen Age,* eds. Roger Ellis and René Tixier, 64–83. Vol. 5. Turnhout, Belgium, 1996.

Walther, Hans. "Zwei unbekannte mittellateinische Gedichte." In *Studien zur lateinischen Dichtung des Mittelalters; Ehrengabe für Karl Strecker zum 4. September 1931.* eds. W. Stach and Hans Walther. Dresden, 1931.

Warner, Marina. *Joan of Arc: The Image of Female Heroism.* New York, 1981.

Wayman, Dorothy G. "The Chancellor and Jeanne d'Arc." *Franciscan Studies* 17 (1957): 273–305.

Wheeler, Bonnie and Charles T. Wood, eds. *Fresh Verdicts on Joan of Arc.* The New Middle Ages, 2. New York, 1996.

Wiesen, David S. *St. Jerome as a Satirist: A Study in Christian Latin Thought and Letters.* Cornell Studies in Classical Philology, 34. Ithaca, N.Y., 1964.

Willard, Charity Cannon. *Christine de Pizan: Her Life and Works.* New York, 1984.

Wood, Charles T. *Joan of Arc and Richard III: Sex, Saints, and Government in the Middle Ages.* New York, 1988.

Wood, Charles T. "Joan of Arc's Mission and the Lost Record of Her Interrogation at Poitiers." In *Fresh Verdicts on Joan of Arc*, eds. Bonnie Wheeler and Charles T. Wood. New York, 1996.

Woodward, Kenneth L. *Making Saints: How the Catholic Church Determines Who Becomes a Saint, Who Doesn't, and Why.* New York, 1990.

INDEX

Printed and bound by CPI Group (UK) Ltd, Croydon, CR0 4YY

09/06/2025

14685774-0001